"Hurd offers fresh insights on familiar topics, moving easily from poets, playwrights, theologians, and spiritual writers. His treatment of Louis-Marie Chauvet makes this contemporary theologian comprehensible and accessible to the average reader. Coming from a person who has spent a lifetime composing texts and music for worship, this book is clearly the fruit of study, personal prayer, and liturgical celebrating. Highly recommended!"

— Judith M. Kubicki, CSSF
Associate Professor of Theology
Fordham University

"Deeply grounded in Scripture and demonstrating deft command of insights provided by Karl Rahner and Louis-Marie Chauvet, Bob Hurd's *Compassionate Christ, Compassionate People* articulates a Christian spirituality that, nourished by liturgical practice, moves with the spirit of God moving within us. Hurd's account of liturgy ties the love that moves Dante's stars with the love that God summons us to practice in the human village."

— Timothy Brunk
Associate Professor of Theology
Villanova University

"You have enjoyed singing Bob Hurd's liturgical music. Here is your opportunity to enter the fruitful mind of this faithful Christian. You will explore not only the workings of worship but also the God whom worship encounters. Hurd's book will help you appreciate why his music so powerfully draws you into Christian prayer."

— Fr. Paul Turner
Pastor, Cathedral of the Immaculate Conception,
Kansas City, Missouri

Compassionate Christ, Compassionate People

Liturgical Foundations of Christian Spirituality

Bob Hurd

Foreword by
Michael Downey

**LITURGICAL PRESS
ACADEMIC**

Collegeville, Minnesota
www.litpress.org

Library of Congress Cataloging-in-Publication Data

Names: Hurd, Bob, author.
Title: Compassionate Christ, compassionate people : liturgical foundations of Christian
    spirituality / Robert Hurd.
Description: Collegeville, Minnesota : Liturgical Press, [2019] | Includes index.
Identifiers: LCCN 2018050946 (print) | LCCN 2019007575 (ebook) |
    ISBN 9780814684870 (eBook) | ISBN 9780814684627 (pbk.)
Subjects: LCSH: Spirituality—Catholic Church—History. | Sacraments (Liturgy)—
    History.
Classification: LCC BX2350.65 (ebook) | LCC BX2350.65 .H865 2019 (print) |
    DDC 264/.02—dc23
LC record available at https://lccn.loc.gov/2018050946

Contents

Acknowledgments

With heartfelt thanks I want to acknowledge the following who in various ways have encouraged and assisted me in the writing of this book:

- My graduate students at Santa Clara University, Seattle University, and the Archdiocese of San Bernadino, who taught me that students of spirituality and worship come from all kinds of church traditions.

- Mary Fay and Joe Zenk, first readers of the earliest part of the book, who encouraged me and offered helpful comments on the writing.

- For seven years, my wife Pia Moriarty and I have lived in the intentional, ecumenical community of Pilgrim Place in Claremont, California. If I have succeeded at all in comparing Roman Catholic and Protestant worship traditions in this book, it is largely due to the generous accompaniment and assistance of my Protestant sisters and brothers. I offer special thanks to Ken Dale, Jean Denton, Jane Douglass, Ron Hines, John Keester, David Lull, Bill Moremen, Steve Smith, and Dwight Vogel; I remember with gratitude the accompaniment of Bill Lesher (1932–2018), my frequent ecumenical conversation partner, who also taught me the importance of interreligious dialogue and cooperation.

- Pastor Lara Martin, Good Shepherd Lutheran Church, Claremont, California, who provided me with texts from her tradition.

- Marty and Linda Haugen, who graciously lived with the writing of this book during several shared vacations; Marty offered helpful suggestions on the eucharistic prayer chapter.

- Timothy Brunk, who read and commented on the manuscript of the book with meticulous care.

- Michael Downey, who has accompanied me all along the way of this book, reading, commenting, offering insightful suggestions, and whose own writing on spirituality continues to inspire me. I am grateful that he accepted my invitation to write the foreword to this book.

- Pia Moriarty, teacher, anthropologist, community organizer, social justice activist, composer, potter, my spouse, my best friend, my treasure, for her unfailing support, encouragement, and practical help on the writing.

It will become apparent to the reader that the primary intellectual influences on this book are Karl Rahner and Louis-Marie Chauvet. In their different ways, each has provided a theological framework for drawing together my own thought along with that of other favorite authors whose writings have nourished me. I am grateful to them all, but especially these two. As a young professor I had the opportunity to meet and interview Karl Rahner at Marquette University's celebration of his seventy-fifth birthday. At that time, I was able to express my personal thanks for how his work has deepened my faith. Similarly, I hope this book may serve as an expression of gratitude to Louis-Marie Chauvet.

Foreword

"A voice like the color of honey." Never mind the mixed metaphor. These are the words I whispered nearly forty years ago when I first heard liturgical composer and musician Bob Hurd sing. The sound was clean and translucent, sweet and invigorating, moving and stilling, penetrating, yes, piercing, but soothing like a balm for the wounded heart.

For forty years and more, Bob Hurd has been composing and singing, spending countless hours in the recording studio, conducting workshops and giving classes, serving the life of parishes and local churches through liturgical ministry. All the while he has gained recognition and a well-deserved reputation throughout the English-speaking world and beyond as one of the finest liturgical musicians of his generation. Occasionally he has found the time to write a scholarly article or an essay on a topic of interest to those who serve the liturgical life of the churches "on the ground."

Since the late 1970s, as many liturgists and liturgical musicians have grown weary to the point of despair in the face of so many obstacles barring the full flowering of the liturgical renewal occasioned by the orientations of the Second Vatican Council, Bob Hurd has kept calm and carried on. Through it all, he would give hints of his dream to write a book on liturgical spirituality. This is it! Bob Hurd's first book.

In circles of liturgical ministry and music, what is not well known is that Bob Hurd was for a number of years a student and a teacher of philosophy. His doctorate in philosophy was focused on the thought of Karl Rahner. This equipped him to pursue his interests in theology, Christology, sacramental theology, liturgy, and spirituality. In teaching a wide range of courses in theology and related disciplines over many years, he has proven to be a careful, reflective, systematic thinker, always attentive to the practical implications of systems of thought, be they classical, medieval, modern, or contemporary. In *Compassionate Christ, Compassionate People*, Bob Hurd brings insights from Scripture, theology, philosophy, the Catholic liturgical tradition—as well as an admirable familiarity with the liturgical practices of other Christian churches—to bear on the task of laying the liturgical foundations of Christian spirituality. Of singular importance here is the theological anthropology and Christology of Karl Rahner, as well as the work of the contemporary sacramental theologian Louis-Marie Chauvet.

It is commonplace to hear that the liturgy is the source and summit of Christian life (*Sacrosanctum Concilium* 10). Properly understood, this is inclusive of every dimension of the Christian life, especially the spiritual life, life in Christ's Spirit, or spirituality. Since the Second Vatican Council, liturgy as source and summit has been repeatedly asserted and affirmed. But rarely has it been explored and explained in a comprehensive and systematic fashion. This is what Bob Hurd sets out to do here. The key to his understanding of the liturgical foundations of Christian spirituality is the *kenosis*, the ongoing self-emptying of God in Christ through the gift of the Spirit of God enlightening, enlivening, guiding, and healing the church, nurturing and sustaining it as the Body of the compassionate Christ, whose members are to be and become a compassionate people in and for the world.

While this may be his first book, Bob Hurd is no novice. After years of study and reflection, prayer and practice, composing music through which he puts words and melodies in people's hearts so that they can open their lips and lift their voices to God in unison, what we have here is the mature work of a quiet scholar who has helped the church to sing rightly—prayerfully, joyfully, heartfully, indeed contemplatively—to the God whose name, beyond all naming, is self-emptying Love. He teaches us words of thanks, praise, lament, forgiveness, mercy, and wonder. He invites us to pause to hear the rhythms of silence. Here we are summoned to participate in the self-emptying of God in Christ in our living, in our worship, in our dying, and in our death. Whether we live or die, we belong to the Lord (Rom 14:8) whose cup runneth over with a fullness that is self-emptying. From that cup we are invited to drink in the mellifluous timbre of these pages.

Michael Downey

Prologue

Before Mystery—An Evocation

We live "the life of a village against the life of the stars," Thornton Wilder wrote in the preface for his play *Our Town*.[1] This is the life of everyday happenings: an early morning birth, households awakening to a new day, the arrival of the milkman and the morning paper, breakfast, the daily journey to school and work, returning home at day's end, sitting down to dinner, having an argument, making love, dying.[2] But generation after generation, these mundane events are played out against the vast horizon of the stars, Wilder's symbol for the eternal.

Visits to Roman archeological sites during his student days gave Wilder a vivid sense of the temporal over against the eternal, of finite human existence against the horizon of infinite mystery. And so, across *Our Town* there are moments in which we are led from everyday village life into the mystery, partly in religious language, partly as a question always confronting human beings.[3] The eternal is always on the brink of peeking through, which is to say that our consciousness

---

[1] Thornton Wilder, "A Preface for Our Town," in *Thornton Wilder: Collected Plays and Writings on the Theater* (New York: The Library of America, 2007), 659.

[2] Ibid., 657.

[3] Wilder's writing reflects both his religious upbringing and modernity's doubts concerning religious faith. He described his religious background to an interviewer as follows: "I came from a very strict Calvinistic father, was brought up partly among missionaries in China, and went to that splendid college at Oberlin at a time when the classrooms and student life carried a good deal of pious didacticism which would now be called narrow Protestantism." Cited by J. D. McClatchy in his foreword to Thornton Wilder's *Heaven's My Destination* (New York: HarperCollins, 2003), xviii. Around the time he wrote *Our Town* he had read Nietzsche but also described himself

somehow reaches not only the mundane but the eternal, not only the ordinary things of life but transcendent mystery.

In act 1, teenager George Gibbs is falling in love with Emily Webb, the girl next door. In the evening, he and his younger sister, Rebecca, are looking at the night sky. Though looking at the far-away moon, George's thoughts focus on something as close as the girl next door. Gazing at the same moon, young Rebecca's thoughts reach out to the eternal:

> REBECCA: I never told you about that letter Jane Crofut got from her minister when she was sick. He wrote Jane a letter and on the envelope the address was like this: It said: Jane Crofut; The Crofut Farm; Grover's Corners; Sutton County; New Hampshire; United States of America.
>
> GEORGE: What's funny about that?
>
> REBECCA: But listen, it's not finished: the United States of America; Continent of North America; Western Hemisphere; the Earth; the Solar System; the Universe; the Mind of God—that's what it said on the envelope.
>
> GEORGE: What do you know!
>
> REBECCA: And the postman brought it just the same.
>
> GEORGE: What do you know![4]

Rebecca is awed by the minister's tracing of earthly and cosmic realities back to their source in the mind of God. But the "mind of God" is clearly not another object lying alongside Grover's Corners, the earth, the solar system, and the universe. Though in Rebecca's telling God appears as the last item in a series, that little word "in," implied in the address (*in* the mind of God), shows that something else is going on. She has climbed up the ladder of beings and found God, not as the final rung, but beyond the entire ladder. There is a leap from a whole chain of conditioned, finite things to their Unconditioned Source. God is not another "thing" in the cosmos; rather, the cosmos and all things are *in* God. In highly abbreviated form, she is

---

as being "under the shadow of Whitehead's philosophy—Christian—Platonic." Cited by Penelope Niven in *Thornton Wilder: A Life* (New York: HarperCollins, 2012), 428.

[4] *Our Town*, in *Thornton Wilder: Collected Plays*, 173.

tracing out the God-ward dynamism of the human heart and mind when its questioning is allowed to run its full course—the ascent to God through the things of the world: this town, this continent, this earth, this solar system, this universe—the mind of God.

George, staring at the same moon, takes a different route. He is awakening to his love for Emily Webb, the girl next door. Instead of carrying him into the cosmos, this love carries him into courtship, marriage, the birth of their first child, and, tragically, the loss of his young wife in second childbirth. His experience of giving himself completely to another, someone who is fragile and can be lost, is also an encounter with the mystery of the eternal. For when we run up against the limits of our finitude, the question of the infinite opens up, as does the question of the abiding value of our earthly commitments. On their wedding day in act 2, Emily tells George that all she wants is for him to love her, adding: "And I mean for *ever*. Do you hear? For ever and ever."[5] Now that she is gone, does his love for her have anything like eternal validity? If so, where is this eternity, this "for ever and ever"? Wilder described *Our Town* as "an attempt to find a value above all price for the smallest events in our daily life."[6] In what would such a value beyond all price be grounded? Is there a Love beyond all loves in which they rest and have their ultimate value? Is there in all our loves, finally, an experience of longing for one knows not what, so that, as C. S. Lewis said, "we remain conscious of a desire which no natural happiness will satisfy"?[7]

George's experience corresponds less to the dynamism of knowing than to the dynamism of freedom and love, that self-donation in which one gives oneself with all one's heart to another. Such love is an act of the heart and the will, affectivity and volition. For to value, to love, is to extend oneself toward another, willing the good of the beloved. This dynamism of the heart has an ethical trajectory as well, because one can give oneself in love more broadly to the welfare of others, to values such as truth, justice, and compassion, and even to the point of risking and sacrificing one's life. Where do we get the sense that finite actions in relation to finite objects or goals have infinite seriousness and eternal validity?

[5] Ibid., 192.
[6] Thornton Wilder, "Preface to Three Plays" in *Collected Plays*, 686.
[7] C. S. Lewis, *The Weight of Glory* (New York: Harper Collins, 2001), 32.

In act 3, the Stage Manager, a character in the play, conducts the audience on a tour of the town cemetery, naming those buried there. Once again, there is a sense of our relation to a mystery beyond ourselves:

> Now there are some things we all know, but we don't take 'em out and look at 'em very often. We all know that *something* is eternal. And it ain't houses and it ain't names, and it ain't earth, and it ain't even the stars . . . everybody knows in their bones that *something* is eternal, and that something has to do with human beings. All the greatest people ever lived have been telling us that for five thousand years and yet you'd be surprised how people are always losing hold of it. There's something way down deep that's eternal about every human being.[8]

In a sense yet to be explored, everyone knows the eternal, yet everyone is prone to lose sight of it. This is the ambiguous terrain on which spirituality is lived—the persistence of mystery, the tendency to "lose hold of it," and the resolve to dwell *with* it intentionally.

The ending of the play delivers us from the village back to the stars, that vast horizon surrounding all human affairs. But we now know that the stars are but sentinels of an eternity that transcends them. And this eternity is somehow related to human beings. The Stage Manager, looking up to the vault of heaven, comments on the strain of village life and the need for sleep. Straining away before the horizon of eternity—this is the life of the village against the life of the stars, the life of the human spirit in the dynamism of its knowing, willing, and loving. Now, we cannot simply live amid the stars; we need the village. But to live *only* in the village is to be less than fully human. If the human being exists as "the mid-point between time and eternity, between the world and God,"[9] then both the village and the stars are valid concerns, and the loss of either side maims our humanity.

Having said that, the people of *Our Town* are mostly and understandably taken up with the village. Dwelling with eyes wide open at the mid-point of time and eternity is a stretch for most of us. Our

---

[8] Wilder, *Our Town*, in *Collected Plays*, 196–97.

[9] Karl Rahner, *Spirit in the World*, trans. William Dych (New York: Herder and Herder, 1968), 407. Rahner is paraphrasing Aquinas, who is paraphrasing the anonymous work *Liber de Causis*.

default position is to turn our backs on the Mystery and concern ourselves solely with the obvious and immediate everyday things over which we have some control. The things we cannot control—well, we leave them aside, not in the sense of honestly acknowledging our own vulnerability before them, but rather in the sense of suppression, denial, flight. This suppression can be merely practical, not so much a question of ideas in our heads, but simply how we live. We flee ultimate questions into the comfort of immediate concerns and goods, distracting ourselves until death. But such suppression can be more theoretically formulated.

When asked about his atheism, the comedian Stephen Fry flippantly quipped that he had no problem with other people having invisible, imaginary friends. The implication: How absurd that a person should have such an invisible and imaginary friend as God. Children play such games but eventually grow out of them. Fry is voicing Freud's suspicion that belief in God is infantile. But consider for a moment the opposite. Imagine God being a directly visible thing in the world.[10] Fry wants a God as visible, say, as the neighbor next door. Or perhaps, since it is *God*, something a little more extraordinary than the neighbor next door, but visible. Then, as Kierkegaard once said, God would be related to humans directly "as the obviously extraordinary to the astonished observer."[11] He elaborates, suggesting that if only God would "take on the figure of a very rare and tremendously large green bird, with a red beak, sitting in a tree on the mound, and perhaps even whistling in an unheard of manner" then people would surely sit up and take notice! But could such a visible thing alongside other things in the world possibly be God? How absurd. Children can't help but think of God in this way but eventually grow out of it. No, God's presence to us must be qualitatively different from our experience of visible things and persons directly present to us in the world.

---

[10] At this point, a Christian believer is thinking: what about Jesus? But Jesus is not God directly present *as God*, Jesus is the divinity present to us through his humanity, God mediated to us through creaturely reality. And in any case, once risen, Jesus is no longer present in an earthly, bodily way. Christ as radically mediating our experience of God is explored in chapter 4.

[11] Soren Kierkegaard, *Concluding Unscientific Postscript*, trans. David F. Swenson and Walter Lowrie (Princeton, NJ: Princeton University Press, 1968), 219.

Spirituality is a countermovement to this narrowing, suppressing tendency. It is concerned with dwelling mindfully in the tension between the village and the stars, the temporal and the eternal. It is "humanity at full stretch," to borrow a phrase from Don Saliers.[12] This requires a certain resolve to move beyond the immediate and obvious, to own the full height and depth of one's humanity. From the perspective of Christian faith, what we are "owning" in this case is not just our full humanity—it is our humanity *graced*. It involves our life with all its human possibilities but also the further gift of God's life moving within us, which necessarily changes the quality of our experience.

John Dunne speaks of this graced deeper life as an "enduring life, a life that could last beyond death." Such a life, he says, would be a life that people "have without knowing it, some current that runs far beneath the surface." He continues:

> The deeper life would be like an undertow, like a current that flows beneath the surface. . . . There is no swelling and breaking in the undertow, no foam, no splash, no sound. Yet it is a powerful current and may move in a direction opposite to that of the waves, may move toward the open sea while they move toward the shore.[13]

Wilder's village is like the shore and his stars are like the open sea. Human knowing, willing, and loving aims at the things of everyday life but in this very movement simultaneously experiences in its depths an undertow or dynamism toward a fullness beyond everything finite—God. Further, this movement of the human spirit is heightened, elevated, magnetized by God's moving toward us (grace). But, Dunne asks, can one really bear to live such a life? Is it not easier to retreat into the immediate and obvious things of life? Why bother with the undertow, which, in any case, might be dangerous? Living the deeper life is an adventure, a stretch, a discipline, a work—the cultivation of a self-possessed, mindful relation to the height and depth of one's existence and all that is met with there. If God moves toward and in us, then spirituality is a responsive answer:

---

[12] Don E. Saliers, *Worship as Theology: Foretaste of Glory Divine* (Nashville: Abingdon Press, 1994), 28.

[13] John Dunne, *Time and Myth* (Notre Dame, IN: University of Notre Dame Press, 1975), 5–6.

moving with the life of God moving within us in ongoing conversion, attunement, and practice.

A friend of mine once speculated on what a dolphin's spirituality would be like, I suppose, because of the high intelligence of this wondrous creature. How would a dolphin experience Mystery? Would it be by going down into the depths, much deeper than dolphins normally go? Would it be, instead, rising up and leaping exuberantly out of the sea? Answer: Yes!

In the end, going up and going down amount to the same thing. They are images for reaching beyond or transcending the immediacy of ordinary experience, especially ordinary experience too narrowly focused. Insofar as the Transcendent Mystery is the ground of all that is, it is "down deep," that is, immanent to creation, including the consciousness of the human creature. Insofar as this Mystery, which sustains each and every being, is not identical with any of them, it remains "above" or transcendent to them. So, our capacity for God as Mystery is engaged when we transcend or go deeper than what is immediately obvious to us in everyday experience. This transcending or going deeper applies both to Rebecca's reaching beyond the cosmos to its transcendent ground and to George's absolute love for Emily. In both cases we have the life of the village, but with an undertow or motion toward the horizon of Absolute Mystery.

The effort required is like the story of Elijah on Mount Horeb. God tells him to leave the shelter of the mountain cave because "the LORD will pass by" (1 Kgs 19:11-13). He has to leave the shelter of the cave, becoming vulnerable in the face of primal elements. The adventure of spirituality involves leaving the various shelters we construct, risking vulnerability in the face of primal mystery. Then, Elijah experiences God not in the obvious and dramatic occurrences of storm, earthquake, and fire, like Kierkegaard's astonished observer, but in "a tiny whispering sound." God is more like a tiny whispering sound surrounding our lives than some dramatic object confronting us. Dramatic events do not introduce us to this experience for the first time but rather bring it out into the open. When you wake up in the morning, you may not be focusing on the sensation in your feet—your attention is elsewhere. But when you stub your toe, a sensitivity that has been there all along becomes uppermost in your awareness!

Elijah's story resonates with another one—the call of Peter in Luke's gospel (5:1-11). Jesus tells Simon Peter to leave the shelter of the shore and "put out into deep water" (v. 4). It is only when Peter *puts out into the deep* that he encounters the miraculous catch of fish and the mystery of God's presence in Jesus. Spirituality is putting out into the deep. What would it mean for you and me, reader, to stand on the mountain top, listening to the "tiny whispering sound" that surrounds us, or to "put out into the deep" instead of just remaining in the shallows of our lives? What would it mean to dwell mindfully at the midpoint between time and eternity, the world and God, and to encounter there the life of God moving within us?

PART ONE

Theological Bearings:
The Life of God Moving within Us

"Godself. Godself I experienced—not human words about God. . . . Indeed, I would say this: you can have the same experience too," Karl Rahner once wrote, assuming the persona of Ignatius of Loyola.[1] Yet, here I am, reader, using *words*, and probably too many, to coax you into reflection on experiencing God. My words presume the Word made flesh; the words of Scripture, ritual, and sacrament; and the many human words of theology, philosophy, and literature responding to the paschal mystery across the centuries. This is an exercise in faith seeking understanding. For I am speaking from within Christian faith about faith and its relation to experience. And though the experience of God is more than just words—more than just *having ideas about*—still, we necessarily receive, interpret, and express these experiences in words, not just after the fact, but all along the way.

That tiny whispering sound surrounding us, that undertow in the depths of our lives, is the experience of the holy Mystery, the life of God moving within us. God's initiative invites and opens up the possibility of our response, our partnership. We learn to move with the life of God moving within us. Led by the Spirit, we learn the steps of the sacred dance. In this movement of God within us and our response we are invited to ongoing change of heart, attunement, and practice. The more this response becomes simply who we are, the

---

[1] Karl Rahner, *Spiritual Writings*, ed. Philip Endean (Maryknoll, NY: Orbis Books, 2004), 38.

more we are practicing spirituality. *Moving with the life of God moving within* us—this is the understanding of spirituality that will animate these pages. As a Christian spirituality, it reaches its most explicit expression in worship, in receiving the Bread of the Word and the Bread and Cup of Christ at the table. Part 2 will explore this in detail. But God's gracious movement within us and our response marks the whole of our lives. So, we must first reflect more deeply on what this *life of God moving within us* is. How do we experience this whisper, this undertow? Part 1 explores this experience in order to give a theological framework for our exploration of liturgical spirituality in part 2.

This experience involves several interrelated ways of sharing in God's life. Distinctions can be made among these different sharings, though our relationship to God "is expressed completely only in and through the whole Christian message," as Rahner says.[2] A line is intelligible in itself but, without ceasing to be a line, can become part of a greater reality—a square. And a square, though intelligible in itself, and without ceasing to be a square, can be taken up into a yet greater reality—a cube.[3] So it is with the Christian mystery. Here, in the light of faith, we can speak of the threefold gift or way in which God moves within us: as Creator, as self-communicating Love (or grace), and as given in radical solidarity with our humanity in the Christ. These modalities of God's life moving within us can be distinguished from each other. But in fact all three have been given and are interrelated. Let us explore each in turn.[4]

---

[2] Karl Rahner, *Foundations of Christian Faith*, trans. William V. Dych (New York: Crossroad, 1982), 75.

[3] I am indebted to C. S. Lewis for this imagery, though I am using it somewhat differently than he does. See *Mere Christianity* (New York: HarperCollins, 2001), 161–62.

[4] Though I draw on many authors in part 1, it is primarily Karl Rahner's theology that I am presenting through these materials as well as direct quotation from his writings. I want to acknowledge this indebtedness at the outset.

Chapter 1

Before the Mystery of Creation: Experiencing Our Createdness

Be still and know that I am God.
Psalm 46:10

Before a word is on my tongue, Lord,
you have known its meaning through and through.
You are with me beyond my understanding:
God of my present, my past and future, too.
Bernadette Farrell, song paraphrase of Psalm 139[1]

To experience the life of God moving within us as Creator is to recognize or "know again" something so primal that it normally escapes us: our createdness, our being sustained by something beyond ourselves. I am reminded of Alec Guinness's memoir in old age, titled, *My Name Escapes Me.*[2] One might just as well say, "My createdness escapes me!" It is like the story of the little fish who swims up to its mother asking, "So where is this ocean I hear so much about?"[3] The most obvious thing can be the most hidden. We must make an effort to bring it to consciousness. Doing this mindfully, day by day, in meditation or prayer is practicing a spiritual discipline. It

---

[1] "O God, You Search Me," Text and Music © 1992, Bernadette Farrell. Published by OCP. All rights reserved. Used with permission.

[2] Alec Guinness, *My Name Escapes Me* (New York: Penguin Books, 1996).

[3] Thomas Keating, "Cultivating the Centering Prayer," in M. Basil Pennington, Thomas Keating, and Thomas E. Clark, *Finding Grace at the Center: The Beginning of Centering Prayer* (Woodstock, VT: Skylight Paths Publishing, 2002), 47.

is less like making something happen than removing blinders and opening ourselves to the ever-present fullness of reality in which we live and move and have our being. Then something happens to us, not of our own making. Our center of gravity shifts from ourselves alone, from our pretense of absolute autonomy, to our relationship with others, all of creation, and the Mystery that grants and holds all in being. This is not a desertion of responsible autonomy but, in the words of John Donne, knowing again that no one of us "is an island, entire to itself."

Despite our impressive autonomy, we are not of our own making; we are existentially indebted. This illusory autonomous self, whether we formulate it philosophically or just practically live it, must die so that a truer self can live. There are many ways in which one must repeatedly lose one's life, as Jesus says, in order to save it (Matt 17:25). This is one of them. Forgetfulness of this giftedness is the beginning of the illusory self of which Thomas Merton once wrote—illusory because it is cut off from the truth of its being:

> When we seem to possess ourselves and use our being and natural faculties in a completely autonomous manner, as if our individual ego were the pure source and end of our own acts, then we are in illusion and our acts, however spontaneous they may seem to be, lack spiritual meaning and authenticity.[4]

Awakening to the giftedness of being, with gratitude and awe, is the beginning of wisdom, the beginning of having a spirituality. Such a discipline belongs above all to liturgical spirituality. The first moment of liturgical worship is not just physically assembling but "gathering" in the spiritual sense of becoming truly gathered within oneself, with other persons, with the whole of creation, with God.[5] The ritual shift into community with God and neighbor in Christ expresses the existential and spiritual shift from being wrongly centered to being rightly centered or gathered, the shift from the false to the true self. For most, it is in worship that we first and explicitly

---

[4] Thomas Merton, *Contemplative Prayer* (New York: Image/Random House, 1996), 48.

[5] All of these relationships are mediated by our relationship to the risen One and the Spirit, but I will take this up later.

learn the language of our createdness: "In the beginning, when God created the heavens and the earth" (Gen 1:1). In worship we learn to profess and pray to God as Creator. Most of our eucharistic prayers feature some variation on these words from Eucharistic Prayer IV:

> you, who alone are good, the source of life,
> have made all that is,
> so that you might fill your creatures with blessings.

Do these words of the liturgy resonate with something in our experience? Does *createdness* enter into our experience of ourselves? Do we have through this some sense of the Creator? To this question, the people of Wilder's *Our Town* provide some important clues. In act 3 the Stage Manager says, "Everybody knows in their bones that *something* is eternal and that something has to do with us human beings." But in the same breath, he also says, "You'd be surprised how people are always losing hold of it."[6] We need to explore both insights, which, taken together, say: this experience of createdness is deeply certain and yet elusive. Let's begin with knowing in our bones that our existence is gift from beyond ourselves. Chapter 2 will then address how elusive this awareness is and why we are prone to lose sight of it.

Knowing in Our Bones

What kind of knowing is this? Experiencing our createdness is not an experience of any particular thing in this world, not even the world as a whole. Yes, the ordinary things of life may awaken this experience, but it is not of *them* but of something *through* them, something more than any of them *are*. The experience of createdness outruns the things directly accessible to us in experience toward that in which all things abide. Coming back from outer space, a Russian cosmonaut said atheism is true because he did not find God "out there." He missed the point, because God *as* creative source in which all things abide cannot be another intracosmic thing alongside them. Karl Rahner puts it this way: "*That* God really does not exist who operates

---

[6] Thornton Wilder, *Our Town*, in *Thornton Wilder: Collected Plays and Writings on the Theater* (New York: The Library of America, 2007), 196–97.

and functions as an individual existent alongside of other existents, and who would thus, as it were, be a member of the larger household of all reality. Anyone in search of such a God is searching for a false God."[7]

Second, this knowing in our bones is not awareness of something that, once upon a time, initiated creation and then receded like an absentee landlord. It is an "in every moment" experience of everything, including ourselves, being granted out of a Mystery that transcends us and yet is closer to us than we are to ourselves. In other words, the existential indebtedness of all creation to its Creator does not refer to one moment in a time past but to every moment of time. "The act of bringing the world into existence," Abraham Heschel wrote, "is a continual process. God called the world into being, and that call goes on. . . . To witness the perpetual marvel of the world's coming into being is to sense the Giver in the given."[8] Though this is not the fullness of the Christian mystery, it is an experiential moment within it.

Witnessing "the perpetual marvel of the world's coming into being" and sensing "the Giver in the given"—this is what we are seeking to lay bare. When I sit on my front porch in early morning stillness, witnessing the world emerging from silence and darkness with birdsong and the gradual lighting up of the horizon, as my past days now give way to this precious new one (how wonderful it is to be able to start afresh!), as I feel the fragility of each breath I draw—for one day I will surely draw my last breath—what leads me to sense through all this "the perpetual marvel of the world's coming into being"? Why does the song "Morning Has Broken" ring so true, connecting this morning's birdsong with the first birdsong of creation?[9] After all, sunrise and birdsong happened the day before, and many

---

[7] Karl Rahner, *Foundations of Christian Faith*, trans. William V. Dych (New York: Crossroad, 1982), 63; emphasis in original. At this point, a Christian believer is thinking: what about Jesus? But Jesus is not God directly present as God, Jesus is the divinity present to us through the humanity—Jesus is God mediated to us through creaturely reality.

[8] Abraham Joshua Heschel, *The Sabbath* (New York: Farrar, Straus and Giroux, 2005), 100–101.

[9] "Morning Has Broken," Text by Eleanor Farjeon, 1881–1965, © 1957, Eleanor Farjeon. All Rights reserved. Harold Ober Assoc., Inc. Music: Trad. Gaelic Melody.

days before that as well. Yet this very morning's experience somehow says to me: in every moment existence is given anew. This givenness of things marks them as existentially indebted. Things are given; they do not give themselves to themselves. Every breath we take is in one sense an exercise of our own autonomy. But we know "in our bones" that with each breath we are living on borrowed power: "When you take away their breath, they die and return to their dust," as Psalm 104 says (NRSV).

How deep does this indebtedness go? One answer is that it goes as deep as nature. Nature is the cause of our being. Without doubt, we exist within nature and are indebted to a series of causes stretching back through all the processes that have led up to our present moment. We too easily forget that "we ourselves are dust of the earth (cf. Gn 2:7); our very bodies are made up of her elements, we breathe her air and we receive life and refreshment from her waters," as Pope Francis says in *Laudato Si'*.[10] To stop here, however, is to presume that nature grants itself existence. But our sense of the sheer givenness of things includes the thing we call nature, the world, the universe. We may be stardust, but that which grants being "ain't even the stars," as Wilder's Stage Manager says.

Whatever theory one has of how past processes have led up to our present moment, these processes do not explain their own existence. Once given, they have unfolded in some manner or another. But all along the way, since they do not carry their cause of existence within themselves, they not only have to be *given* but continually *sustained*. So, foundational energy, matter, and the things to which they give rise, including time itself, are indebted in the same way. The big bang, however true it may be, doesn't explain the *existence* of something to bang; evolution, however true, doesn't explain the *existence* of something to evolve. Creation "out of nothing" is a more radical concept than causality because causality presumes something already existing to undergo change.

This "in every moment" dependence of ourselves and all creation on the Creator is perhaps best described by Herbert McCabe, who says this process is "not like a sculptor who makes a statue and leaves

---

[10] *On Care for Our Common Home: Laudato Si'*, Encyclical Letter of the Holy Father Francis (Washington, DC: United States Conference of Catholic Bishops/Vatican City: Liberia Editrice Vaticana, 2015), par. 2.

it alone, but like a singer who keeps her song in existence at all times."[11] Dwell on that image for a moment. In every second of the song's sounding, over its whole life span, it's "being there" is projected by something beyond itself. Its emerging out of the silence, unfolding in the present, and future completion when its sounding ceases—in other words, it's *being* and its *time*—all this is created and carried by something beyond itself. Once it is given, the musicologist may discern its structure, duration, the relation of intervals, tempo, and how this or that note evolves from the preceding note. But none of these account for the song's existence. And one who looks only at these aspects of the song will not find its creative source among them. For the Singer who projects it into existence is neither the song nor some particular note within the song and yet is intimately present all along the way as its creative source. Where the song is sounding, the Singer is! Without the Singer, the song is not. Once we recognize this, we can experience the power, even the shock, of the ancient philosophical question: Why is there something rather than nothing? Things might not be at all, we might not be at all! Yet here we are. To his credit, Stephen Hawking, never shy to announce his atheism, admits that this is a question his scientific understanding can't answer: "What is it that breathes fire into the equations and makes a universe for them to describe?"[12]

Now let us go a step further. Suppose the song has self-awareness. If the Singer-Creator is singing and upholding the song in every moment of its sounding, might not this "being created and upheld" enter into the song's self-awareness? Not in the sense that the song would exhaustively comprehend its source, but rather in the bare sense of experiencing that it is *sourced* or given to itself out of it knows not what. Might this not be what *everybody knows in their bones*, as Wilder has it, if only they would attend to it?

The anonymous author of *The Cloud of Unknowing* and *The Book of Privy Counselling* speaks similarly. He echoes Augustine's notion that God is closer to us than we are to ourselves. God "is your being and in him, you are what you are, not only because he is the cause and

---

[11] Herbert McCabe, *God, Christ and Us*, ed. Brian Davies (New York: Continuum, 2003), 103. Cited in Elizabeth Johnson, *Ask the Beasts: Darwin and the God of Love* (New York: Bloomsbury Continuum, 2015), 123.

[12] Stephen Hawking, *A Brief History of Time* (New York: Bantam Books, 1988), 174. Cited in Johnson, *Ask the Beasts*, 138.

being of all that exists, but because he is *your* cause and the deep center of *your* being."[13] So he bids us to "go down to the deepest point of your mind and think of yourself in this simple, elemental way . . . do not think *what you are* but *that you are*."[14] This is the purpose of centering prayer. Stepping back from everyday knowledge of everyday things, one attends to the primal feeling of *existing*. Here we encounter something deeper than our ego and its limited autonomy. Here we let go of doing and attend to being. We encounter our createdness—that we quite impressively *are* but *we are not* the fullness of Being in which we abide. Simultaneously, we experience that everything else that enters our purview is less than the fullness of being. Normally, "my createdness escapes me," but in this contemplative act I reel it back in! In this experience of our givenness we encounter the Giver in the given. Do not shrink, says the author of the *Cloud*, "from the sweat and toil involved in gaining real self-knowledge, for I am sure that when you have acquired it you will very soon come to an experiential knowledge of God's goodness and love."[15]

As I said earlier, one can use either *going up* or *going down deep* imagery for recapturing our sense of createdness. Thomas Merton *goes up*, saying, "There exists some point at which I can meet God in a real and experimental contact with His infinite actuality. This is the 'place' of God, His sanctuary—it is the point where my contingent being depends upon His love. Within myself is a metaphorical apex of existence at which I am held in being by my Creator."[16] Merton then uses a striking image, reminiscent of the Singer-song relation referred to above: "God utters me like a word. . . . A word will never be able to comprehend the voice that utters it."[17] Heschel provides an interesting variation on this theme: "If an idea had the ability to think and to transcend itself, it would be aware of its being at this moment a thought of my mind." The religious person, he continues, "has such an awareness of being known by God."[18]

[13] *The Cloud of Unknowing and The Book of Privy Counselling*, trans. and ed. William Johnston (New York: Image/Random House, 2014), 138.

[14] Ibid., 140.

[15] Ibid., 58.

[16] Thomas Merton, *New Seeds of Contemplation* (New York: New Directions, 2007), 37.

[17] Ibid.

[18] Abraham Joshua Heschel, *Man Is Not Alone: A Philosophy of Religion* (New York: Farrar, Straus and Giroux, 1976), 128.

A Paradoxical Knowledge:
"You Are with Me Beyond My Understanding"

The awareness of our createdness is a strange kind of knowing. It is not knowledge as mastering the known object. A word will never, as Merton says, be able to comprehend the voice that utters it, and a song cannot comprehend the Singer who voices it. But we do experience, if we do not repress it, that our existence is thought or spoken or sung. We do sense that the whole world does not account for itself. We understand the meaningfulness of the question: Why is there something rather than nothing? This is a kind of negative knowledge analogous to Socratic ignorance: to know that there is something that escapes one's knowing. But it is also a kind of positive knowledge in the sense that our consciousness stretches beyond any finite limit toward—without reaching—the fullness of Being. The highest kind of knowledge, then, is to experience that there is something to know that is greater than my capacity to know. I comprehend that my knowledge falls short in the face of . . .? Drawing on Heidegger's way of speaking, Louis-Marie Chauvet expresses this paradoxical awareness by saying we are "to let ourselves go to this demanding letting be in which we find ourselves out of our depths."[19] Yes, there are indeed things that I do not yet know but can come to know. But there is also an experience, and so a kind of knowledge, of something ever in process of escaping while sustaining my experience. This is Merton's apex of existence or the *Cloud of Unknowing*'s deep down center of existence. This is Bernadette Farrell's perceptive reading of Psalm 139 quoted at the head of this chapter: "You are with me beyond my understanding." If God is with us beyond our understanding then our response, our spirituality, consists of the practice of letting "ourselves go to this demanding letting be in which we find ourselves out of our depths."

Experiencing this Mystery, which sources all beings, would be to experience a presence "running through everything, yet not contained by anything," and "lying at the heart of everything," as Benedictine Gregory Collins says, citing a line from the *Upanishads*: "There

---

[19] Louis-Marie Chauvet, *Symbol and Sacrament: A Sacramental Reinterpretation of Christian Existence*, trans. Patrick Madigan and Madeleine Beaumont (Collegeville, MN: Liturgical Press, 1995), 51.

is something beyond our mind which abides in silence within our mind."[20] *Beyond* our mind yet *abiding in silence* within our mind. Let us take "mind" in the broadest, most truthful sense. The human self is not just a knower but one who loves and wills. What we are looking for, then, is the sense that in every act of our own agency, acts of knowing, loving, and willing, we also experience being enabled by something beyond ourselves. "Within our mind" says this something is somehow interior to our awareness of self and all that we relate to in knowledge and freedom. "Beyond our mind" says this same something is mysterious—literally mysterious—because it is more than our mind and exceeds the mind's power to grasp. Its "abiding in silence" is the silence or barely audible whisper of God passing by Elijah on Mount Horeb, so easy to overlook unless we practice attentiveness to it. Not a particular thing of experience but the abiding basis of all experience. Not this or that fact but the basis of all facts. So, we are brought back to our two statements from *Our Town*: a paradoxical awareness of something deeply certain and yet elusive. When Augustine asks who God is in the *Confessions*, he answers: "most hidden yet intimately present."[21]

To do justice to this mind that, in knowing, loving, and willing anything at all, stands before Mystery, we must go a bit further. How to experience that our being is a being-with something beyond our understanding? Consider the complex structure of human consciousness. We may summarize it as an unfolding dynamism of *being a self—in relation to others—within the whole of reality.* Another word for this is "transcendence." The verb "transcend" means to move beyond. Human knowing, loving, and willing is a movement beyond the self into encounter with others and the world. But this self that continually goes out from itself does not thereby lose itself in the other it knows, loves, or wills. Rather, it possesses itself in the very act of relating to others; it holds itself in distinction from what it knows. *Relating to* is not simply *mirroring* the other. A mirror is not aware of itself as it reflects the other on its surface. But human knowing is self-aware while also knowing the other. It holds these two together,

---

[20] Gregory Collins, *Meeting Christ in His Mysteries* (Collegeville, MN: Liturgical Press, 2010), 27–28.

[21] *The Confessions of St. Augustine* 1.4, trans. Maria Boulding (New York: Vintage/Random House, 1997), 5.

in their relation to and distinction from each other, in a single consciousness. We are never just self-aware but also other-aware. Every encounter with the other—what is not the self—is simultaneously a deepening in self-knowledge. Aquinas expresses this by saying that in every act of going out of oneself to the other there is simultaneously a *complete return* to the self.[22]

As I write these words, I have before me the room in which I sit, the desk and paper on which I am writing, the pen moving across the page, my hand, my arm, in fact, my body moving the pen. I am simultaneously aware of all of these things (other-awareness) and aware of myself being aware of them (self-awareness). Human self-consciousness does not have itself first and then build a bridge "out" to the world; rather, it has itself in relation to the other and the world from the very beginning, though this relation obviously develops and deepens over time.

This is the famous *subject-object* or *self-other* characteristic of the human spirit.[23] But there is another crucial, though often overlooked, element. Awareness of self in relation to others also includes a sense of "the whole show," whatever that might be. The transcendence by which one has a self in relation to others occurs within a reach toward the whole of reality. In knowing-loving-willing any particular thing, we always hold it and ourselves within a broader horizon of reality. And this transcending movement of the human spirit toward the whole of reality is not just an add-on to having a self in relation to others. It is what makes possible being a self in relation to others. We must still explore what this means. But this orientation, this transcendence, as Elizabeth Johnson says, "is what constitutes us as spiritual subjects, or persons, properly so called."[24]

---

[22] *Summa Theologiae* I, q. 14, a. 2.

[23] Some traditions of spirituality see this unity of self- and other-awareness as a problem to be overcome. Meditation aims to abolish this distinction in favor of an undifferentiated union with all that is. But in the subject-object model we are presenting here, what makes us distinctively human is that we are neither lost in the *other* nor locked up in the *self* but a communion of both grounded in a reach toward Transcendent Mystery. Because this reach toward Transcendent Mystery underlies all our knowing, willing, and loving, there can be extraordinary experiences in which the object recedes so much and the Mystery is so intensely present that something approaching sheer unity with all that is may be glimpsed. But this entails a much more nuanced view than that we simply overcome the supposedly regrettable subject-object nature of human consciousness.

[24] Elizabeth Johnson, *Quest for the Living God* (New York: Continuum, 2007), 34.

Human Transcendence:
A Reach Always Exceeding Its Grasp

This transcending reach toward the whole of reality, which underlies and makes possible awareness of self and other, is what Karl
Rahner has in mind when he writes, "What it really means to have
a created origin is experienced basically and originally in the process
of transcendence."[25] The key point is that this movement of human
spirit toward the whole is both its act and at the same time an act
enabled by that toward which it moves. Think of a magnet drawing
what is magnetized toward itself. In one way the movement is *in* the
things being drawn; it is their action. But simultaneously this very
movement is granted by something beyond them—the magnet. In a
similar way, God, as creative source and goal, is interior to our very
being and agency as knowers, lovers, and free agents. Our very personhood, even with its impressive autonomy, is not absolute; it is
given to itself from beyond itself. This ever-present enabling source,
which Rahner prefers to call the holy Mystery,[26] is not an innate idea,
as though we were born with the idea of God as part of our human
equipment. Nor is it a direct intuition of God, separate from our
everyday knowledge. It is, rather, an awareness that emerges with
our ordinary experience of ourselves in relation to the world around
us.

The gist is captured in a line from the poet Robert Browning, who
said that a person's "reach should exceed his grasp, else what's a
heaven for?"[27] Human consciousness is always granted to itself out
of the Transcendent Mystery because in the course of ordinary experience it necessarily reaches out toward this Mystery. And the
Mystery as Creator is continually granting and sustaining this very
action of reaching.

How can we envision this more concretely? By way of illustration,
Rahner uses the notion of the horizon. When you reach out to grasp
an object, you necessarily reach into a space or horizon *in which* the
object *is* and *is to be grasped*. You can't grasp this surrounding space—
it exceeds your grasp—but you nevertheless reach into it on your

---

[25] Rahner, *Foundations*, 77.

[26] Ibid., 65–66.

[27] Robert Browning, "Andrea del Sarto," line 98. Available online at www.bartlby
.com.

way to grasping anything else. It is *beyond all grasp* but necessarily present if you are going to grasp anything else. Notice that both the subjective act of reaching and the object's "graspability" are indebted to the surrounding space. Without it, you could not reach, nor could the object be grasped.

Similarly, when you see a tree on the hilltop, you not only see the tree but your vision also extends beyond the tree toward the horizon. Without the "more" of the horizon, you could not perceive the edges, the outline, and therefore the tree as an individual thing. One must see *beyond* the tree in order to see it for what it truly is—a single, limited object in relation to one's act of seeing. Your eye does not create the visual horizon but is a capacity to extend toward it and participate in it. We could say that the horizon, manifesting itself to you, allows you to experience yourself experiencing the thing seen! But this horizon is a very strange thing. It is not another object along-side the tree. Rather, it's a kind of non-object or emptiness surround-ing the tree. It is present to me and yet remains beyond me and the tree I perceive. If I walk toward the horizon, what happens? It recedes. I cannot attain it as an object possessed. It is beyond grasp. Yet I ex-perience my movement toward it as I profile the tree against it. So, a *something beyond all grasp* "lets be" the human process of *being a self— in relation to others—within the whole of reality.*

Now the visual imagery I have used so far—the eye seeing the tree within the broader horizon—is only an analogy for what happens in human knowing, loving, and willing. And every analogy limps. This one limps because spatial-visual horizons (as well as temporal hori-zons) are finite. Our experience includes all sorts of finite horizons: a particular painting within the horizon of the wall, a particular task within the horizon of the workplace, an individual moment within the temporal horizon of the day, a particular epoch within the horizon of history, a specific idea within the horizon of a general theory, a feeling within the horizon of our psychological history. The very fact that we know the finitude of these various horizons implies, however, that we transcend them, that we are not rigidly locked within any of them.

My examples, drawn from sensory experience, have been some-what artificial. For pedagogical reasons, I have left out the intellectual component. Human sense knowledge is permeated and transformed by intellectual operations. Human knowing-loving-willing, though indebted to sense experience, is qualified by spirit or intellect. Humanly speaking, I not only *sense* the tree as a discreet "something" (sensation) but *understand* the tree (intellectual knowing) to be a finite, individual *being*—a finite instance of *Being*. In other words, it is not just an experience of "this-here-now" but an experience of "this-here-now-as-a-finite-instance-of-Being." And in knowing the other as a finite instance of Being—whether this is an individual thing or a finite horizon—I also know and possess myself as the finite one having this experience. All of our particular experiences of individual things (including ourselves) within finite horizons are held within a reach toward *more being than any finite thing or finite horizon is.*

What supplies the *more* of this reach beyond finite things and finite horizons? Does the mind create this *more* for itself? Rahner answers: "The movement of transcendence is not the subject creating its own unlimited space as though it has absolute power over being, but is the infinite horizon of being making itself manifest."[28] We use words such as Being, the Absolute, the Infinite, the Creator, God, even the Abyss, for this ultimate horizon. Such words are fingers pointing to the moon because it is the paradoxical *experience* of something that necessarily *escapes our experience.* Like bats flying into the sun, Aristotle said. It is an understanding flowing from being with something that is beyond understanding. "You are with me beyond my understanding." We experience all that we can comprehend by being with or reaching toward the Incomprehensible. It is really nameless, though we have to name it when talking about it. That is why its presence to us as enabling cause of our being as knowers and free agents is named *Mystery.* This is not a vague, pietistic term but a precise philosophical and theological one. The horizon of human spirit is unrestricted, unlimited—the very fullness of Being. And Being with a capital *B* is code for Mystery. This fullness of Being, ever beyond our reach yet that toward which we always reach, is the Creator or holy Mystery in whom we live and move and have our being. We experience it as something out of which and toward which our knowing-loving-willing dynamically tends in every act of awareness.

---

[28] Rahner, *Foundations*, 34.

This Mystery is *beyond* our mind yet *abiding in silence* within our mind, as we heard the *Upanishads* say. Aquinas's way of putting this is: "All knowing beings implicitly know God in any- and everything that they know."[29] Elsewhere, he will say that human consciousness is *quodammodo omnia*, "in a way everything," because while it is not the power to grasp the fullness of Being, it is by its very nature always dynamically coming from and tending toward this mysterious fullness. It is *capax dei*, a capacity for God. And it's very *tending toward*, it's dynamic self-actualization, is its being sourced and drawn forward by the Mystery that transcends it. As Thomas Merton writes, "God approaches our minds by receding from them."[30] In this dynamic process of transcendence, Karl Rahner says, "which necessarily and inescapably orients us toward the ineffable and holy mystery, we experience what creatureliness is and we experience it immediately."[31]

What from our side is a dynamic transcendence toward the horizon of Infinite Mystery is, from God's side, God continually creating us in each moment as conscious, personal beings. Which is to say, along with Psalm 139, that God encompasses us on all sides:

> O Lord, you search me and you know me.
> You yourself know my resting and my rising;
> You discern my thoughts from afar.
> You mark when I walk or lie down;
> you know all my ways through and through.
> Before ever a word is on my tongue,
> you know it, O Lord, through and through.
> Behind and before, you besiege me,
> your hand ever laid upon me.
> Too wonderful for me, this knowledge;
> too high, beyond my reach.

The psalm tells the paradox we have been exploring: an awareness of God's presence that is "too high, beyond my reach" and yet which has, in fact, reached into the psalmist's awareness and is described in great detail:

---

[29] Aquinas, *On Truth* (*De Veritate*) q. 22, a. 2, ad. 1.
[30] Thomas Merton, *No Man Is an Island* (New York: Harcourt, 1955), 239.
[31] Rahner, *Foundations*, 76.

O where can I go from your spirit,
or where can I flee from you face?
If I climb the heavens you are there.
If I lie in the grave you are there.
If I take the wings of the dawn
or dwell at the sea's furthest end,
even there your hand would lead me;
your right hand would hold me fast.

If I say, "Let the darkness hide me
and the light around me be night,"
even darkness is not dark to you,
the night shall be as bright as day,
and darkness the same as light.[32]

[32] *The Revised Grail Psalms*, Copyright © 2010, Conception Abbey / The Grail, admin. GIA Publications, Inc., www.giamusic.com. All rights reserved.

Chapter 2

About Resistances

Something as small as a hand held
over the eye can blot out the sun.[1]

Too High, Beyond Our Reach:
Losing Sight of the Mystery

The people of *Our Town* may know in their bones that something
is eternal, but they can also have their doubts. This is what humans
do: "You'd be surprised how people are always losing hold of it."[2]
Our situation is like a story I recently heard during a Sunday homily.
It concerns twins in the womb, a boy and a girl. The time of birth is
drawing near, and the girl says to the boy: "You know, I have this
feeling that there is a Mother. I think there is a Mother." And the boy
says: "A Mother? How do you know that? How could you possibly
know that?" "Honestly," the girl says, "I really think there is a
Mother." "Where did you get that infantile idea?" asks the boy. The
girl says, "Can't you feel it? Can't you feel that something is happening? I just have this sense that there is a Mother and someday we are
going to see her face to face."[3]

---

[1] This is a paraphrase of a statement Heschel cites from Baal Shem: "Replete is the
world with a spiritual radiance, replete with sublime and marvelous secrets. But a
small hand held against the eye hides it all." See Abraham Joshua Heschel, *God in
Search of Man: A Philosophy of Judaism* (New York: Farrar, Straus and Giroux, 1976), 85.

[2] Thornton Wilder, *Our Town*, in *Thornton Wilder: Collected Plays and Writings on the
Theater* (New York: The Library of America, 2007), 197.

[3] This story in its original form can be found in Benjamin A. Vima, *Sonday Sonrise:
Homilies for Sundays and Solemnities of Years ABC* (Bloomington, IL: Trafford Publishing, 2011), 363.

I'm not suggesting that the girl represents people of faith and the boy people without faith. If we are honest, I think most of us are both. Spirituality takes us out of conventional shelters and comforts. It takes us into the territory of wonder, yes, but also struggle, like Jacob wrestling with the angel, or Jesus going out into the desert, or John of the Cross writing about the dark night of the soul. Even a person of faith can experience dark moments of feeling "left altogether without God in the world."[4]

Given that the Mystery that sustains us cannot be directly experienced or controlled like things in the world, it is not surprising that people are always losing awareness of it. But I think Wilder's observation implies more. Always losing awareness of it suggests something about ourselves in our freedom. So does Psalm 139:7: "Where can I go from your spirit? From your presence, where can I flee?" There is really nowhere we can flee from the Mystery in which all things abide, but still we try. There is such a thing as hiding from our createdness and so from God. God's first question in the Bible occurs after Adam and Eve eat the forbidden fruit (Gen 3:9). God asks: "Where are you?" Commenting on this scene, Heschel says: "It is man who hides, who flees, who has an alibi. God is less rare than we think; when we long for Him, His distance crumbles away."[5] This shows that our experience of createdness is determined in part by our free response to it. Knowledge steers freedom, but freedom also steers knowledge. With freedom comes a spectrum of ways in which we lose sight of the Mystery in which all things abide, ranging from a lack of mindfulness to evasion to rejection, so that, as Rahner says, "what is most basic and original and self-evident can also be what is most able to be overlooked and is most able to be suppressed."[6] Something as small as a hand held over the eye can blot out the sun.

I once heard a comedian present a vignette of someone on a plane who was upset because he had not received his bag of peanuts. The comedian said: "My God, man, you are sitting in a chair thirty

---

[4] Soren Kierkegaard, *Concluding Unscientific Postscript*, trans. David F. Swenson and Walter Lowrie (Princeton, NJ: Princeton University Press, 1968), 220. Kierkegaard is paraphrasing Ephesians 2:12.

[5] Abraham Joshua Heschel, *Man Is Not Alone: A Philosophy of Religion* (New York: Farrar, Straus and Giroux, 1976), 153.

[6] Karl Rahner, *Foundations of Christian Faith*, trans. William V. Dych (New York: Crossroad, 1982), 29.

thousand feet up in the air and you are worried about a bag of peanuts?" We are quite capable, in other words, of shutting out the awe-
some in favor of the small, manageable details of life. We withdraw
from the full range of what is open to us, including not just immediate
experience but reflection on experience. Henri Nouwen wrote, "Half
of life is reflecting on what is being lived."[7] But reflecting on what is
being lived can cause anxiety. Sitting in a chair thirty thousand feet
in the air is not what we want to contemplate—watch the movie
instead and ask for another bag of peanuts.

The human situation is this vignette writ large. We bear a psychological burden that other animals are spared. To be made a little lower
than the angels, as Psalm 8 says, means that we are *animal* enough to
be mortal but *spirit* enough to be conscious of our own mortality. This
consciousness, which encompasses our own finitude, encompasses
much more. It encompasses everything else that it is possible to question and think about. As we have seen above, our consciousness
includes an overreach that outruns limits toward the holy and infinite
Mystery. In awareness of self and other we reach out beyond any
limited thing or meaning toward the whole. This very ability to en-
tertain reality as a whole, questioning the meaning of our place within
it, is our glory and our anguish. Beholding the stars might be awe-
inspiring, but it is also frightening, because the apparent infinity of
the heavens dwarfs us and reveals our finitude to us. "When we
become aware of this radical finitude," John Shea says, "we might
experience pain and be tempted to look away. Our ego does not want
us to take into account this basic condition of being human. It urges
us to get on with life with little or no knowledge of what life itself is
all about."[8]

Repressing Our Mortality and Creatureliness

Some years ago the cultural anthropologist Ernest Becker described
this tendency to withdraw from the full horizon of life as *partialization*: "narrowing down the world, shutting off experience, developing

---

[7] Henri Nouwen, *Can You Drink This Cup?* (Notre Dame, IN: Ave Maria Press, 1996,
2005), 29.
[8] John Shea, *Following Jesus* (New York: Orbis Books, 2010), 72.

an obliviousness" to the full shock and mystery of existence.[9] For as soon as a person "lifts his nose from the ground and starts sniffing at eternal problems like life and death, the meaning of a rose or a star cluster—then he is in trouble." By "partializing the world for comfortable action" we live only in that smaller area where we can exert control and autonomy.[10] One lives only for the village and ignores the stars. We occupy ourselves, Rahner says, with the grains of sand along the seashore but never look up "at the edge of the infinite ocean of mystery."[11] As this constricted posture becomes habitual, it becomes less and less conscious, less and less an explicit choice. Becker writes, "Most of us—by the time we leave childhood—have repressed our vision of the primary miraculousness of creation."[12]

Thornton Wilder's *Our Town* provides a poignant example of *partialization* in act 3. Though her dead companions in the cemetery try to dissuade her, the dead Emily returns to the past to relive her twelfth birthday. Seeing how things really are from the perspective of mortality, she is appalled by how narrowly people live their lives, not really noticing each other, the village, the earth, the stars, life itself. The pathos of the scene comes from the fact that what she feels and says *now*, fourteen years on and dead, cannot really make a dent in how her family speaks and acts in the past she is revisiting. She is aware of the miracle and fragility of existence, but they are focused only on the little details of the daily life. The situation becomes unbearable. She returns to the graveyard. The dead Mrs. Gibbs asks: "Were you happy?" To which Emily replies, "No . . . I should have listened to you. That's all human beings are! Just blind people."[13]

As a young child I once woke in the night to find my parents comforting my brother David, who was only fifteen months older than I. On the verge of tears, he kept saying, "I'm going to die someday." I don't remember how my parents calmed him, but somehow he got over it; he repressed this disturbing realization. To some extent such repression is psychologically healthy and necessary. "The great

---

[9] Ernest Becker, *The Denial of Death* (New York: Free Press Paperbacks, 1997), 178.
[10] Ibid.
[11] "The Experience of God Today," *Theological Investigations*, vol. 11, trans. David Bourke (New York: Seabury Press, 1974), 159.
[12] Becker, *Denial*, 50.
[13] Wilder, *Our Town*, 207.

boon of repression," Becker says, "is that it makes it possible to live decisively in an overwhelmingly miraculous and incomprehensible world, a world so full of beauty, majesty and terror that if animals perceived it all they would be paralyzed to act."[14]

The Return of the Repressed: Putting God in All the Wrong Places

Suppressing the overreach of consciousness, however, comes at a price. For this overreach is but another name for the transcendence by which we experience our createdness and the holy Mystery in which all abide. Suppressing this is suppressing the truth of our being. Not only that but since "the truth will out," this suppressed dimension usually returns in disguised and distorted forms. We make something in our lives, especially where we have control, our "everything," our "Absolute." The Divine is displaced onto something that is not divine. One flees the fragility of existence and mortality by placing the source of being and fulfillment either within oneself, or at least in something one can control. The result is the building up of a false ego or character. False, because we are not the source of our own being. False, because this strategy does not abolish mortality or grant us absolute autonomy. It can take many forms, personal and communal. It might be our own ego, our love interest, our tribe, work, wealth, or possessions. It can be a political ideology, which in the extreme results in a Third Reich or the Khmer Rouge. Hitler's Third Reich was supposed to last for a thousand years—in other words, forever, like the kingdom of God. What is happening here? The Divine is displaced onto something that is not divine. Even faith, as Karl Rahner says, "can be drawn into the half-light of ideology."[15] When we make God serve our own purposes, we have "godded" something—our own will?—but we are no longer serving the living God. In each case we serve idols of our own making. To such idols we devote all our energies; in them we anchor our autonomy, absent true recognition of limits.

---

[14] Becker, *Denial*, 50.
[15] Karl Rahner, *Do You Believe in God?*, trans. Richard Strachan (New York: Paulist Press, 1969), 25.

This need not be a theoretically held position. We may think we believe in God, but if in the daily round we rest solely in ourselves, serving only the finite idols of our own making, then we are living a practical if unacknowledged atheism. So, over the time of our lives we come into our own, achieving some autonomy and agency in the world. Across this flow of life, many things become "attached" to this apparently enduring core of autonomy in us: knowledge, relationships, work, home, family, political and religious alignments, and all the material things we acquire. All of this feeds the illusion that we simply stand on our own two feet, until some crisis arises, especially the final crisis when the whole thing goes under, as Georgian Tashjian's poem so poignantly puts it:

> *Resting Place*
> Up-ended in a shallow stream was a forked stick
>   which an errant water motion
>   had pinned quite firmly
>   in the sand.
>   A leaf caught on it
>   and was held there by the current
>
> a piece of gray moss was snagged by a tatter
>   and stayed.
>   A red bird feather
>   riding a quiet ripple
>   came close and remained
>   as did a ridge of bark from far up the river.
>
> Black leaves, lately unbedded, and more green ones
>   drifted by;
>   many of both kinds
>   held with the stick.
>   This structure
>   made a firm resting place
>   for a blue dragonfly before it all went under.[16]

The people of *Our Town* live a village life and attend to village matters, even while having the stars. Can one really have both? The

[16] Georgian Tashjian, *The Quiet Noise of Remembering* (Palo Alto, CA: Altoan Press, 1976), 19.

ial issue seems to be one of balance: standing on one's own two
hile acknowledging that "we are living in a mystery, from
creatures we did not make and powers we cannot comprehend," as
poet Wendell Berry writes.[17] Can we live decisively without shrinking back from our mortality and existential indebtedness, our createdness?

Two Waves

We began this chapter with a story of twins in the womb. Listen now to the Story of Two Waves:

> Two ocean waves were racing from Hawaii across the Pacific. They were having a hilarious time, seeing who could jump the highest, who could dash the fastest. Then they came to the shores of Japan. One wave was horrified: "Did you see what happened to the waves? They rushed in to shore, got smashed on the rocks, and disappeared!"
>
> The other wave said, "No sweat."
>
> "What do you mean, 'No Sweat?' Don't you see the waves rushing in to shore, getting smashed on the rocks and disappearing? 'No Sweat!'
>
> What do you mean, 'No Sweat?' Don't you know that's what's going to happen to us? We're going to rush into shore, get smashed on the rocks, and disappear."
>
> "No sweat! We are the ocean."
>
> Two waves racing across the Pacific. They look exactly alike. But one wave was just a wave. The other wave had already become ocean while he was still a wave. How? By insight into his true nature. What do I want to do before I die? I want to become ocean while I am still a wave—by insight into my true nature.[18]

One way of reading this story: However imperfectly, before I die—and especially in the hour of death—I want to entrust myself to the Mystery in which I and all things abide. While still a wave, I want to move freely and trustingly with the ocean of Mystery that sustains

---

[17] Wendell Berry, "The Pleasures of Eating," in *What Are People For?* (Berkeley, CA: Counterpoint, 2010), 152.

[18] Dickson Yagi, in *The Dialogue Comes of Age*, ed. John Cobb and Ward McAfee (Minneapolis: Fortress Press, 2010), 164. This is Yagi's particular version of this story, but it seems to have appeared in numerous versions and places.

and moves within me. This is achieved, the story says, by *insight into our true nature*. What does that mean? One interpretation, I suppose, could be that my existence as a distinct wave is an illusion: I *am* the ocean in which I will apparently disappear as I crash into the rocks. Let go this illusion of separateness and "No sweat."

I understand it differently: My real and distinct being exists by the grace of a plenitude that transcends me yet bears me up from within and draws me forward toward union. I am not myself this plenitude, but my being is a participation in it. The illusion of separateness, then, is the illusion of complete autonomy from within oneself instead of as gift from beyond oneself. Ernest Becker dubbed this illusion the *causa sui* project, the desire to be completely self-causing, to be one's own creator, one's own god. He offered this analysis as a revised reading of Freud's Oedipal project: to be author or father of oneself, to stand aloof from any dependency, not because of the sex drive, but out of fear of one's creatureliness and mortality. "The prison of one's own character is painstakingly built to deny one thing and one thing alone: one's creatureliness. The creatureliness is the terror."[19]

The story of the two waves suggests, however, that there can be *insight into our true nature* that brings not terror but wonderment and peace. Thich Nhat Hanh writes, "When the wave knows that its ground of being is water, it overcomes all fear and sorrow. The moment we surrender our entire being to God, all of our fears vanish."[20] Christian spirituality has words for this kind of insight. First, *purification*: liberation from the illusory self, from the attempt to be one's own creator or god, whether this is formulated theoretically or lived out practically. Dorothee Sölle wrote about the positive side of this, namely, the recovery of "radical amazement" or wonder. Purification recovers our true nature (or better, our graced nature) by removing blinders from our eyes, so that we may experience the mysterious goodness and giftedness of creation.[21] Second, *enlightenment* or *illumination*: initial wonder, opened up by purification, brings clarity and truth. Dying to the false self opens a way to a truer self, a self

[19] Becker, *Denial*, 87.

[20] In his introduction to Thomas Merton, *Contemplative Prayer* (New York: Random House, 1996), xii.

[21] Dorothee Sölle, *The Silent Cry: Mysticism and Resistance*, trans. Barbara and Martin Rumschiedt (Minneapolis: Fortress Press, 2001), 88–93.

both autonomous *and* dependent on others and the Holy Mystery. Finally, *union*: communion with the Mystery in which all things abide, a communion embracing other persons and creation as well. Now, hidden, as it were, in every step of this process, is the summons to move with the life of God moving within us. This *insight into our true nature* is not simply self-produced. It is God's movement within us, impelling us toward purification, illumination, and union. Jean Vanier writes, "Holiness does not come as we stretch out towards God, but as we welcome the Holy One who comes to dwell in us."[22]

All of this reaches articulate expression in liturgical spirituality. Those undergoing the rite of initiation at the Easter Vigil pass through stages of purification and enlightenment on their way toward union with the ecclesial and sacramental Body of Christ. Everyone who acknowledges rather than hides from their createdness must confront mortality. But those who learn to trust rather than fear or resent the Mystery are like the Wave that keeps saying, "No sweat," because in death they see more than death. They see the dying and rising of Jesus. Reflecting on how the practice of centering prayer is a kind of rehearsal for our own death, Cynthia Bourgeault writes, "Something has held us and carried us. And this same something, we gradually come to trust, will hold and carry us at the hour of our death. To know this—really *know* this—is the beginning of the resurrection life."[23]

The paschal mystery of Christ's *kenosis* or self-emptying teaches us two great renunciations. The first renunciation is captured in John's gospel when Jesus says, "I can do nothing on my own" (John 5:30; NRSV). It is also enacted in Matthew and Luke when Jesus rebuffs the tempter in the desert (Matt 4:1-11; Luke 4:1-13). In both cases Jesus, true God and true human being, renounces the temptation to be god *in place of God*. He comes to do the will of the One who sent him, not to replace it with his own. In effect, he renounces the *causa sui* project. In a similar vein, Thomas Merton wrote of "the renunciation of all deluded images of ourselves, all exaggerated estimates of

---

[22] Jean Vanier, *Drawn into the Mystery of Jesus* (Ottawa: Novalis, 2004), quoted in *Give Us This Day* (May 2017): 290.

[23] Cynthia Bourgeault, *Centering Prayer and Inner Awakening* (Lanham, MD: Cowley Publications, 2004), 81.

our own capacities, in order to obey God's will as it comes to us."[24]
And this brings us to the second great Christic renunciation. Louis-
Marie Chauvet describes it as "consent to his *human 'autonomy,'* and
thus the rejection of the temptation to use God to unburden himself
of the full human responsibility he had to assume."[25] Doing God's
will freely rather than slavishly implies human autonomy and responsibility, which cannot be shirked in the name of dependence on
God. Such is the Christic pattern of spirituality for those who follow
Jesus. Our autonomy is not a solo performance but a duet with the
Mystery in which we live and move and have our being. Performing
this duet requires recovering rather than hiding from a sense of our
createdness. And so what Chauvet says is true: "We do not come to
ourselves if we do not renounce ourselves and thus abandon the attempt to found ourselves on ourselves."[26]

---

[24] Merton, *Contemplative Prayer*, xiii.

[25] Louis-Marie Chauvet, *Symbol and Sacrament: A Sacramental Reinterpretation of Christian Existence*, trans. Patrick Madigan and Madeleine Beaumont (Collegeville, MN: Liturgical Press, 1995), 301.

[26] Ibid.

Chapter 3

Behind and Before, You Besiege Me:
The Mystery Comes Near

"God loved us first," says John. That first loving is God's making
love our climate, in which we find ourselves, come to ourselves,
and then obscurely sense the infinite unknown as the soul's beloved.

Sebastian Moore[1]

Moving within the Climate of Love

Let us now return to Psalm 139. While this psalm expresses God
as Creator encompassing us on all sides, it expresses much more:
"you search me and you know me . . . Behind and before you besiege
me . . . your hand ever laid upon me." Beyond the closeness of the
Creator to the creature, an even greater intimacy is possible and meant
by *the life of God moving within us*. The experience of our createdness
is taken up into a greater one. The God in whom we live and move
and have our being seeks us out: "you besiege me." To recall earlier
language, that reality lying in the depths of our lives like an undertow
is not only the primal experience of being held in being but also of
being held by "the Love that moves the sun and the stars."

But like a wheel in perfect balance turning,
I felt my will and my desire impelled
by the Love that moves the sun and the other stars.[2]

---

[1] Sebastian Moore, *The Fire and the Rose are One* (New York: Seabury Press, 1980), 20.
[2] Dante, *The Divine Comedy*, vol. 3: *Paradise*, trans. Mark Musa (New York: Penguin
Books, 1986), 394 (Canto 33, lines 143–45).

Spirituality is *moving with the life of God moving within us*, but now this is moving within the circle of gratuitous love, God's love for us and our responsive love for God. "Creation," Pope Francis says, "is of the order of love. God's love is the fundamental moving force in all created things." He prefaces this sentence with a profound psychological insight: "The universe did not emerge as the result of arbitrary omnipotence, a show of force or a desire for self-assertion."[3] Narcissistic self-assertion, domination over others, imposing human ideologies by grotesque murderous force—these all too human "values" are polar opposites to God's creating and upholding of all things in love. In Julian of Norwich's vision of God's "familiar love," creation is seen as a tiny hazelnut compared to the Creator. "I wondered how it could last," she says, "for it was so small I thought it might suddenly have disappeared. And the answer in my mind was, 'It lasts and will last for ever because God loves it; and everything exists in the same way by the love of God.'"[4] Abraham Heschel writes, "There is a care that hovers over Being. . . . Being would cease to be were it not for God's care of Being."[5]

Now love is above all the giving of oneself. This is not a military siege. God besieges us the way a lover besieges the beloved. Julian captures this succinctly: "God's good wish is to have us."[6] This is "deep calling unto deep" as Psalm 42 says, freedom calling unto freedom. So God's self-offer is not subsequent to creation but its very motive, as we pray in Eucharistic Prayer IV: "you . . . have made all that is, so that you might fill your creatures with blessings." The blessing, ultimately, is sharing in God's life. The response of the beloved is the free return-gift of oneself, that is, *moving with the life of God moving within us.*

Jesus speaks of this mutual indwelling, expressing the deepest possibilities of the self in freedom, in John's gospel. He prays that all who come to believe may be one "as you, Father, are in me and I in

---

[3] On Care for Our Common Home, *Laudato Si'*, Encyclical Letter of the Holy Father Francis (Washington, DC: United States Conference of Catholic Bishops, 2015), par. 77.

[4] Julian of Norwich, *Revelations of Divine Love*, trans. Elizabeth Spearing (New York: Penguin, 1998), 47 (Long Text, 5).

[5] Abraham J. Heschel, *Who Is Man* (Stanford, CA: Stanford University Press, 1965), 92.

[6] Julian, *Revelations*, 50 (Long Text, 6).

you" (John 17:23). Or, when conversing with Nicodemus, Jesus says, "no one can see the kingdom of God without being born from above" (John 3:3). To be *born from above*—this seems to mean living our lives from God instead of merely from ourselves. God is the Life of our life rather than our ego, our tribe, our work, our possessions, our status. In so many ways we continually backslide into these "less than God" realities—all well and good in themselves—but not so good if we turn them into ultimates.

"Grace" is the theological word for *God's good wish to have us.* "Grace," Karl Rahner says, "is the nearness of the *abiding* mystery."[7] God's self-offer is both the motive and the fulfillment of our being: "From the outset God is lovingly seeking in freedom to bestow himself, and because he so wills in freedom, because he wills grace, he must create a 'nature' to which he can impart himself as free love. Nature is, because grace has to be."[8] If we ask when and where this offer of shared life happens—God living in us, us living in God—the short answer is *always and everywhere.* As the motive for creation, God's self-offer accompanies all of creation and history and is ever-present, already shaping one's existence, awaiting a free human response. Rahner uses the term "self-communication" to describe the nearness of the abiding Mystery offering itself:

> When we speak of God's self-communication, we should not understand this term in the sense that God would say something *about* himself in some revelation or other. The term "self-communication" is really intended to signify that God in his own most proper reality makes himself the innermost constitutive element of the human person.[9]

Something that is gift radicalizes and magnetizes our nature from the center outward. That is the meaning of the remarkable phrase that God's self-communication is "the innermost constitutive element of the human person." So we must amend all our previous reflections

---

[7] Karl Rahner, "The Concept of Mystery in Catholic Theology," trans. Kevin Smyth, *Theological Investigations*, vol. 4 (New York: Seabury Press, 1974), 56.

[8] Karl Rahner, "On the Theology of Worship," trans. Edward Quinn, *Theological Investigations*, vol. 19 (New York: Crossroad, 1983), 143.

[9] Karl Rahner, *Foundations of Christian Faith*, trans. William V. Dych (New York: Seabury Press, 1978), 116.

on experiencing our createdness. For we never in fact experience our createdness in isolation from God's loving self-communication. God's self-offer is freely given in the very act of creating us. However dimly recognized, interior to the experience of our givenness is the experience of being the object of God's love. When we retrieve the felt sense of our createdness in reflection, meditation, and prayer, we head into "God loved us first" territory. In the quotation heading this chapter, Sebastian Moore describes this as "God's making love our climate, in which we find ourselves, come to ourselves, and then obscurely sense the infinite unknown as the soul's beloved."

Earlier, we heard Thomas Merton speak of a real experience of the Giver at the point where one's being is dependent on God, which he called the apex of one's being. Elsewhere he calls it the center of one's being. But he qualifies this by saying "it is the point where my contingent being depends upon His love."[10] That word, "love," means God's offer of self-bestowal or simply grace. To recover the center of our being in its dependence, its createdness, is to encounter the Love that made us and wishes to impart itself to us. "We only know Him," Merton says, "in so far as we are known by Him."[11]

Mediated Immediacy

The paradox of Psalm 139 is this innermost accompaniment of God who is "too high, beyond my reach." This accompaniment is not any less intimate for being mediated by the ordinary things of life. In the psalmist's experience of *having a self—in relation to others—within a reach toward the whole of reality*, it is the otherness of nature that most obviously paradoxically mediates the immediacy of God. Through the heavens, the grave, the sea's furthest end, the light, and the darkness of night, "you, God, are there." God, who is not the heavens, the sea, the light, and the darkness, is present here and now through them. They are not signs of an absent and elsewhere reality but one that is intimately present. That is the paradox of mediated immediacy.[12] But

---

[10] Thomas Merton, *New Seeds of Contemplation* (New York: New Directions, 2007), 37.

[11] Ibid., 39.

[12] Rahner, *Foundations*, 83–84.

the mediating factor may veer more toward the subjective, self-aware pole of this complex. We experience not only that our being is given but that the Mystery touches the deepest part of the self. The very root of the psalmist's subjectivity, that which knows, loves, wills (rather than that which is known, loved, willed), becomes that through which the God who besieges is disclosed: "Before ever a word is on my tongue, O Lord, you know it through and through." This is God as "the innermost constitutive element" of the human person, as we heard Rahner say.

Whether the experience leans more toward the objective pole of consciousness (the things we attend to) or the subjective pole (our self-aware act of attending), it is a matter of mediated immediacy. Through one reality another reality is rendered immediately present.

To understand this notion of mediated immediacy, consider interpersonal relationships. You can't see another person's consciousness directly, but you do experience the other's interiority immediately through the mediation of the body—in gestures, facial expressions, words spoken, deeds done. The body as mediator, though distinct from the spirit, is the *being-forth* or *self-expression* of the spirit. As we saw in chapter 1, every finite thing we know, love, or will mediates to us our transcending reach beyond these objects toward the Infinite Horizon. If we now conceive of this Infinite Horizon as granting and upholding this transcending reach and, beyond this, drawing near as self-bestowing Love, then, whether we attend to it or not, every finite thing we know, love, and will, including ourselves, can mediate the "in every moment" immediacy of Transcendent Love. As noted in chapter 1, Aquinas says, "All knowing beings implicitly know God in any- and everything that they know."[13]

C. S. Lewis recounts several peak experiences of this type from his childhood, saying, "The central story of my life is about nothing else."[14] These were experiences of intense piercing desire, suddenly and surprisingly triggered by particular objects such as nature, romantic poetry, and music. They opened up "something quite different from ordinary life and even from ordinary pleasure; something, as

---

[13] Aquinas, *On Truth (De Veritate)* q. 22, a. 2, ad. 1.
[14] C. S. Lewis, *Surprised by Joy: The Shape of My Early Life* (New York: Houghton Mifflin Harcourt, 2012), 17.

they would now say, 'in another dimension.' " And yet this something "was not *in* them; it only came *through* them, and what came through them was longing. . . . They are not the thing itself; they are only the scent of a flower we have not found, the echo of a tune we have not heard, news from a country we have never yet visited."[15]

Lewis's imagery is fascinating in more ways than one. First, it captures the paradoxical nature of this awareness—experiencing something that transcends our experience. "We cannot tell it because it is a desire for something that has never actually appeared in our experience. We cannot hide it because our experience is constantly suggesting it."[16] This is clearly an example of mediated immediacy. Second, the *something more* disclosed through the finite object is not a further, graspable object but rather points back to a dynamism within ourselves reaching forward through and beyond any finite object of experience: "what came through them was longing." The locus of the heightening in this case is the heart's desire, so that we are made restless for more being than any finite being is, for something in another dimension. This is Augustine's restless heart. This is Psalm 42's "deep calls to deep," the depth of divine Love calling unto the depths of the human heart. The psalmist's heart answers, even from a place of distress: "As the deer longs for streams of water, so my soul longs for you, O God."

In a remarkable paper, Bill Moremen explores the spirituality of racewalking, especially the altered state of "being in the zone." Here, I think, we have another example of mediated immediacy. Through all the specifics of sustained training, disciplined activity, and highly focused attention to detail, there can arise in the act of racewalking an experience of transcending one's limits, merging with the "whole," opening toward the ground of being. While all the particulars one attends to seem to drop away in the moment of transcendence, it is not by bypassing them but by passing through them that one comes into this experience. Moremen says, "I think of walking in the zone as walking into the apophatic depth of God or in awareness of the kenotic nature of God emptying into each moment of creation.

---

[15] C. S. Lewis, "The Weight of Glory," in *The Weight of Glory and Other Addresses* (Grand Rapids, MI: Eerdmans Publishing Company, 1965), 4–5.

[16] Ibid.

Experiences of being in the zone are most often experienced as a gift or as a surprise."[17]

The racewalker's preparation and effort does not itself produce this heightened experience of transcendence. Not unlike Lewis's experiences, "being in the zone" comes as a gift, a surprise. One does not master and possess this Mystery but rather is possessed by it. Rahner's reflection, "On Movement," closely parallels Moremen's racewalking imagery. He says, "In the simplest act of movement—for acts presuppose knowledge and freedom—what it is to be human is in fact fully present, and we are faced with our own existence." He elaborates as follows:

> We exist as unending movement, conscious of itself and of its unfinishedness. . . . We move; we cannot but be seeking. But the Real and the Ultimate is coming to us, and seeking us out. . . . And when the time comes that we have found—found because we have been found—we will discover that our very coming-toward was already being carried (this is what we call grace) by the power of the movement that is coming upon us, by God's movement toward us.[18]

In such experiences a decentering occurs: my center of gravity is no longer my own ego but rather in my relation to what is given from beyond myself. My truest self and autonomy is precisely in this relation to another autonomy, another freedom that, far from diminishing me, heightens my being and self-possession. But especially in moments of "being in the zone" this heightened self-possession is, paradoxically, marked more by coming to rest than by striving, by union rather than seeking, by pure reception rather than grasping.[19]

---

[17] Bill Moremen, "In the Zone and Step by Step: A Theology of Racewalking and Other Walks of Life," unpublished paper delivered at Pilgrim Place, Claremont, California (2017), 5.

[18] *Karl Rahner: Spiritual Writings*, ed. Philip Endean (New York: Orbis Books, 2008), 55.

[19] Such anticipations of ultimate union coincide well with Aquinas's understanding of the beatific vision. In the vision, we do not by conscious striving and activity "take God in." Rather, God takes us in. Our freedom, desire, and knowledge are not erased but so elevated and fulfilled by the Holy Mystery that we come to rest. See *Summa Contra Gentiles*, chapter 51, where Aquinas says God is not only the object but the *medium* of the vision; also, *Summa Theologiae*, 2a-2ae, q. 27, art. 3, where Aquinas, quoting Matthew 25:21, says *not that a person grasps this joy, but rather enters into it.*

Shaped by Love for Love

One may discern in this gift character not just the gift of *being* but of *being borne* by a Love that seeks us out. Nothing frees us from our self-absorption more powerfully than being loved by another. Nothing that we can do for ourselves is a substitute for how expansively another's love makes us grow. So, across the spectrum of finite things and events mediating the approach of God toward us in love, it is above all through other persons and communities that this experience touches our lives.

Jesuit Gregory Boyle's book *Tattoos on the Heart* brims over with such examples. There is simply no way of summarizing this remarkable book in a few paragraphs (message to reader: read this book!). But quoting the poet Galway Kinnell, Boyle gives us the key to his work with former gang members. The poet says: "Sometimes it's necessary to reteach a thing its loveliness."[20] There is a very practical side to learning one's loveliness—acquiring skills, receiving counseling, getting a high school diploma, going to college, getting a job—all things that Homeboy Industries provides. But at the heart of all of this is a deeper dimension of reteaching a person his or her loveliness. Gregory Boyle says, "As misshapen as we feel ourselves to be, attention from another reminds us of our true shape in God."[21] The gang life is both a haven and a hothouse of the misshapen life. This is the life of mostly absent or abusive fathers (and sometimes mothers), of children whose parents are already gang members, of us versus them, of "We are the guys who hate those guys," of drive-by shootings, of early deaths and inconsolable mothers.[22]

How does a gang member move out of such misshapenness into a newly shaped life? How does one find the resilience to make this move and stick with it, despite apparently overwhelming obstacles? Transformation seems to involve a twofold realization. First, persons need to be retaught their loveliness, something that happens both person-to-person and in the context of communal affirmation. "What is the delivery system for resilience?" Boyle asks. "In part, it's the

---

[20] Gregory Boyle, *Tattoos on the Heart: The Power of Boundless Compassion* (New York: Free Press, 2010), 87.

[21] Ibid., 55.

[22] Ibid., 130.

loving, caring adult who pays attention. It's the community of un-
conditional love, representing the very 'no matter whatness' of
God."[23] Second, this discovery of one's goodness and loveliness—
really seeing oneself through God's eyes—opens the reconfigured
heart to compassion for others. A profound experience of kinship
replaces the us-versus-them groupthink of gang life. Gustavo
Gutiérrez writes, "God loves us first (1 John 4:19). Everything starts
from there. The gift of God's love is the source of our being and puts
its impress on our lives. We have been made by love and for love.
Only by loving, then, can we fulfill ourselves as persons; that is how
we respond to the initiative taken by God's love."[24]

This love of God, ever offering itself, is mediated through persons
and communities. That is what the Homeboy network and other
communities of compassion do. This is the job description of the
church. In fact, God's approach as Love is what opens up such possibilities of mediated transformation. Against all that demeans the
human person, all the individual and collective ways that we harm
and demonize each other, there is the healing countermovement and
resistance of God who is love: "If we choose to stand in the right
place, God, through us, creates a community of resistance," Boyle
says.[25] Further, "God is compassionate loving kindness. All we're
asked to do is to be in the world who God is. Certainly compassion
was the wallpaper of Jesus' soul, the contour of his heart, it was who
he was. . . . This was how Jesus was moved, from the entirety of
his being."[26]

Why does the human heart resonate so deeply with such experiences? Why does whatever responsive contribution we make feel like
rhyming with something beyond ourselves? In the more traditional
language of Ignatius's spiritual exercises, "It belongs to the Creator
to go in and come out and cause a movement in the soul."[27] Commenting on this passage, Rahner says, "It is that coming and going

---

[23] Ibid., 86–87.

[24] Gustavo Gutiérrez, *We Drink from Our Own Wells*, trans. Matthew J. O'Connell
(New York: Orbis Books, 2010), 109–10.

[25] Ibid., 177.

[26] Ibid., 62–63.

[27] Karl Rahner, *The Dynamic Element of the Church* (New York: Herder and Herder,
1964), 142.

in which God himself as such is given (and nothing else), and that movement in which the soul is 'wholly' drawn to the love of God."[28] Spirituality as *moving with the life of God moving within us* is a matter of keeping vigil, of attending and responding to these comings and goings. Like the daily regimen of the racewalker, daily practices of prayer and meditation, culminating in and flowing from Sunday liturgy, prepare us to explicitly receive and embrace God's self-communication through various mediations: the events of everyday life, the gathered Body of the church, the minister, the Word, the Bread and Cup, and the sending forth to build kinship with one's neighbor. To anticipate what will be addressed later, these examples of mediated immediacy are another way of speaking about sacramentality.

The decentering surprise and gift character of God's self-communication is uppermost in W. H. Auden's account of a summer evening in 1933. He was sitting on a lawn with several colleagues. They were not intimate friends, just acquaintances:

> We were talking casually about everyday matters, when, quite suddenly and unexpectedly, something happened. I felt myself invaded by a power which, though I consented to it, was irresistible and certainly not mine. For the first time in my life I knew exactly—because thanks to the power I was doing it—what it means to love one's neighbor as oneself.[29]

Auden's consent to this experience illustrates the partnership of divine and human freedom in the grace relationship. There is God's wish to impart divine life to us in terms of offer or invitation, and our free response in terms of acceptance or rejection, or perhaps a conflicted combination of both. One thing to notice in all of these examples, however, is that the offer of self and relationship changes the situation of the addressee, even before any response. The approach of the other in the offer is now part of one's consciousness and opens up a new situation for one's freedom: do I accept or reject this offer? This awareness and choice is not of my own making; it is indebted to the approach of the other. This gratuitous offer has

---

[28] Ibid., 143.

[29] Alexander McCall Smith, *What W. H. Auden Can Do for You* (Princeton, NJ: Princeton University Press, 2013), 81.

changed the situation of my existence. This is what it means to say that God's gracious self-offer shapes human existence.[30]

 Imagine that you have been invited to someone's home for a festive meal. The possibility of sharing in the meal and life of this person is now a factor in your self-awareness and freedom. You may say yes or no, you may go or not go, but with respect to the person who has issued the invitation, you have a relationship that you did not previously have. A kindness has already been extended toward you. Your knowing-loving-willing capacities now exist within a new horizon of possibilities.

In this way, Rahner holds that God's self-offer to humanity or, in other words, God's grace-as-offer, coming before any human response, already changes the situation of our existence. To use Kierkegaard's language, we have a different and new inwardness evoked by God's approach, which is more than God's act of holding us in existence. We exist by God's gift, but more than that: we exist *as invited to communion with God*. Depending on how we actually respond to this invitation, we live either in acceptance or rejection of the friendship offered. If we go to the festive meal, we begin to actually share in the life of our host.

Like the air we breathe, it may be taken for granted. God's self-offer, not an afterthought to creation, but its very motive, is always there, surrounding us. We don't give it a thought. Nonawareness does not mean, however, that the invitation is not a real ongoing factor shaping the quality of one's life. A baby can be surrounded by love from birth and yet only gradually become aware of how it has been carried and shaped all along by such love. With growing awareness, the child can make a return of love.

Often, consciousness-expanding experiences do not mean the arrival of something utterly new in our lives but rather recognition of something that has been true all along. The newness or change is in us because we now have a depth of awareness we did not previously have. Sometimes the change is quite dramatic. "Then who can explain this next moment," Boyle says, "when the utter fullness of God rushes in on you—when you completely know the One in whom

---

[30] Rahner's term for this shaping is the "supernatural existential," meaning that our existence is modified by the supernatural offer of sharing in God's life, culminating in the beatific vision. See *Foundations*, 126–33.

'you move and live and have your being,' as St. Paul writes. You see, then, that it has been God's joy to love you all along. And this is completely new."[31]

Spirituality, especially liturgical spirituality, takes us from inattentive forgetfulness to articulate naming and acknowledgment, even if such naming is directed to what is ultimately nameless. Having explicitly owned this truth, we become more fully self-possessed participants in the circle of gracious love—God's love for us and our return-gift of love for God and neighbor.[32] Being in love comes into its own only when lovers engage in rituals of naming and acknowledging their love to each other. It is only in saying, "You are my only one—I give myself to you," that love really lives. Transposed into theological terms, God's self-offer accompanies us from the beginning, shaping our experience, and such experience is intensified and more fully actualized insofar as we welcome and grow in awareness of it. We play our part, actualize a free response, "make a return," as Psalm 116 says: "I will lift up the cup of salvation and call on the name of the LORD" (v. 13; NRSV). In the spiritual disciplines of prayer, meditation, and the liturgy, culminating in service to our sisters and brothers, we open ourselves to the life of God moving within us. We overcome our congenital forgetfulness of that which is closer to us than we are to ourselves and explicitly actualize a return of love. Bernard Lonergan expresses it this way:

> There is in the world, as it were, a charged field of love and meaning; here and there it reaches a notable intensity; but it is ever unobtrusive, hidden, inviting each one of us to join. And join we must if we are to perceive it, for perceiving is through our own loving.[33]

Both Boyle and Auden describe their experiences of being besieged by agapic Love in the language of the Gospel. Each in his own context knows what it means to love one's neighbor as oneself. In other words, it is in Christ that the meaning of our createdness and being

---

[31] Boyle, *Tattoos*, 25.

[32] The expression "return-gift" is borrowed from Louis-Marie Chauvet. In chapters 8 and 9, I treat it in detail.

[33] Bernard Lonergan, *Method in Theology* (New York: Herder and Herder, 1972), 290.

approached by Love comes fully out into the open. Our own articulate naming, acknowledgment of, and response to this Love, both in and beyond the liturgy, is made possible by God's Incarnate Word, embodying, mediating, articulating God's way with us in an earthly time and place. Not only that—in his true humanity, Jesus expresses our response to God's way with us. The path for spirituality begins to emerge: Jesus enacts God's way with us and enacts human response in self-emptying love or kenosis. Our spirituality, our *moving with the life of God moving within us* must then be moving in and with the self-emptying of Jesus. And to the Mystery of Jesus, God's kenotic way and our kenotic response, we now turn.

Chapter 4

Before the Mystery of the Incarnation

For in him all the fullness of God was pleased to dwell,
and through him God was pleased to reconcile to himself
all things, whether on earth or in heaven, by making peace
through the blood of his cross.

Colossians 1:19-20, NRSV

God's descent into the flesh will explain to us the secret and
blessed meaning of our all-transcending spirit. . . . God's distance
is but the incomprehensibility of his all-penetrating nearness.

Karl Rahner[1]

Kierkegaard once said that the miracle of creation is "not the creation of something which is nothing over against the Creator, but the creation of something which is something."[2] This goes against our normal habit of thought: the more one thing is dependent on another, the less it has a reality and autonomy of its own. This is true of many causal relationships within nature. And so, since the creature is utterly dependent in every moment on the Creator for its very being, we assume it should follow the same rule. But the opposite is true in the Creator-creature relationship. "We and the existents of our world," Karl Rahner says, "really and truly are and are different from God not in spite of, but because we are established in being by God and

---

[1] Karl Rahner, "The Little Word God," in *Grace in Freedom*, trans. Hilda Graef (New York: Herder and Herder, 1969), 200.

[2] Soren Kierkegaard, *Concluding Unscientific Postscript*, trans. David of Swenson and Walter Lowrie (Princeton, NJ: Princeton University Press, 1941, 1968), 220.

not by anyone else."[3] Only God as Creator can "cause to be" something other than God and, while continually upholding it, set it free in its own autonomy.[4] In the previous chapter, we have seen that at the level of love, there is a nearness of one to another which, rather than limiting freedom, opens up its deepest most genuine possibilities. The capacity for individuation and community go hand in hand. Above all, this is true of the Creator-creature relationship. We have seen this dynamic at work in our createdness, our being given to ourselves in every moment out of the holy Mystery that transcends us. Our very being as personal, autonomous subjects is established and carried by the horizon of Infinite Mystery, which enables all our acts of knowing, loving, and willing. Yet these are our acts, our very personhood in action.

But we have also seen that this gift of creaturely autonomy belongs to a deeper gift. Creation is of the order of love and grace. Creation *is* so that the grace of love and communion *can be*. Creation is within, not before, God's will to bestow God's self on us. In Christ, Ephesians 1:4 says, we were chosen "before the foundation of the world" and destined to become children of God. Gustavo Gutiérrez cites this passage to underscore the point that God's gratuitous self-bestowal in love "is a gift we receive before we exist, or, to be more accurate, a gift in view of which we have been created."[5] So the human creature, continually established and sustained by Infinite Mystery, has always been enfolded in the approach of this Mystery as gracious self-bestowing love. This self-communicating nearness of God, even in the mode of offer, radicalizes our freedom and autonomy as creatures. What God sustains "in every moment" of creating us is not simply the capacity to exist consciously and freely, but the more profound inwardness and possibility of reaching out in love to the Love that approaches. Or not! "This love," Elizabeth Johnson says, "experienced as the ground of our being, is nothing other than the gift of God's own self. It is freely offered to everyone without exception as light and the promise of life, and becomes visible in history wherever love of neighbor, faithfulness to conscience, courage for

---

[3] Karl Rahner, *Foundations of Christian Faith*, trans. William V. Dych (New York: Seabury Press, 1978), 79.

[4] Ibid.

[5] Gustavo Gutiérrez, *We Drink from Our Own Wells*, trans. Matthew J. O'Connell (New York: Orbis, 2010), 110.

resistance to evil, and any other human witness to what is 'more' takes place."[6]

In Him the Fullness of God Was Pleased to Dwell

In light of this we can begin to understand the incarnation in a genuinely theological way. God's creation of and gracious self-bestowal on genuinely autonomous human creatures is a lesser instance of a still higher possibility. God can cause to be a creature genuinely other than God, who is so infused with God's self-communication as to also be God. The experiential correlative of this is unique to Jesus. It is the experience of being continually given to oneself so intimately and lovingly out of the holy Mystery that one's humanity belongs to this Mystery as its own self-expression. "The Word became flesh and lived among us" (John 1:14; NRSV). This humanity is the very humanity of God, God with us, truly God, truly human. And so, in Eucharistic Prayer IV of the Roman Rite we pray:

> in the fullness of time
> you sent your Only Begotten Son to be our Savior.
> Made incarnate by the Holy Spirit
> and born of the Virgin Mary,
> he shared our human nature
> in all things but sin.

Consider, then, three imaginings: how Jesus is like us, how he is unlike us, and, finally, how we might begin to understand the knowledge and self-consciousness of Christ. All three "imaginings" are fingers pointing to the moon, faith seeking understanding of the mystery of God's presence in Jesus. Scripture invites us to make these imaginings, as does the Council of Chalcedon in its "One Person, Two Natures" formula.[7] These imaginings do not propose full comprehension but, in the manner of negative theology, keep us in

---

[6] Elizabeth Johnson, *Quest for the Living God: Mapping Frontiers in the Theology of God* (New York: Continuum, 2011), 41.

[7] Karl Rahner explores this Chalcedonian formula in depth in two essays: "Current Problems in Christology," in *Theological Investigations*, vol. 1, trans. Cornelius Ernst (New York: Seabury Press, 1974), 149–200; "Dogmatic Reflections on the Knowledge and Self-Consciousness of Christ," in *Theological Investigations*, vol. 5, trans. Karl-H. Kruger (New York: Seabury Press, 1966), 193–215.

the right neighborhood of this mystery. Tendencies to end up in the wrong neighborhood take two forms historically: overplaying the divinity so that Christ is no longer recognizably human or overplaying the humanity so that Christ is no longer recognizably divine.[8] To be in the right neighborhood means that Christ's divinity does not diminish or replace his humanity. At the same time, Christ's fully realized humanity truly belongs in a unique and unsurpassable way to God.

First Imagining: How Jesus Is Like Us

Because Jesus is truly human, we must imagine a likeness between his humanity and ours: "he shared our human nature in all things but sin." According to John's Prologue, not only Jesus' humanity but every human being is related to the Logos-Word. For all things came to be through the Word—the Word that was with God from the beginning and was God (John 1:1-3). A word is an utterance. The divine Word is God's self-utterance. To borrow a human analogy from Yves Congar, "We say ourselves to ourselves."[9] God's eternal saying of God's self is the divine Word or Logos, or Only Begotten. When God wishes to say (create) something that is *not* God, it is through the Word that *is* God that it comes to be and continually exists. Eucharistic Prayer II of the Roman Rite echoes this, speaking of Christ as "your Word through whom you made all things." To be a creature is to have one's being through the Word, the divine Logos. Not only human creatures but the whole of creation has being through the Word. Speaking of the "Gospel of Creation," Pope Francis cites Psalm 33: "By the word of the Lord the heavens were made."[10] Ilia Delio

---

[8] From the perspective of process theology, John B. Cobb Jr. plots in detail the emergence of the issue in chapters 8 and 9 of *Christ in a Pluralistic Age* (Eugene, OR: Wipf and Stock Publishers, 1998), 136–73. In one respect, on page 140, he reaches a conclusion similar to that of Rahner: the human selfhood of Jesus "is not lost by identifying with the Logos but perfected thereby."

[9] Yves Congar, *The Word and the Spirit*, trans. David Smith (San Francisco: Harper and Row, 1986), 10.

[10] *On Care for Our Common Home: Laudato Si'*, Encyclical Letter of the Holy Father Francis (Washington, DC: United States Conference of Catholic Bishops/Vatican City: Liberia Editrice Vaticana, 2015), par. 77.

gives beautiful expression to this: "Every leaf, cloud, fruit, animal, and person is an outward expression of the Word of God in love."[11]

But as we have seen, this dependence of creatures on God does not diminish but rather guarantees their real though finite autonomy. So too with the humanity of Christ in its unique dependence on and union with the Logos of God. The simultaneous unity of creatures with and distinction from the Creator is realized in the highest possible way in Jesus as true God and true human being.[12] From the standpoint of his humanness, his presence to self and to all he knows, loves, and wills is similar to that of every other human being. It occurs within a self-transcending reach toward Infinite Mystery, a reach that in every moment is created and borne by this same Mystery, through the divine Logos.

When Eucharistic Prayer IV says, "he shared our human nature in all things but sin," it is paraphrasing Hebrews 4:15. In Christ, Hebrews says, we have a high priest who, like us, "has similarly been tested in every way, yet without sin." Consider that word "tested" for a moment. It means that in his human freedom, Jesus faces and takes real decisions. He is tempted in the desert, tempted as we are. This is Jesus having to muster the resolution to go into danger— Jerusalem—even when his disciples try to dissuade him. If we are faithful to the *truly human* dimension of the incarnation, the sinlessness of Jesus cannot mean that he is simply and automatically "above it all." "The New Testament," says Dermot Lane, "never says that Jesus could not sin; it states rather that Jesus in fact did not sin. The sinlessness of Jesus, therefore, should be understood as the achievement of a rich response by the man Jesus to the gift of God's grace throughout his life."[13] Negatively put, in understanding how Jesus is like us, we must not imagine that in his human nature he is less free than we are. Positively put, we should imagine that he is the freest of human beings.

[11] Ilia Delio, *The Unbearable Wholeness of Being* (New York: Orbis Books, 2013), 121.

[12] Karl Rahner, "On the Theology of the Incarnation," in *Theological Investigations*, vol. 4, trans. Kevin Smyth (New York: Seabury Press, 1974), 109–10.

[13] Dermot Lane, *The Reality of Jesus* (New York: Paulist Press, 1975), 123.

Second Imagining: How Jesus Is Unlike Us

Insofar as Jesus is truly God, we must also imagine a difference between him and ourselves. Jesus' humanity, while having a truly human mode of consciousness and freedom, is unique because it belongs to God uniquely. God, source of our being, makes us "something rather than nothing," something real and free over against God. Similarly, the divine Logos, creating and supporting Christ's human reality in union with itself, makes it "something rather than nothing," something real and free in relation to the divinity. Rahner explains it this way: "Only a *divine* Person can possess as its own a freedom really distinct from itself in such a way that this freedom does not cease to be free even with regard to the divine Person."[14]

Now, because this unique "belonging to the Logos" is that of a truly human reality, it shares continuity with the rest of us who are not the incarnation of God. For in its very uniqueness it completes the trajectory of transcendence that belongs to every human person. From our side this is experienced as a movement toward union with the incomprehensible Mystery in every act of knowing, loving, and willing particular things and purposes in the world. And the Holy Mystery, which grounds this movement, has from the beginning radicalized it by moving toward us in self-bestowing love. Another way of expressing this is to say, with Augustine, that God is closer to us than we are to ourselves—most transcendent and yet most intimate to our being. By this closeness, Rahner says, God "is not a force competing with others in the world" but "the ground which establishes the world in its own reality. Consequently, it should be clear that God's closer proximity does not absorb the creature but makes it more independent."[15] In Jesus this closeness amounts to union, so much so that the humanity of Jesus, in all that he is, says, and does, is the expression of the Word of God, the revelation of God's presence. This expression comes not at the cost of his human knowing, loving, and willing, but through it. The basis and mysterious horizon of Jesus' human being and consciousness is the Logos of God. In Rahner's words, "When the Word becomes man, his hu-

[14] Rahner, "Current Problems," 162.
[15] Karl Rahner, *Encyclopedia of Theology: The Concise* Sacramentum Mundi, ed. Karl Rahner (New York: Seabury Press, 1975), 769–70.

manity is not prior. It is something that comes to be and is constituted in essence and existence when and insofar as the Logos empties himself."[16] This brings us to our third imagining: how to understand the knowledge and self-consciousness of Jesus.

Third Imagining: A Truly Human Self-Consciousness

Imagining the self-consciousness of Jesus sounds incredibly presumptuous. But we are not pretending to know the specific personality of Jesus. The only proper way to "know" Jesus in this way is through the Scriptures, meditation, personal and liturgical prayer, the sacramental life, and service to all for whom Jesus lived, died, and rose. It comes from being clothed in Christ (Gal 3:27), from "undergoing Christ" as Ronald Rolheiser says.[17] Were not their hearts burning as he spoke to them on the way? Was he not made known to them in the breaking of the bread (Luke 24:32-35)?

Through all of these mediations, which also come to expression in the liturgy, the Risen One speaks to us and accompanies us here and now. But in this third imagining we are only trying to describe minimally what a truly human consciousness must be like if it also belongs to God as God's humanity. In doing so we are trying to move beyond a typical misunderstanding of the "One Person, Two Natures" formula of Chalcedon. It is a very understandable misunderstanding! This formula says that, in the union of the human and divine natures in the Person of the Logos, these natures exist without confusion and without separation. They are not mixed together to produce some new third reality. Specifically, as I said above, human knowing, loving, and willing are not displaced by divine omniscience and freedom. Needless to say, this is hard to imagine. And it is very easy to imagine it wrongly. We do this first by imagining the human nature of Jesus as a self-enclosed reality that is held in being by another self-enclosed reality, which is the divine Logos. They are united because they are "stuck together," unconfused because they are cordoned off from each other. Unintentionally, we are thinking in physical terms about spiritual realities—freedom, love, and knowledge.

---

[16] Rahner, "On the Theology of the Incarnation," 116.

[17] Ronald Rolheiser, *The Holy Longing: The Search for Christian Spirituality* (New York: Doubleday, 1999), 74.

This unintentional mode of thinking poses serious problems. If the divine Logos is really going to act and speak through the humanity of Jesus, and come out into the open of history, then it seems that the cordon must be removed and divine consciousness must override the human consciousness. While one gives a verbal bow to the human nature of Jesus, one is really imagining this humanity "like a puppet of the divine subject who alone would be active, although in the livery of man," as Rahner says.[18] In short, we understand the humanity of Jesus "as a thing and as an 'instrument' which is moved by the subjectivity of the Logos."[19] Not only does this not fit with the Jesus we know from Scripture, but it is also, according to church teaching, a heresy.[20] Again, this unconscious mode of thought results in a further problem. It makes room for the salvific activity of the Logos through the passive instrument of Jesus' humanity, but it does not make room for the agency and partnership of Jesus' humanity with the Logos in this activity. A truly human mediating role is removed from the man Jesus. The mediator is not the God-man but the God part of the God-man. The humanity, in this conception, does not actively mediate the divinity to us.

This, in turn, places a roadblock in the way of Christian spirituality. If Jesus' humanity is but a passive instrument, if his human knowing and willing are not actively engaged in doing the will of the One who sent him, it is hard to see how followers of Jesus can actively imitate him and participate in his reality as Mediator. How can we—both as church and as individuals—actively, intentionally, strive to move with the life of God moving within us if the human reality of Jesus did not actively do so? As the one who radically mediates this partnership with God to us, Christ must himself, as truly divine and truly human, be the fullest possible actualization of this partnership. Unconsciously, the idea persists that God's radical presence to Christ's humanity must somehow impede or limit his creaturely reality and consciousness. But, as we have already seen, "closeness to God and active independence of a creature increase in direct, not in inverse proportion. . . . Consequently, Christ's human nature is the most

---

[18] Rahner, *Foundations*, 249.
[19] Ibid., 287.
[20] Monotheletism: only one divine will operative in Christ.

independent, the freest and in the modern sense, the most 'personal' in its actual humanity."[21]

As soon as we realize that the human person is not a self-enclosed autonomous being but always exists as oriented toward and borne by its divine ground, then we move beyond this false way of thinking and its attendant difficulties. We can now make room for Jesus as truly and fully human, "who, standing before God on our side in free human obedience, is Mediator, not only in virtue of the ontological union of the two natures, but also through his activity, which is directed to God (as obedience to the will of the Father) and cannot be conceived of *simply* as God's activity in and through a human nature thought of as purely instrumental."[22] Rahner writes,

> the human nature of Jesus is a created, conscious and free reality to which there belongs a created "subjectivity" at least in the sense of a created will, a created *energeia*. This created subjectivity is distinct from the subjectivity of the Logos and faces God at a created distance in freedom, in obedience and in prayer, and it is not omniscient.[23]

On the face of it, attributing a created subjectivity or psychological personhood to Christ's humanity may seem to contradict Chalcedon's "One Person, Two Natures" formula. But affirming, as it certainly does, a human knowing and willing in Jesus, Chalcedon necessarily implies the possession of a human "I" in Jesus. The intention of this teaching, then, is not to exclude full reality from the humanity of Christ but to underscore that this reality in its truly human actualization really belongs to the Person of the Logos. Anything short of this lands us back into the heresy of Monothelitism, which proposed two natures but only one divine will operative in Jesus. In 1951 Pope Pius XII issued the encyclical *Sempiternus Rex*, which celebrates Chalcedon's accomplishment. In the initial draft of this document, it was recommended that he condemn as error the notion of a human psychological subject in Jesus. He refused to do so and removed such wording from the final form of the encyclical.[24]

---

[21] Rahner, *Encyclopedia of Theology*, 768.
[22] Rahner, "Current Problems," 161.
[23] Rahner, *Foundations*, 287.
[24] Rahner, "Current Problems," 159; Lane, *The Reality of Jesus*, 116.

Now if Jesus has a truly human self-consciousness, and yet in his depths "lives and moves and has his being" in the divine Logos, does this preclude development in Jesus' human knowledge or, in fact, require it? Humans grow in awareness of the world and themselves through time and experience. Parents and teachers witness the marvel by which young persons "come into their own," growing toward greater self-assurance and self-possession. Can we imagine such a growth "[in] wisdom and age and favor" in Jesus, as Luke 2:52 says? Can we imagine a growing awareness of his unique Sonship?

If we envision Jesus as omniscient from the womb, with perfect knowledge of his identity and mission as Son of God, then we are imagining only a divine, omniscient consciousness in him. If we imagine him, by human effort alone, being a bit more God-conscious than the rest of us, then we have forgotten that his humanity belongs to the Person of the Logos, the enabling horizon of his human being and consciousness.[25] If he has a unique experience of God, so much so that he is God's Word to us, it is because God is uniquely (compared to the rest of us) the ground of his being. This is where the analogy between our createdness and that of Jesus becomes helpful. God's ongoing creation of and approach to us in self-bestowing love is the innermost condition of our being and consciousness, though it remains a gift and something less than incarnation. The incarnation or union with the Logos means that God's ongoing creation of and self-bestowal on the humanity of Jesus is the innermost condition of his human reality. As we are only self-aware and other-aware insofar as we are also given over to the horizon of Holy Mystery, Jesus' knowing, loving, and willing come to him out of his being radically given over to the Logos.

Though in our depths we experience being continually given to ourselves from beyond ourselves, this experience can remain hidden just because it is so basic. It rises up into our conscious life to the extent that we recognize and freely own it rather than repressing it. We grow in awareness of having been created by and for Love as we grow in awareness of everything else through our lives. Analogously,

---

[25] This inadequate understanding of Jesus is what is meant by "consciousness Christology" in some forms of liberal Protestantism. By contrast, Rahner's "consciousness Christology" flows from and expresses ontological union with the Logos.

in the depths of his humanity, Jesus experiences himself and all else within his belonging to the Logos of God. But this experience comes more and more to the fore in his awareness over the course of his personal history. As he grows in age and wisdom and favor, he recognizes and owns the identity that has been his from the beginning. This is the meaning of Congar's phrase "we say ourselves to ourselves" or, as Rahner puts it, Jesus experiences a humanly recognizable "temporal process of translating his radical self-awareness into language through encounter with his open history."[26] Elsewhere Rahner writes, "He prays, he is obedient, he comes to be historically, he makes free decisions, and in a process of genuine historical development he also has new experiences which surprise him, and these are clearly in evidence in the New Testament."[27]

Jesus: God's Homily to Humanity

As truly divine, Jesus is God acting in history. As truly human, Jesus is humanity responding fully and unconflictedly—"sinlessly"—to God. And this brings us directly to our concern with spirituality. If spirituality is *moving with the life of God moving within us*, then Jesus is the highest actualization of a human life freely moving with the life of God within. The pattern of spirituality is Christic. It is the pattern of Jesus' being and life, in a specific historical time and place. As Elizabeth Johnson said above, wherever human persons respond to God's love in service to neighbor and fidelity to conscience, they "make visible" this God of love. Human mediations of this holy Mystery spring up all over this earth wherever human beings, addressed by God's gracious self-communication, welcome, interpret, and attempt to walk in the way of this Love. Despite human weakness, failure, greed, violence—in short, sin—such responses, enabled and carried by God's self-communication, are a yes to grace. They

---

[26] Rahner, *Encyclopedia of Theology*, 769.

[27] Rahner, *Foundations*, 292. Raymond Brown agrees with Rahner's assessment. After reviewing gospel passages that show limitations in Jesus' knowledge, Brown says that those who want to claim omniscience for Jesus "have a difficult task" and must explain away these passages in ways that are not credible. See Raymond E. Brown, *An Introduction to New Testament Christology* (New York: Paulist Press, 1994), 59.

are always mediated by spatial-temporal-historical events. The more explicitly aware we become that we are addressed and approached by the holy Mystery, the more explicitly religious we become. Our lives generate a religious self-understanding, a religious narrative, an explicit spirituality in response to God's self-communication.

This does not happen in isolation. When we respond according to our better angels, we usually understand this in the inherited categories supplied by familial, religious, philosophical, and cultural traditions. But it is also possible that our graced experience leads us to break with such categories or view them in a new way. In this dialectic between person and community, some respond to God's self-communication so profoundly that their lives generate a religious narrative for others. Their lives illustrate spiritual paths embodying transformation, compassion, mercy, and justice that become socially effective. These are spiritual-social embodiments of God's grace humanly interpreted and enacted. God's self-communication and the human response "takes place historically at ever definite points in time and space and from there it is addressed to others as a call to their freedom."[28]

In other words, persons responding profoundly to God's accompaniment become light for others. What happens to the "one" is meant for the "many." Their experience awakens "the holy longing"[29] that abides in persons and communities, evoked by God's gracious self-communication. It can be the experience of the prophets, or Buddha, or Francis of Assisi, or in our own time, that of a Gandhi, Mother Teresa, Oscar Romero, Nelson Mandela, or Dorothy Day. In other words, we have religions and spiritual traditions. We have prophets, religious and moral leaders, holy women and men, saints. But in Jesus, "making visible" the God of Love in a human life by *moving with the life of God within* comes to the fullest possible expression within history. For this narrative is not only a human one evoked by God's approach in gratuitous love. This narrative is written by God in the God-man Jesus. The human reality of Jesus, belonging to the divine Logos, mediates who God is for us uniquely because he belongs to God uniquely. In him, God's offer of self-communication

---

[28] Ibid., 193.
[29] The title of Rolheiser's book, cited earlier.

and the free human acceptance of it occurs "once for all," as Romans
6:10 says (NRSV).

Over the centuries, theologians have spoken of creation as a book
in which we may read the Creator's intention. The deepest intention
of creation is the successful partnership of God and humanity, historically manifested in the Word through whom all things were made
becoming flesh. Paul's Second Letter to Timothy speaks of God's
"own design and the grace bestowed on us in Christ Jesus before
time began, but now made manifest through the appearance of our
savior, Christ Jesus, who destroyed death and brought life" (2 Tim
1:9b-10). Christ, then, is God's own interpretation of the book's meaning and purpose. Christ is God's "homily" to humanity, as Oscar
Romero once said.[30] A good homilist, commenting on a text, opens
up its true meaning to the listeners. The Christ event, happening
within creation and history, opens up the meaning of the whole. To
put it another way, one may liken creation and history to a poem.
Christ, a word within that poem, crystallizes and discloses the meaning of the words coming before and after. Earlier I quoted Ilia Delio
partially in order to emphasize how creation is related to the Logos.
But to complete the picture, we may now quote her more fully, with
emphasis on the incarnate Logos:

> Because creation is centered on incarnation, every leaf, cloud, fruit,
> animal, and person is an outward expression of the Word of God in
> love. . . . As the motif or pattern of creation, Christ is the perfect
> divine-human-cosmic communion who exemplifies the meaning and
> purpose of all creation, namely, the praise and glory of God in a com-
> munion of love.[31]

Note that it is because Jesus *is* this communion that he *exemplifies*
it. Christ does not simply reveal history's intended goal. He does not
simply show what has been true all along—God's approach in self-
bestowing love. God's will to bestow God's self as our beatitude is
not only revealed but fully and successfully enacted by the yes of
Jesus' human freedom. It truly comes to pass. The promise of communion with God is accomplished "once for all" and now exists

---

[30] Oscar Romero, *The Violence of Love* (New York: Orbis Books, 1998), 182–83.
[31] Delio, *Unbearable Wholeness*, 121.

historically as God's irrevocable pledge calling to the freedom of all.[32] That this communion of love has the last word, despite all the harm humans do each other, is verified in the resurrection. This is not a glib *deus ex machina* consolation but one that comes at great cost, as Brian Wren's profound hymn text reminds us:

> God remembers pain, nail by nail, thorn by thorn,
> hunger, thirst, and muscles torn.
> Time may dull our griefs and heal our lesser wounds,
> but in eternal Love yesterday is now,
> and pain is in the heart of God.[33]

Highlighting the "for all" character of the paschal mystery, Wren's hymn text ends by paraphrasing Colossians 3:3: "Our lives are hid with Christ in God." In his death and resurrection, Christ takes all of us, including the whole creation, with him. "When the vessel of his body was shattered in death," Rahner says, "Christ was poured out over the whole cosmos."[34] In *Laudato Si'*, Pope Francis echoes this theme of the cosmic significance of Christ's death and resurrection: "Christ has taken unto himself this material world and now, risen, is intimately present to each being, surrounding it with affection and penetrating it with his light."[35] If being created means being related to the Logos of God, being re-created or redeemed means being related to the crucified and risen Christ who surrounds our being "with affection."

The self-emptying or kenosis of Jesus is not just about death but about new, transfigured life. Our lives are hidden with this Christ in God. This is the *alreadyness* of the kingdom. He is eternally the mediator of our relationship to the Holy Mystery, the mediator of who we are meant to be. And because of this, by the grace of his Spirit, we can, in the *not-yetness* of history, move with the life of God moving within us.

---

[32] Rahner, *Foundations*, 193.

[33] "God Remembers Pain." Words: Brian Wren. © 1993 Hope Publishing Company, Carol Stream, IL 60188. All rights reserved. Used by permission. Marty Haugen has set this text to a haunting melody, © 2003, GIA Publications, Inc.

[34] Karl Rahner, *On the Theology of Death*, 66.

[35] *Laudato Si'*, par. 221.

Transition to Part 2

To conclude this chapter and part 1, let us consider a series of statements that provide a bridge to part 2.

1. *Christian spirituality is Christic and, because Christic, trinitarian.* Because Christ belongs to God and to us, because in Christ this human-divine partnership is actualized "sinlessly" and "once for all," we say: In his paschal living, dying, and rising, and in the gift of the Spirit, Christ radically mediates God to us. That is why there is a specifically Christian spirituality. To *move with the life of God moving within us* means having our being in Christ. To do so is to receive his Spirit and live as sons and daughters of his Abba.

2. *Christian spirituality is kenotic.* As Philippians 2:5-12 says, Jesus moves with the life of God moving within him by self-emptying love for his Abba, humankind, and all creation. To move Christianly with the life of God moving within us is to participate in the self-emptying love of Christ. That is the discipline of Christian spirituality.

3. *Christian spirituality is ecclesial.* Dwelling in Christ means standing with him in his relationships—toward his and our Abba, other human beings, and all creation. It is an inherently communal endeavor, flowing from the fact that Christ gathers people to himself, making them coworkers. It finds expression in Jesus' prayer for his disciples, "that they may be one, as we are one, I in them and you in me" (John 17:22-23; NRSV). It follows that Christian spirituality is *ecclesial.* It is a mutual indwelling—Christ in us and we in him. So much so that we are members of his body. So much so that when one member suffers, all the members suffer with it, as Paul says, and when one member is honored all are honored with it (1 Cor 12:25-27). This is no "lone ranger" spirituality. Communion with the holy Mystery is also communion with neighbor. "Just as you did it to one of the least of these who are members of my family, you did it to me" (Matt 25:40; NRSV).

4. *Christian spirituality is liturgical.* Christ's paschal living, dying, and rising begets a narrative and a ritual for participation: "Do this in memory of me." By undergoing Christ as Word and as Feast we put on Christ and enter into his self-emptying love for God and the world. It is in fact only through the church and its liturgy that the Christian story has been carried forward in history and is available

for elaborations in other nonliturgical and nonecclesial contexts. And this leads us to our final point and the subtitle of this book.

5. *The liturgy is foundational for Christian spirituality.* Surely, it is Christ himself who is foundational for Christian spirituality. True, but this Christ is only mediated to history through the lived faith of his Body, the church. And this lived faith comes to its fullest, most participatory expression in the liturgy. To paraphrase Louis-Marie Chauvet, Christians gathering for worship have kept Christ's presence in the middle of the world by keeping his memory alive.[36] Everything else is tributary to this. Scripture scholars, theologians, ethicists, artists—all have a Christian content on which to exercise their craft thanks to the persistence of the worshiping community from age to age. The liturgy has been and continues to be the original and most potent delivery system of the Christian story. But this means that the liturgy is foundational for Christian spirituality. It is "source" and "summit."[37]

Of the Eucharist, Karl Rahner once wrote, "In this sacrament the enduring basis for our own Christian thought is constantly re-asserted and made tangibly present in symbol."[38] The conviction of this book is that in the liturgy as a whole the enduring basis for Christian spirituality is constantly reasserted and made tangibly present in symbol: in gathering as the Body of Christ, proclaiming and preaching the Word, praying the eucharistic prayer, receiving Communion, and being sent. Rahner's phrase, "tangibly present in symbol," applies both to Word (Liturgy of the Word) and Sacrament (Liturgy of the Eucharist). Though it is customary to distinguish them, they also partake of each other, because the risen Christ, present in and through each, unites them. Sacraments mediate the Word and the Word is

---

[36] Louis-Marie Chauvet, *The Sacraments: The Word of God at the Mercy of the Body,* trans. Madeleine Beaumont (Collegeville, MN: Liturgical Press, 2001), 137.

[37] Constitution on the Sacred Liturgy (*Sacrosanctum Concilium*) 10. All quotations of documents from the Second Vatican Council are taken from Austin Flannery, ed., *Vatican Council II: Constitutions, Decrees, Declarations; The Basic Sixteen Documents* (Collegeville, MN: Liturgical Press, 2014). The paragraph number is provided for each quotation.

[38] Karl Rahner, "The Eucharist and Our Daily Lives," in *Theological Investigations,* vol. 7, trans. David Bourke (New York: Seabury Press, 1977), 211.

sacramental. Through fragile, historically conditioned human words, the Word of God in Christ and the Spirit is truly communicated to us. The Word, therefore, is symbolic or sacramental: through a finite human reality the infinite mystery of God is truly present and communicated. On the other hand, the sacrament celebrated in the eucharistic prayer and Communion is *word-full*—it is the crystallization of the Word, as Louis-Marie Chauvet says.[39] Both modalities of the Word-made-flesh in our midst are foundational for Christian spirituality because they mediate the story and presence of the risen One from age to age.

Certainly, Christian spirituality may be encountered in other ways, religious but also secular, and this is all to the good. It may be encountered in literature, music, the visual arts, architecture. It may be encountered in dialogues with Buddhists (and other faiths), for whom the self-emptying of Jesus is of great interest. Whether explicitly named as such or not, the spirituality of Jesus' compassionate self-giving may be experienced in serving the poor, working for social justice, loving another person selflessly, raising children with great care and love. These less "churchy" but truly graced human performances of spirituality provide a healthy antidote to what is often an overly constricted viewpoint on the part of us who are "churched." The liturgy throws light on all of these "beyond liturgy" experiences. In turn, they throw light on how we understand what we are doing liturgically.

So, regarding Christian spirituality, the liturgy is not the only show in town. But historically, it is the show from which all the other shows are derived. Referring to Word and Eucharist as mediators of the Christian story, John Shea says they "are not secondary expressions upon the experience; they are the very embodiment of the experience. They are the privileged creations that carry the experience through time and history and make it available to each new generation."[40] To put this dynamic simply, gospel singers may enter the secular music industry and have great success there singing both religious and secular songs. But they learned to sing Gospel in church.

---

[39] Louis-Marie Chauvet, *Symbol and Sacrament*, trans. Patrick Madigan and Madeleine Beaumont (Collegeville, MN: Liturgical Press, 1995), 221–22.

[40] John Shea, *An Experience Named Spirit* (Chicago: Thomas More Press, 1983), 62–63.

For various reasons, many people today pursue their spiritual lives without institutional church involvement. If they remember the Christian story from their childhood, or meet fragments of it in other contexts, holding it in their hearts and practicing it in their dealings, they are holding something inherited from the church and its risen Lord. It would not be present for them without the ecclesial matrix Christ called into being and in which the Scriptures and sacraments were formed and passed on from age to age. Once again, the liturgy is foundational for Christian spirituality. It is where, in sacramental word and word-full sacrament, we explicitly tell the story and participate in the paschal mystery of Christ.

PART TWO

Exploring the Liturgical Script:
The Letter and the Spirit

Jesus' humanity is immersed in God. That is why his words and deeds mediate or communicate God to others. That is why his humanity is both Word and Sacrament of God. He is the unity underlying both, as the Emmaus story shows. Word and Sacrament immerse us in the risen One who is immersed in God. Another way of saying this: Christ's living, dying, and rising beget a narrative and a ritual for participation. Those initiated and gathered into such participation are made members of the Body of Christ, the church. The liturgy is preeminently where this church is immersed in the risen One, learning the narrative (Word) and sharing in the breaking of the bread (Sacrament). In this way, we become his word, his sacrament for others. So, once again, the liturgy is foundational for Christian spirituality, for moving with the life of God moving within us Christically.

Part 2, then, explores the letter and the spirit of the liturgy. Studying the letter means learning the script, becoming more reflective and intentional about the texts and actions we enact in worship. Discovering the spirit means discerning the spirituality embedded in these rites—gathering, Word, eucharistic prayer, Communion, and sending. Each ritual segment provides a particular avenue of approach to the paschal mystery and its spirituality. What does it mean to be truly gathered? to find ourselves in the Word? to enter with Christ into his self-offering in the eucharistic prayer? to commune with the risen One and be sent forth as his presence to others? Is there a single thread of spirituality woven through all of these?

67

Starting from my Roman Catholic tradition, I want to address these questions in conversation with my Protestant sisters and brothers. Thanks to the ecumenical movement and decades of historical studies, recent years have seen a remarkable convergence in patterns of worship between Roman Catholic and some Protestant churches. This convergence has borne fruit in two significant ways. First, we now share substantially the same lectionary readings across the liturgical year. Despite our differences, we all hear the same Scriptures each Sunday. Second, in the wake of Vatican II, Catholics and Protestants alike created new eucharistic prayers that essentially share the same structure, strongly influenced by the tradition of the Eastern churches. So, despite differences, we are also praying similarly structured eucharistic prayers. Because this structure is not neutral but actually embodies a spirituality, Catholics and Protestants are drinking from the same well.

A few qualifications, however. I am conversing with Protestant traditions whose orders of service, reflecting ecumenical progress, are closest to Roman Catholic liturgy. Better to say we have moved closer to each other. The reforms of Vatican II brought the Catholic Church closer to many of the values the reformers insisted on, including the centrality of the Word in the liturgy and the priority of baptism and Eucharist among the sacraments. The ground has been shifting beneath all of us for the good. We are gradually overcoming the cliché that "Protestants took the book and Catholics took the sacraments," with the result "that both groups were impoverished," as John Shea says.[1] The convergence between Catholic and Protestant orders of service "on paper" does not, however, automatically spell convergence in practice. The Roman Missal and Lectionary are strictly normative for Catholics. Among Protestant churches, orders of service can range from being fairly normative (Episcopal and Lutheran) to being merely suggestions that ministers can take or leave. Finally, there are, of course, forms and offshoots of Protestant worship that are quite different and do not allow for the comparisons I am proposing here. With sincere respect for both the remaining diversity and the growing unity among Christians, let us now undertake our study.

---

[1] John Shea, *An Experience Named Spirit* (Chicago, IL: Thomas More Press, 1983), 61.

Chapter 5

Learning the Script:
Ritual Structures and Texts

Elie Wiesel prefaces one of his books with the following story:

> For trying to precipitate the redemption, Baal Shem Tov was punished. Exiled to a faraway land, he was deprived of his powers and his knowledge. He turned to Reb Tzvi-Hersh Soifer, his faithful servant and disciple, who never left him. Help me, said the Baal Shem Tov, do you remember *anything*—a prayer, even a *word*, from before? No, Tzvi-Hersh did not. He too had forgotten everything. Everything? Really? No, said Tzvi Hersh, I still remember the alphabet. Then what are you waiting for, exclaimed the Master of the Good Name, start reciting! *Aleph—Bet—Gimmel—Daled*, Tzvi Hersh began. And with great fervor they both recited all twenty-two letters, repeating them again and again until their memory was restored to them.[1]

The obvious question: Why should reciting the twenty-two letters of the Hebrew alphabet restore their memory of tradition and, with this, their lost powers? Psalm 119 provides the answer. Each of its twenty-two stanzas begins with one of the twenty-two letters of the alphabet. The mechanism at work here: remembering the part triggers memory *aha!* of the whole. A small thing, a compact thing, a letter, word, or phrase evokes the whole.

Our Memory Alphabet

And so it is with Christian liturgy. Individual ritual texts of the liturgy function as our memory alphabet of the whole faith. These

---

[1] Elie Wiesel, *Wise Men and Their Tales* (New York: Schocken Books, 2003), ix.

texts vary across Catholic, Protestant, and Eastern rite churches, but the principle is the same. Here are some examples. "In the name of the Father, and of the Son, and of the Holy Spirit." Saying these words as we make the sign of the cross on our bodies evokes the entire paschal mystery: the Word made flesh, living, dying, and rising; the sending of the Spirit; the mystery of the Triune God; and our call to move with this life of God moving within us. "Lamb of God, you take away the sins of the world, have mercy on us"—again the entire story is somehow encoded in this short phrase. These letters, phrases, sentences of our memory alphabet are not end points but rather windows into the Holy Mystery of God, who approaches us as self-bestowing mercy and love. Reciting these parts of our memory alphabet mindfully and "with great fervor," as did the Master of the Good Name and his companion, we are brought back from forgetfulness to the whole identity-forming story. And it is not simply a story of past events, though it includes these; it is the paschal mystery in person, the risen Christ, addressing us now. With this remembering-by-reciting comes the recovery and deepening of our "powers," that is, our capacity for moving with the life of God moving within us, our spirituality.

Entering a Symbolic World

Louis-Marie Chauvet affords us another perspective on liturgy as our memory alphabet. When the part, say, the sign of the cross, somehow evokes the whole paschal mystery, then we are experiencing symbol and symbolic language. Symbols and symbolic language operate broadly across human experience, not only in the liturgy. For example, I hold a piece of concrete in my hand. From one point of view it is just and only that—a piece of concrete. But if it happens to be a fragment of the Berlin Wall, it also symbolizes something beyond itself. In fact, this small thing evokes a whole complex reality: the Berlin Wall, the Communist dictatorship that built it, the fall of the Berlin Wall, and an opening toward freedom. "The symbolic element," Chauvet says, "*crystallizes* in itself the whole world to which it belongs."[2] Now, if we say this piece of concrete on its own is the

---

[2] Louis-Marie Chauvet, *The Sacraments: The Word of God at the Mercy of the Body*, trans. Madeleine Beaumont (Collegeville, MN: Liturgical Press, 1995), 71–72.

real thing but the world it opens up as symbol is somehow not real or less real, this is just plain nonsense. Precisely in its symbolic function it brings the real world into view. The Berlin Wall was real; its demise was a real historical event. This is the rich power of symbol—it both is and is not what it evokes. The fragment is not actually the whole physical wall, just a small piece of it. But as symbol it not only presents itself *as a fragment* but makes present the whole wall and all that it stands for. In this sense it *is* the wall.[3]

It is important to grasp this truth because to undergo the liturgy and its spirituality is to inhabit a world of symbols—symbolic words and actions. And for the believer this is hardly less real for being symbolic. Rather, it evokes what is most real: God's way with us and our response, or, as Chauvet writes, "the communication of the gratuitous gift of God, entrance into the mystery of Christ's passover."[4]

Consider another example, this time a liturgical one. Under Khrushchev's leadership during the height of the Cold War, Christians in the Soviet Union were persecuted with renewed vigor. Arriving at a church in Riga, Khrushchev's henchmen began removing the community's treasured icons, throwing them into a truck. In great distress, the priest and people gathered round to witness the desecration. But the truck got caught in the mud. To get it moving, some of the icons were removed and thrown under the wheels. One of the henchmen spat out these words to the priest: "So, what do you think of that, priest?" Surrounded by his people, he replied, "I have only one thing to say, 'Christ is risen. Alleluia!'" And the people answered: "Truly the Lord is risen. Alleluia!"

What has happened? Against the attempt to erase the religious memory and identity of a people, a short phrase or two, in this case a ritual text, summons them to remember and reclaim their faith in the paschal mystery of Christ. It works because this phrase on their lips, prayed over a lifetime, lives deeply in their hearts: "The word is near you, in your mouth and in your heart" (Rom 10:8). Expressing his own Jewish faith, Abraham Heschel said, "To believe is to remember."[5] This is no less true of Christian faith and spirituality. For

---

[3] Ibid. Chauvet elaborates these ideas fully in chapters 4 and 5.

[4] Ibid., 87.

[5] Abraham Joshua Heschel, *Man Is Not Alone* (New York: Farrar, Straus and Giroux, 1976), 161.

Christians, what is remembered through symbolic ritual texts and actions is not only the paschal mystery but our identity as graced and free participants in it. The symbolic phrase or gesture evokes the whole to which it belongs (the paschal mystery) and also discloses our identity as sharing in it with each other. It mediates to us our personal and communal identity as followers of Jesus.[6]

There is an interesting addendum to the Riga story. After I had shared it in a presentation, a man approached me. His relatives, he said, had been members of that church in Riga. After this horrible incident, their problem was to figure out how they would celebrate liturgy on the next and following Sundays until they could replace their lost icons. The priest gathered his people and assigned some of them special roles. On the next Sunday, a mother and her baby would "stand in" for the now missing icon of Mary and the Child Jesus. Two men would "stand in" for the missing icon of Saints Peter and Paul, and so on, wherever an icon was missing throughout the entire church. Active participants in the mystery!

The icon, like our liturgical memory alphabet, presents a particular subject of the Gospel, "written in line and color," as iconographers say. It opens us toward the whole Christian mystery. Gazing upon the specific richness of this "part," we are brought through it into the whole. How appropriate, then, that members of this church should assume the role of living icons, for that is the job description we receive in baptism—that is, spirituality! We learn and rehearse the liturgical script so that we can perform it and welcome the self-bestowing mercy and love of God. We become living icons, embodying, however imperfectly, this Presence to others. We become the Body of Christ.

But to remember, we must first have learned. Actors bring a play to life by learning the script "by heart." Rehearsing the words over and over prepares them to perform. A key word at the beginning of a line can then unlock the whole. So it is with the script of the liturgy. We learn it so that we can remember and enact it together. From the perspective of spirituality, the true significance of the liturgy in the vernacular lies in this: every baptized person learns the script of the liturgy in order to enact it communally as the Body of Christ. And this *ritual* performance is for the sake of *existential* performance. We give ourselves to sacramental gestures of the love of God because

---

[6] Chauvet, *The Sacraments*, 73–74.

these empower us to enact God's love in this world. This existential performance, in turn, deepens our understanding of the rite's symbols. Holy Thursday's washing of the feet forms the church for service to others. Concrete acts of service such as caring for the homeless, welcoming refugees, or standing with one's Muslim neighbors when their mosque is threatened throw light back on what it means to wash each other's feet. Imbibing and acting on the paschal story over time forms the content of our character. It makes a home in us: the word is near you, in your mouth and in your heart.

"Christ is risen. Alleluia!" "Truly, the Lord is risen. Alleluia!" Our liturgical script or memory alphabet is composed of such words and phrases—microunits, if you will. Some are longer and more complex, while others are shorter and fairly straightforward. Each one evokes in some way the paschal mystery. But the prayer of the liturgy is a unity as well as series of such microunits. Taken together, these evocative "letters" or microunits fall within major ritual units of meaning (macrounits) that structure the entire liturgy. These macrounits are the gathering, Liturgy of the Word, eucharistic prayer, communion rite, and sending. To discern liturgical spirituality means finding the spirituality embedded in these micro- and macrounits of meaning. Before beginning to do this with the gathering rite, let us note two further aspects of the liturgical script: (1) the distinction between the Word in the rite and the Word in the readings and (2) the dialectic of objectivity and subjectivity in the liturgy.

The Word in the Readings and the Word in the Rites

It is useful to distinguish between the liturgy's ritual texts, which are mostly fixed, though with some options, and the readings, which vary from celebration to celebration. True, the Scriptures proclaimed and preached follow a ritual pattern and form a major ritual unit of the celebration. True, the ritual texts are not simply something other than Scripture. They quote, paraphrase, and are deeply shaped by Scripture. Granting this, in what follows I will speak of fixed ritual texts as *the Word in the rite* and the Scriptures of the day or season as *the Word in the readings*. If we ask how the gospel or paschal mystery is communicated across the liturgy, the answer is: through the Word in the rite and the Word in the readings. Word is capitalized to indicate that through the words in each case we encounter the Person of the Word, the Christ. We could just as well say the *Gospel* in the rite and the *Gospel* in the readings or the *paschal mystery* in the rite and the *paschal mystery* in the readings.

At any one point in the liturgy we are engaged in one of these linguistic streams, one relatively fixed, the other offering great variation and detail. Together, they communicate the one Gospel or paschal mystery across the entire liturgy. The part-whole mechanism discussed above is at play here as well: through this particular ritual text or this particular gospel story and other readings, we are led into the one paschal mystery.

It is not simply that the Liturgy of the Word is distinct from the fixed ritual texts that come before and after it. Rather, the Word in the readings informs the Word in the rite throughout the whole liturgy. Within the gathering rite, for example, the Word in the readings can be anticipated at several points: the gathering song or entrance antiphon, the presider's opening introduction, the penitential act with invocations, and the opening prayer or collect. All of these may and often do anticipate the Scriptures of the day or season. Later, a song for preparation or communion may echo the day's gospel. During certain seasons, the preface of the eucharistic prayer reiterates the day's gospel. The readings are just not content to live solely in the Liturgy of the Word segment of the liturgy! They spill backward into the gathering rite and forward into the succeeding rites. Experiences of the fixed and the variable are interwoven throughout the entire liturgy.

This distinction provides a spectrum of possibilities for enactment. At any one moment of the liturgy, emphasis may fall primarily on either the Word in the rite or the Word in the readings or some combination of both. Options for music can build on this spectrum. An opening song, such as Owen Alstott's "Gather Us Together," reminds us what it means to be the Body of Christ, speaking primarily to the Word in the rite of gathering:

> *Refrain:* Lord, Jesus Christ, gather us together. Make us one bread, one body, in your love.
>
> *Verse:* Gather your people, who long to be one, one in you, O Lord, in truth and love.[7]

---

[7] "Gather Us Together," Owen Alstott, © 1980, OCP. All rights reserved. Used with permission.

By contrast, a gathering song anticipating the day's gospel speaks primarily to the Word in the readings. Consider the First Sunday of Lent, featuring the temptation of Jesus in the wilderness (Matt 4:1-11). In the second of three temptations the devil urges Jesus to leap from the temple parapet: "If you are the Son of God, throw yourself down." If you do so, says the tempter, perversely quoting Psalm 91, God will command the angels to "support you, lest you dash your foot against a stone." In effect, this and the other temptations consist in using God for one's self-aggrandizement. But Psalm 91 is really about the mutual fidelity of God and those who "dwell in the shelter of the Most High" (v. 1). In this moment of temptation Jesus is faithful to God and God is faithful to Jesus. As Psalm 91 says: "He will call upon me and I will answer; I will be with him in distress; I will deliver him and give him honor. With length of days I will satisfy him" (vv. 15-16). This is the Roman Missal's entrance antiphon on this Sunday, with verses drawn from the rest of the psalm. Singing this text for gathering brings the assembling church into the day's gospel from the outset, inviting worshipers to step into the shoes of Jesus.[8] An equally valid option is to sing a hymn such as "The Glory of These Forty Days" or "Led by the Spirit,"[9] both of which anticipate the gospel story and invite us to imitate the fidelity of Christ.

Heightening what has begun in song, the presider may introduce the liturgy through the lens of the gospel: "Sisters and brothers, today we begin our Lenten journey. With Jesus, we go out into the desert, we undertake fasting, prayer, and service to those in need. With Jesus, we confront temptation so as to become true disciples and abide in the shelter of the Most High." While this dovetails nicely with the penitential act that follows, it quotes the Word in the readings (the gospel) to shape our consciousness as the assembling church. All of this is to say that as we explore the spirituality embedded in the liturgy's texts and actions, we do so with an eye toward both the Word in the rite and the Word in the readings.

---

[8] The Collegeville Composers Group has provided a responsorial setting, "Those Who Love Me, I Will Deliver," in *Psallite* (Collegeville, MN: Liturgical Press, 2005). Used with permission.

[9] "Led by the Spirit," Bob Hurd, © 1996 Published by OCP. All rights reserved. Used with permission.

Objectivity and Subjectivity

The chapter title, "Learning the Script," bids us to think of our relation to the liturgy with the analogy of an actor performing a script or, for that matter, a singer performing a score. To do so illustrates the objective and subjective nature of the worship. Normally, actors do not make up their own script but receive and follow it. Performing Shakespeare means learning his lines rather than making up our own. We do this because we are convinced that Shakespeare's words embody a depth and wisdom worth repeated visits. Lines flowing spontaneously out of our own subjectivity probably will not carry such depth and wisdom. Instead, we receive and make our own something handed on from the past—tradition. The words of the gospel and the liturgy are like that, but even more so. As St. Paul says, "I received from the Lord what I also handed on to you, that the Lord Jesus, on the night he was handed over, took bread, and, after he had given thanks" (1 Cor 11:23-26). The phrase "from the Lord" is not a reference to Paul's vision of the risen Christ, as though "the Lord" communicated details of the Last Supper to him in this encounter. The tradition is indeed originally from the Lord but mediated to Paul through the very church he once persecuted. From the community of believers who are "in the Lord" he learns the eucharistic rite and now shares it with others.[10]

To make a home in us, the rite must be relatively fixed, not continually changing and shifting. The fixedness of the script or rite makes possible personal and communal internalization by repetition over time. How could Shakespeare's *Hamlet* become anchored in the actor's or theatergoer's psyche if the script changed radically with each performance? How could a teacher or student acquire profound familiarity with, say, the fiction of Virginia Woolf, if those writings did not remain fixed on the page? Repeatability over time also means that the rite can be shared from one generation to the next. "Tradition," G. K. Chesterton writes, "means giving votes to the most obscure of all classes, our ancestors. It is the democracy of the dead. Tradition refuses to submit to the small and arrogant oligarchy of those who merely happen to be walking about."[11]

---

[10] Jerome Kodell, *The Eucharist in the New Testament*, ed. Mary Ann Getty, Zacchaeus Studies (Collegeville, MN: Liturgical Press, 1991), 71.

[11] Gilbert K. Chesterton, *Orthodoxy* (New York: Dodd, Mead and Company, 1943), 85.

This objective character of the liturgy, however, is not above history and change. It has been formed and reformed in different historical periods. The work of the Second Vatican Council represents the most recent reconfiguration within Roman Catholicism, a work that was also coordinated with revisions in some churches in the Protestant tradition. So tradition always has a growing edge, like a tree that is green all year round. While keeping some of its leaves it is always putting forth new ones too. The tree does not reinvent itself each spring but just continues to grow, both renewing and changing itself. Still, these historical reconfigurations produce a normative liturgical script, a reconfigured objectivity, if you will. This objectivity, density, and otherness of the liturgy as a received text resists the narcissistic temptation to reduce worship to an expression of our own subjectivity or current ideologies.

On the other hand, consider the crucial role of the actor or singer in bringing a received text to life. Making the text our own means not only receiving and internalizing it but bringing the inner authority of our own graced experience to its enactment. The text needs our subjectivity to live! What Louis-Marie Chauvet says of proclaiming the Scriptures can just as well be said of voicing the whole liturgical text. There is, he writes, "the writing laid down there, flat, as a testament of the earthly history of the believing people; the *voice* which, in proclaiming the writing from the pulpit bestows life on it and lifts it up from its prone position as a 'dead' text."[12]

Liturgical spirituality is the objectivity of received tradition and the subjectivity that animates it in this time and place, personally and communally. We not only receive and follow it but inhabit it. We bring our subjectivity into play. A joyful text (or song) calls forth our experiences of joy and gladness in the voicing of it. A text (or song) of lamentation bids us bring our experiences of lament to performing it. Many actors play Shakespeare's *Hamlet* well, but each somewhat differently because their personal histories are unique and, more broadly, their shared *today* differs from that of previous generations. Each brings a different set of personal and social experiences to enacting the role. So there is a sense in which the play (including the play of the liturgy) is different each time it is performed even though the text is relatively stable. In this sense, current affairs must find a home

[12] Louis-Marie Chauvet, *Symbol and Sacrament*, trans. Patrick Madigan and Madeleine Beaumont (Collegeville, MN: Liturgical Press, 1995), 212.

in worship, but they cannot be the sole determinant of its script. By contrast, imagine the "to be or not to be" soliloquy spoken mechanically with no feeling, as though one's graced personhood were completely repressed. Mechanical repetition of liturgical words and actions, without the gift of our subjectivity, our very lives, leaves them prone—a dead letter.

Liturgical spirituality, then, is the interplay of our unique subjectivity and history, personally and communally, with the objectivity of the rites. This interplay engenders a spirituality of self-donation and self-transcendence on our part. It is an expression of our subjectivity, but as transcending ourselves to meet the received script of tradition. Good actors do not use the script as a platform for their egos; rather, they both lend and transcend themselves in bringing the character to life. The character they play is not themselves but someone else. And so it is when we enact the liturgy: "it is no longer I who live, but it is Christ who lives in me" (Gal 2:20; NRSV). This reaching out toward nothing less than the paschal mystery ultimately means we are learning to inhabit the character of Christ. Or better, we "undergo Christ," to borrow a phrase from Ronald Rolheiser,[13] because it is by grace that we participate in this holy play. It is true, as the poet Gerard Manley Hopkins wrote, "What I do is me," but spiritually speaking you and I, reader, do more.

> I say more: the just man justices;
> Keeps grace: that keeps all his goings graces;
> Acts in God's eye what in God's eye he is—
> Christ—for Christ plays in ten thousand places,
> Lovely in limbs, and lovely in eyes not his
> To the Father through the features of men's faces.[14]

This is much more than mechanical repetition of the script or conformity to rubrics. To play the game of golf, you must study and follow the rule book. To play the game well, you must also study the skill book. Enacting the liturgy skillfully actualizes its evangelizing potential. In the end, liturgy is not just text but enactment of text. And

---

[13] Ronald Rolheiser, *The Holy Longing* (New York: Doubleday, 1999), 74.

[14] Gerard Manley Hopkins, "As Kingfishers Catch Fire." Available online at www.poetryfoundation.org.

enactment entails embodied gestures or action as well as text. The action of singing communally enacts the very "gatheredness" that the lyrics of such a song are trying to communicate. We are doing what we are saying.

A final word before turning to the gathering rite. Our procedure will be to let the rites *as they are* guide us into their spirituality. I am less concerned with their historical background, how they were formed, or what compromises and tensions lay behind the texts as they now stand. We will meet some of this information along the way. In any liturgical tradition there is a certain amount of arbitrariness and imperfection. Given the Second Vatican Council's reform of the liturgy—a reform that intended both to preserve the essential and remove obscuring accretions—it is enough to consider how these rites presently function and what they now communicate.

Chapter 6

The Spirituality of Gathering

Summoned by the God who made us,
Rich in our diversity,
Gathered in the name of Jesus,
Richer still in unity.
Delores Dufner[1]

Gathering as a Spiritual Task and Journey

Gathering—this word for the opening of the liturgy speaks to the depths of our graced humanity. What it "says" may be described in a series of questions—really three interrelated dimensions of one question. How shall I be in relation to my own existence? How shall I/we be in relation to others? How shall I/we be in relation to the mystery of God? In each case the spiritual journey is toward being rightly gathered instead of being un-gathered or wrongly gathered. These three questions may be combined into one, which is the spiritual import of the gathering rite: According to Christian faith, what does it mean to be truly gathered?

In Relation to Oneself

I can be un-gathered in myself. Like the prodigal son, I can be un-gathered in the sense of not yet having much of a self, driven more by external pressures and attractions than inner conviction. In the process of individuation every young person must leave home and negotiate the journey toward autonomous selfhood. But as every parent knows, this journey can be fraught with misdirection, awkwardness, and even peril. "Of all forms of genius," Thornton Wilder has one of his characters say, "goodness has the longest awkward age."[2]

Lacking self-possession, the willful but unwise youth is easily manipulated from without, quickly squandering his inheritance in a distant country. This *away from home* geography symbolizes his *away from self* alienation. Ultimately, his most important inheritance, his own self, is what he squanders on unworthy external things. When his un-gatheredness has brought him to a dead end, he comes to himself (see Luke 15:17). This marks the beginning of a new inwardness. The return journey mirrors the internal move toward a gatheredness or self-possession he previously lacked. But only when he is gathered in the arms of his father does he find his true center. It is in relation to the other that he gains an authentic self. And even this, one senses, is just the beginning of an open-ended process.

Symbol [margin annotation]

This story features another form of un-gatheredness: inner dividedness. Having come to himself, the prodigal must now choose between two selves or lives, the one he began with and something radically new. What will he do—stay in his lost-ness and shame or acknowledge his fault and go back to face the consequences? But one can persist in such inner dividedness for quite a while, avoiding the decision between these two lives. "For I do not do the good I want," Paul writes, "but I do the evil I do not want" (Rom 7:19). So, one lives a divided, un-gathered life. In the saying, "Let the one among you who is without sin be the first to throw a stone at her" (John 8:7), Jesus highlights something we all know. None of us is without sin, which means we continually carry some un-gatheredness, some inner dividedness, within ourselves. And the liturgy's gathering rite speaks to this existential situation.

In contrast to these forms of personal un-gatheredness, one may be *wrongly* gathered within oneself. We can, in other words, project a strongly organized self but in service to unworthy or even inhumane goals. We can serve our own self-interest with impressive calculation

---

[2] Thornton Wilder, *Heaven's My Destination* (New York: Harper and Brothers, 1935), title page.

[à la 3 temptations in desset]

and discipline, going after status, wealth, or power with little regard for others. What does it profit us to gain the whole world, Jesus asks, if we lose our souls in the process (Mark 8:36)? Personal aggrandizement at the cost of authenticity is ultimately a bad deal. The story of the Rich Man and Lazarus comes to mind. Or the farmer who builds a larger barn to hoard crops and secure his future only to die that very night. To the bumper-sticker that says, "The one who dies with the most toys wins," the reply (another bumper-sticker) is, "But you still die and you can't take it with you." "Thus will it be for the one who stores up treasure for himself but is not rich in what matters to God" (Luke 12:21).

Consider the elder brother in Luke's parable (Luke 15:11-32), alienated from both his younger brother and his father. As long as he remains wrongly gathered within himself, wanting to be a completely self-made man rather than receiving anything as gift, he cannot gather rightly with others. The temptation to found one's identity absolutely in oneself or in things one can control is great. But none of these can really deliver freedom from limits and mortality. We saw this temptation earlier in Ernest Becker's account of the *causa sui* project, so characteristic of modernity and postmodernity (chap. 2). Personal gain and autonomy with no acceptance of limits as the answer to life's meaning is, finally, too narrow and simply untrue.

A common thread runs through these forms of un-gatheredness or being wrongly gathered: disordered love. We give our hearts, our passion, wrongly or to the wrong things. Yes, we can delight in and even love many things. The disorder lies in giving highest devotion to a lesser good or even a disvalue. "Where your treasure is, there also will your heart be" (Matt 6:21). The right ordering of one's loves is an important part of the spiritual journey toward gatheredness. And the gathering rite speaks to this.

[margin note: Where your time is]

② *In Relation to Others*

How shall I/we be in relation to others? This is the question of the neighbor. It applies not only to interpersonal relationships but to relationships between communities and nations. In the parable of the man beaten by robbers and left to die at the roadside, the real question, says Jesus, is not *who is my neighbor* but *who was I neighbor to* (see Luke 10:25-37). The call is to be neighbor to anyone and everyone, especially the most vulnerable. Neighboring implies a profound sense of belonging to each other, of communion or gatheredness with others. We met this notion earlier in Auden's account of his sudden overwhelming experience of knowing what it means to love one's neighbor as oneself. We met with it too under the name *kinship* in Greg Boyle's work with former gang members. Serial killers, terrorists, gang members, as well as the robbers in our parable have become psychologically incapable of empathy, of recognizing their victims as persons. But recognition of kinship makes coworkers and bread bakers out of people who once shot at each other. People thrive in communities of kinship, which is to say, love, one for another.

Gatheredness in this sense is a wider kind of love than close friendships or the intimacy of lovers, though it may animate these. It is an agapic love of neighbor—everyone—flowing from the love of God. Auden's love of neighbor and Boyle's kinship are human mediations of the love of God, a love that wills the healing and well-being of all. Despite its universality, this love is not abstract. We meet it daily in the concrete other, who may well be a mere acquaintance or even a stranger to begin with. The Samaritan and the victim he rescues are complete strangers to each other. Not only that, they belong to communities estranged from each other—Samaritans and Jews. Reaching toward gatheredness is a challenge for communities as well as for individuals.

Gatheredness toward others includes still more, it reaches toward the whole of creation. The word human means *of the earth*. To be human is to share a world with other creatures. In *Laudato Si'*, Pope Francis reminds us that mistreatment of creation is a vice. Genesis bids us not only to *till* but to *care for* the earth: " 'Tilling' refers to cultivating, ploughing or working, while 'keeping' means caring, protecting, overseeing, and preserving."[3] But further, degradation of the environment endangers our human sisters and brothers as well as future generations. You cannot really be gathered to others while at the same time undermining them! Pope Francis writes that "everything is interconnected, and . . . genuine care for our own lives and our relationships with nature is inseparable from fraternity, justice

[3] *On Care for Our Common Home: Laudato Si'*, Encyclical Letter of the Holy Father Francis (Washington, DC: United States Conference of Catholic Bishops/Vatican City: Liberia Editrice Vaticana, 2015), par. 67.

and faithfulness to others."[4] The gathering rite is concerned with just this issue: how shall we be with each other?

③ *In Relation to God*

Sadly, history is replete with wrong kinds of communal gathered-ness: people gathered round all too human idols and ideologies. Think of the Nazi state, the killing fields of the Khmer Rouge, apart-heid, the violence of ISIS, the mistreatment of Palestinians. Closer to home, think of society and economics organized around slavery. Think of the displacement of Native American peoples and destruc-tion of their cultures. Think of the continuing institutionally sup-ported discrimination against blacks and people of color, which the Civil Rights Movement began to address in the 1960s. Think of the current vilification and mistreatment of refugees and immigrants. Can human communities be truly gathered without being gathered rightly to the Holy Mystery in which they and all things abide? It seems we can even use the Holy Mystery to legitimize the mistreat-ment of others.

I have tried to portray this Mystery experientially, that is, from the side of the human subject undergoing it. The faith-engendered notions of theology—creation, grace, and Christology—have expe-riential correlates. The experiential correlate of the notion of creation is the lived sense that we are given to ourselves out of a Mystery that both transcends us and is closer to us than we are to ourselves. Spiri-tuality as *moving with the life of God moving within us*, then, lies in practicing a meditative-reflective recovery of this sense and gratefully entrusting oneself to the Mystery in which all things abide. A practi-cal ethics of respect and care flows out of such a sense. But for Chris-tian faith this experience is permeated by the further gift of grace or God's self-communication.

The experiential correlate of the notion of grace is the sense that we are made by Love for love. The gift of creation *is* so that the grace of love and communion *can be*. In the face of all the brokenness, pain, and suffering of our world, love is what we are here for and is our ultimate beatitude. It breaks out in surprising and transformative

[4] Ibid., par. 70.

ways, as when the hated enemy, the Samaritan, rescues the Jew, left for dead by his own. Or when the community whose children were cruelly taken by bullets steps forth to offer the gunman forgiveness. What comes to the surface in such acts of loving-kindness is the call of Love, which, like a hidden undertow, accompanies all creation. It is "like a seed, already put in the soil; it is like yeast working in the dough; it is like the ferment that makes the beer bubble; it is like the treasure hidden in the field."[5]

Spirituality as *moving with the life of God within us*, then, entails a double participation in this Love: inwardly, moving from hearts of stone to hearts of flesh and compassion; outwardly, loving God and neighbor. Agapic love in action is the only credible response to evil. We cannot love God whom we cannot see if we do not love and act for the sister or brother whose need we do see (1 John 4:20). The love by which we love and seek the well-being of others is not simply our own but a participation in God. God is love, John's first letter says, and those who abide in love abide in God and God in them (1 John 4:16). For Christians, acts of love and justice are thus a witness to the love of God. But this love, accompanying all creation from the beginning, has also entered into history in Jesus and his Spirit and so our witness is through and about the Christ-event.

The experiential correlate of the Christ-event is twofold. It is the lived experience of Jesus our brother, who marks out in the highest way possible the pattern of spirituality. In his humanity he moves *radically* with the life of God—the divinity—moving *radically* within him. Still, unique as Jesus' lived experience is, he is like us in all things but sin (Heb 4:15); his living, dying, and rising is *for us*. Love and communion between humanity and God, enacted once for all, now exists within the stream of history as God's pledge and call to the freedom of all. Christ, in whom we were chosen before the foundation of the world (Eph 1:4), unlocks the meaning of our own created-ness, and calls us to agapic love. The life, death, and resurrection of Jesus reveal "the secret and blessed meaning of our all-transcending spirit."[6] For us, then, spirituality as *moving with the life of God moving*

---

[5] Joseph G. Donders, *Jesus the Stranger: Reflections on the Gospels* (Maryknoll, NY: Orbis Books, 1999), 84; quoted in *Give Us This Day* (July 2017): 334.

[6] Karl Rahner, "The Little Word God," in *Grace and Freedom*, trans. Hilda Graef (New York: Herder and Herder, 1969), 200.

within us means living this Christic pattern of self-offering to God and neighbor.

The heart of this Christic pattern, as the Philippians hymn says, is self-emptying: "though he was in the form of God . . . he emptied himself" (Phil 2:5-8). As we shall see, each ritual stage of the liturgy engages us in this motion, this paschal pattern, in a particular way. And so it is with the gathering rite: moving in and with the self-emptying of Jesus, we are gathered rightly to God, within ourselves, to others, and to creation. Christ and his Spirit mediate our walk with God. This is how we "undergo Christ," to borrow Ronald Rolheiser's beautiful expression.[7]

But there is likewise the possibility of not being gathered. Where are you? This is God's first question in the Bible, Heschel told us, because the human pair are hiding from God.[8] Hiding from God, even if we profess to be believers and are members of Christ's Body, is always a possibility. A different kind of motion, withdrawal from gatheredness, animates the human pair. The spirituality of the gathering rite calls us from various forms of hiding to being with God. Jesus puts the issue negatively in what he says of Jerusalem. His words could equally apply to Christian believers and communities today: "How often have I desired to gather your children together as a hen gathers her brood under her wings, and you were not willing" (Luke 13:34; NRSV).

Far from being superficial ceremonial items on the way to the rest of the liturgy, the individual moments of the gathering rite answer in specific ways what it means to be truly gathered. That is why *gathering* is the most appropriate name for the opening rites of the liturgy.

An Ecclesiology of Gathering

Roman Catholic documents on the liturgy do not hesitate to call this opening rite *gathering*. So too do the explanatory notes of various Protestant orders of worship. The *United Methodist Book of Worship* says: "This time is both an outward and visible gathering of the

---

[7] Ronald Rolheiser, *The Holy Longing* (New York: Doubleday, 1999), 74.

[8] Abraham Joshua Heschel, *Man Is Not Alone: A Philosophy of Religion* (New York: Farrar, Straus and Giroux, 1976), 153.

people and an inward and spiritual gathering—a focusing of awareness that they are a people gathered in the presence of God known
to us through Jesus Christ in the power of the Holy Spirit."[9] "On the
day of Christ's resurrection, and at other times, God gathers us in
Christian assembly," says *Evangelical Lutheran Worship* service book.[10]
According to the Presbyterian *Book of Common Worship*: "In the name
of Christ we answer God's call and assemble as the community of
faith."[11]

The General Instruction of the Roman Missal says the introductory
rites are "to establish communion."[12] It describes this communion as
"a local gathering" in which the promise of Christ is fulfilled: "For
where two or three are gathered together in my name, there am I in
the midst of them" (Matt 18:20). Christ is truly present "in the assembly gathered in his name," the same document says.[13] What is
gathered is the local church as the unified celebrant of the liturgy,
animated by diverse roles and ministries. The Orthodox theologian,
Alexander Schmemann, writes,

> When I say that I am going to church, it means I am going into the
> assembly of the faithful in order, together with them, to *constitute the
> Church*, in order to be what I became on the day of my baptism—a
> *member*, in the fullest, absolute meaning of the term, of the body of
> Christ.[14]

For Roman Catholics, the term "the faithful" sometimes distinguishes the laity from the ordained. But here "the assembly of the
faithful" means the people and presider together. Even the distin-
guishing sacramental mark of ordination presumes the baptismal
call shared with all the baptized. By baptism, ordained ministers are
members of Christ's Body; by ordination, servants of that Body. The

---

[9] *The United Methodist Book of Worship* (Nashville, TN: United Methodist Publishing
House, 1992), 16.

[10] *Evangelical Lutheran Worship*, Pew Edition (Minneapolis, MN: Augsburg Press,
2006), 92.

[11] *Book of Common Worship* (Louisville, KY: Westminster John Knox Press, 1993), 34.

[12] *General Instruction of the Roman Missal* (GIRM), Third Typical Edition (Washington DC: United States Conference of Catholic Bishops, 2011), par. 46.

[13] Ibid., par. 27.

[14] Alexander Schmemann, *The Eucharist* (Crestwood, NY: St Vladimir's Seminary
Press, 2003), 23.

lesson here is that a distinction is not a separation. When the priest and people gather, they are one church, not two. The "assembly of the faithful" is Paul's single body with many parts, different gifts and roles for the upbuilding of the body. It follows that the priest is not *the* celebrant. The celebrant is, rather, the local gathering—the church—with the priest as the *presider* of the celebration. The *Catechism of the Catholic Church* says it is "the whole *community*, the Body of Christ united with its Head, that celebrates," and "it is thus the whole assembly that is *leitourgos*."[15] Despite remaining differences in other respects, this official teaching reveals a point of convergence between Catholic and Protestant understandings. The significance of the gathering rite is that it assembles the local church as celebrant of the liturgy.

Beginning from the very ordinary act of going to church, gathering is a spiritual passage. It is physically manifested by assembling in the local church building. But it is also a journey of heart and mind. For both clergy and laity, this journey toward gatheredness becomes formal ritual with the liturgy's opening. It is a passing over into Christ. The many, coming from varied places and circumstances, coalesce into the one Body of Christ. It is thus a renewal of our baptismal identity.

The *Catechism* describes this passage as *heightened actualization*. The church, it points out, means various things simultaneously—the liturgical assembly, the local community, the universal community of believers. But it "is made real as a liturgical, above all a Eucharistic, assembly." *Eucharistic* because the assembly draws its "life from the word and the Body of Christ and so herself becomes Christ's Body."[16] For the Protestant reader, it is important to note the referent of the word "eucharistic" here. It is not just Holy Communion but the unity of the Liturgy of the Word and the Liturgy of the Eucharist.[17] Karl Rahner understood the Eucharist in just this way, "as the fullest actualization of the essence of the church. For the church neither is nor

---

[15] *Catechism of the Catholic Church* (New York: Doubleday, 1997), pars. 1140, 1144.

[16] Ibid., par. 752.

[17] In other contexts "Eucharist" sometimes means more specifically the consecrated bread and wine received in communion. The broader meaning is the entire celebration as a unity of what Protestants often call Word and Sacrament and what Catholics call the Liturgy of the Word and the Liturgy of the Eucharist.

wants to be anything else but the presence of Christ in time and space."[18]

As heightened actualization, liturgical gathering/celebrating is like a family reunion. We are family not only at the reunion but before and after it as well. But the family is most itself when it regathers, *YES!* sharing its story around a meal. The reunion not only reminds us of an identity received in the past but actualizes and deepens it anew today and for the future. Never just a repetition of what the family once was, it is a new event in which new things happen: the healing of old hurts, the bonding of siblings, family members befriending each other in a new way. So it is with the liturgy. The gathering rite is the opening act of an ecclesial reunion. To become ever more deeply what we became on the day of our baptism—immersed in Christ— that is what is new each time we gather and celebrate the liturgy. That is what the liturgy, our memory alphabet of the faith, does. That is what was happening when the Russian priest proclaimed: "Christ is risen. Alleluia!" and his distressed people, regathered to their identity by these words, answered, "The Lord is truly risen. Alleluia!"

But in addition to all this, the gatheredness or communion so attained is a sign, a sacrament for others. These others obviously include those gathered for worship. But in its very character of gatheredness, the local assembly signs something for the world—a sign that will be deepened as the liturgy unfolds. Ultimately, it signs Christ. But what is the church signing when it signs Christ through whom "God was pleased to reconcile to himself all things" (Col 1:19-20; NRSV)? The opening paragraph of Vatican II's Dogmatic Constitution on the Church (*Lumen Gentium*) expresses it this way: "The church in Christ, is a sacrament—a sign and instrument, that is, of communion with God and of the unity of the entire human race" (LG 1). To sign Christ *sacramentally* is to embody the content of his redemptive presence and action: reconciliation and communion with God, reconciliation and communion with the neighbor (everyone). Ritually, this begins with the gathering rite, for "Christ is really present in the very liturgical assembly gathered in his name."[19] The local church's own heightened in-house unity, first signaled in this rite, is meant

[18] Karl Rahner, *Foundations of Christian Faith*, trans William V. Dych (New York: Crossroad, 1982), 427.
[19] GIRM, par. 27.

for others. Kenan Osborne writes, "The Church is Church only if and to the extent that it brings to presence Christ and his Spirit."[20] Christian liturgical spirituality entails this practice of being a sign of Christ to others.

Like the practitioner of sign language, the gathering church stands up and signs communion with God and neighbor (everyone). In a world torn by war and tribalism, the gathering church signs peace borne of mutual respect and compassion, one person for another, one community for another, one religion for another, one nation for another: "they shall beat their swords into plowshares, and their spears into pruning hooks; nation shall not lift up sword against nation, neither shall they learn war any more" (Isa 2:4; NRSV).

The gathering church as instrument and sign of love of God and love of neighbor has a backward and forward reference that belongs to its very nature as a sacrament. Backward, because here and now it heightens what we became on the day of our baptism. And what we became on the day of our baptism refers back to the life, death, and resurrection of Jesus. In him God has definitively transformed the world. Into this "once for all" reality we are plunged in the water of baptism.

But the worshiping church is also forward-leaning. Even in its highest ritual actualization it is not the fullness of God's reign but its symbol or sacrament.[21] This is what the Dogmatic Constitution on the Church (*Lumen Gentium*) means when it says that the church is "the kingdom of Christ already present in mystery" (LG 3). This "present in mystery" should be read as "present *but* in mystery." This is no ordinary presence. It indicates the already/not yet nature of what the church *signs* when it signs communion with God and the unity of humanity. Not only must what happens liturgically be embodied existentially as agapic love in action, but we must accept that even this pair—liturgy and its verification in ethical engagement—is not the fullness of the reign. This fullness, definitively begun in Christ, is not an exclusively human work to be finished and controlled within history. It is a divine-human work, growing "visibly in the world through the power of God" (LG 3). "In the Eucharist," writes William

---

[20] Kenan Osborne, *The Christian Sacraments of Initiation* (Mahwah, NJ: Paulist Press, 1987), 88.

[21] Louis-Marie Chauvet, *The Sacraments*, trans. Madeleine Beaumont (Collegeville, MN: Liturgical Press, 2001), 29.

Cavanaugh, "the church is 'straining forward to what lies ahead' (Phil. 3:13)."[22] What lies ahead is not only what we may accomplish tomorrow and in the days following but something that outruns all human days and times. That is why Paul says our citizenship is in heaven (Phil 3:20).

This is not abandonment of the world but a way of being in the world truthfully rather than in illusion. The illusion of all ideologies, personal and communal, is that within worldly time we can create a final perfection safe from mortality. But the Eucharist, Cavanaugh says, "keeps the church in tune with a different time. The endless uniform march of the world's time is denied by the promise and the realization of history's end in the Eucharistic celebration."[23] And so, yes, there is the ethical call to bend the arc of history more and more toward justice. Real though unfinished and imperfect embodiments of the reign are like leaven raising human history toward its absolute future in God. But the urgency of "thy kingdom come, thy will be done on earth" in the Lord's Prayer is counterbalanced by sober acknowledgment of our neediness and failures: "Give us this day our daily bread and forgive us our trespasses. . . . Deliver us from evil." We are not masters of the situation but followers of Jesus, who, in worldly terms, failed miserably in his own time and place! But God raised him from the dead. So our worldly time is taken up into God's time. Our life is hidden with the risen Christ in God (Col 3:3).

If Christian spirituality is *moving with the life of God moving within us, mediated by Christ and his Spirit,* then the liturgy is the preeminent place of remembering, rehearsing, and deepening this identity, this *moving with.* The Roman Catholic Eucharistic Prayer for Various Needs II captures the whole movement: "Blessed indeed is your Son, present in our midst when we are gathered by his love and when, as once he did for the disciples, so now for us, he opens the Scriptures and breaks the bread." Here we are gathered into Christ's self-emptying love for God and humankind so that we may become more deeply who we are as members of his Body—sacraments or mediators "of communion with God and of the unity of the entire race" (LG 1). All this begins with the gathering rite. In light of this, our task now is to descend into the particular elements or microunits of the rite to see how they speak to the question: what does it mean do be truly

---

[22] William T. Cavanaugh, *Torture and Eucharist* (Malden, MA: Blackwell, 1998), 228.

[23] Ibid., 227.

gathered? But even before this, we must consider the fact that gathering begins even before the gathering rite.

Informal Gathering: Going to Church

Before the formal liturgical procession there is an informal one. This very ordinary action of going to church embodies a spirituality. It is a gift of self to the assembling church, an act of love, a first step along the avenue of gathering. It becomes more so the more mindfully we undertake it. Do we sufficiently recognize our importance to others, who are incomplete without us? Or their importance to us, who are incomplete without them? The second-century *Didascalia of the Apostles* says: "Let no one deprive the Church by staying away; if they do, they deprive the body of Christ of one of its members. . . . Do not, then, make light of yourselves, do not deprive our Savior of his members, do not rend, do not scatter his Body!"[24]

Of course, we can in our freedom stay away. For just that reason, going to church truly is a gift. This offering of self anticipates the central act of the liturgy, the self-offering of Christ and our participation in it. In going to church we pass over more consciously into a circle of gracious love—God's gratuitous love for us in Christ and the Spirit, and our grace-enabled response of love for God, neighbor, and creation. What Pope Francis says about our relation to all creatures is equally true of the simple act of going to church to be with our sisters and brothers. In contrast to the *self as center* character of modernity, heightened by individualism and consumerism, Francis reminds us that "our openness to others, each of whom is a 'thou' capable of knowing, loving and entering into dialogue, remains the source of our nobility as human persons."[25] "We are always," he says, "capable of going out of ourselves toward the other."[26] Going to church is going out of ourselves toward the other, that is, toward God and neighbor.

This act of going out of ourselves to church varies culturally. It may not be as simple as a short walk or drive. In one of my classes,

---

[24] "Didascalia of the Apostles," in Lucien Deiss, *The Springtime of the Liturgy*, trans. Matthew J. O'Connell (Collegeville, MN: Liturgical Press, 1979), 177.

[25] *Laudato Si'*, par. 119.

[26] *Laudato Si'*, par. 208.

a Ugandan student described how his village would go to church, located miles away in a distant town. Every Sunday, the whole village rises in the darkness before dawn to make the several-hours-long journey. Singing along the way, they fall into a kind of dancing procession, as they go. Approaching the church, they meet people from other villages who have enacted the same procession. Some time is given over for mutual greeting and singing together. Then, like converging streams, they flow together into the church, and the formal rite begins as they sing the gathering song. Whether this preliturgical procession is simple or taxing, it is an exercise in self-transcendence, the gift of self, personally and communally, to the gathering assembly. It begins our participation in the self-emptying love of Christ.

Processing or going to church embodies another dimension of self-transcendence. There is a leave-taking, a relinquishing of something. And if we do not do this we never really arrive. What is it? To say we leave "the world" is dangerously misleading, because the liturgy is not on another planet! It has everything to do with our world: "the bread that I will give is my flesh for the life of the world" (John 6:51). Recognizing that God's self-communicating presence is active everywhere, we must resolutely reject the old dualism of the profane world and the sacred sphere of liturgy. To say we leave behind our personal concerns is also misleading, for we bring our concerns to the liturgy.

What we leave behind, I believe, is our workaday posture, that posture of feeling responsible and autonomous—so much so that we easily fall into the illusion that we are in charge of existence. There is, in other words, a passing beyond the *self as center*, the self narrowly focused on individual agendas and needs. We may experience this workaday dimension as a stressful burden or a source of satisfaction in our accomplishments, or some combination of both. But when we operate at the level of "it's all up to me" we take up a very limited and potentially illusory viewpoint.[27]

Wayne Muller describes this trance of our limited, everyday posture brilliantly in his beautiful book, *The Sabbath*. Two of the dubious features of modernity are the twin tyrannies of work and the marketplace. G. K. Chesterton once wrote about the madness of virtues

---

[27] Chapter 2 on resistances explored forms of this illusory self-understanding in detail.

run wild. Living to work rather than working to live is a case in point.[28] Modernity says only the self that produces, accomplishes, and consumes is worthy. As evidence, one need only observe how the Sabbath fares in today's marketplace—just another day for working and consuming. Producing, accomplishing, and consuming are not evil. They are normal parts of human flourishing. But, they can run wild. As Muller says,

> We can, over time, become enthralled in the trance of our work. It is all-important, it must be done right away, it won't get done without me, I cannot stop or it will fall apart, it is all up to me, terrible things will happen if I don't get this done. I have to keep working because I have things to buy and there are bills to pay for those things I need to buy to help me get these things done.[29]

The wisdom of the Sabbath is to break the spell, saying: "*Stop now.*" Truth be told, it is not all up to me, "the galaxy will somehow manage without us for this hour, this day."[30]

The first reading on the First Sunday in Advent, Year A (Isa 2:1-5), provides an image of leaving behind the "it's all up to me" posture. Isaiah has a vision concerning the mountain of the Lord: "Come, let us go up to the LORD's mountain . . . That he may instruct us in his ways, and we may walk in his paths." This is an image of gathering toward God with others: "All nations will stream toward it." We exchange the limited viewpoint of the valley for that of the mountain top. The higher we go, the more encompassing our view and the closer we come to each other. We begin to see as God sees. "What really happens in the soul's union with God in terms of liberation and healing?" theologian Dorothee Sölle asks. "It is an exercise in seeing how God sees, the perception of what is little and unimportant; it is listening to the cry of God's children who are in slavery in Egypt. God calls upon the soul to give away its own ears and eyes and to let itself be given those of God."[31]

---

[28] See "The Suicide of Thought," in Gilbert K. Chesterton, *Orthodoxy* (New York: Dodd, Mead and Company, 1943), 52–55.

[29] Wayne Muller, *The Sabbath* (New York: Bantam Books, 1999), 210.

[30] Ibid., 83.

[31] Dorothee Sölle, *The Silent Cry: Mysticism and Resistance* (Minneapolis: Fortress Press, 2001), 293.

Climbing the mountain of God is climbing out of one's ego *insofar as it claims to be the center of reality*. We relinquish the immediacy of the self-absorbed ego for fuller reality and truth. Important as my immediate concerns and agendas are, they are not the center of reality. My true center is not myself, but God above and within, who made me and continually sustains me and all other creatures. As a Christian, my true center is not myself but the Christ-self, with which I have been clothed in baptism: "I am the vine, you are the branches" (John 15:5). We are rooted in a reality deeper than our own ego. Gathering as climbing the mountain of God is not a question of leaving the world behind but of "a different relationship to the world—one that has borrowed the eyes of God."[32] In Western spirituality this decentering corresponds to the way of purification: the movement toward God begins with letting go of the little constricted self so that a truer, greater life may take hold. And this opening to God is at the same time an opening to the neighbor, near and far, every human being, and the whole of creation.

"To leave, to come . . . This is the *beginning*, the starting point," Schmemann says.[33] All this is in continuity with what follows in the formal gathering rite. Going to church begins the *transitus* toward the paschal mystery that animates the whole liturgy. For in going out of ourselves toward others and relinquishing the *self as center* for God as center, we practice a paschal spirituality. We undergo dying to an illusory self so that a truer self might be born. We practice the kenosis, the self-emptying, that marks the Christian mystery.

The Formal Gathering Rite and Its Spirituality

"What we need more than anything else," Abraham Heschel once wrote, "is not text-books but text-people!"[34] Singers, poets, actors, and teachers all know what it is to become text-people. Through repeated readings of scores, scripts, or books, they develop an internal

---

[32] Ibid., 293.

[33] Alexander Schmemann, *For the Life of the World* (Crestwood, NY: St Vladimir's Seminary Press, 1973), 28.

[34] Related by Abraham Heschel's daughter, Susannah, at a UCLA Conference, 2016. For the extended essay in which this quotation occurs, see Abraham Joshua Heschel, "The Spirit of Jewish Education," *Jewish Education* (Fall 1953): 9–20.

repertoire. They *eat the book* and become themselves carriers of a tradition to others. A missionary serving a preliterate hill tribe in Southeast Asia once told them how sorry he was that they didn't have books. Books, he explained, are such important storehouses of a community's treasured history, stories, and wisdom. They answered, "Oh, we once had books like the Chinese, but one day they fell into our rice and we ate them." Again, the missionary expressed sorrow at their loss. But they responded: "We didn't lose them, we ate them—they are inside us."[35]

In the biblical paradigm, God requires the prophet Ezekiel to eat the scroll: "Open your mouth and eat what I am giving you . . . eat this scroll, then go, speak to the house of Israel" (Ezek 2:8; 3:1). Echoing this understanding, Paul says, "The word is near you, in your mouth and in your heart" (Rom 10:8). To have a spirituality in the concrete is to have such an internal repertoire. Gustavo Gutiérrez wrote a book on spirituality titled *We Drink from Our Own Wells.*[36] What *well* do I drink from in my spirituality? What repertoire do I draw on? Having a liturgical spirituality means that over the time of our lives and repeated prayings of the liturgy, the Word in the rite and the Word in the readings, including related songs and hymns, become the well from which we drink. We internalize them, and they become part of our being. The words on the page, then, remind us of what we already know in our hearts.

My wife's parents, John and Pat, brought communion to Mary, John's dying sister. He tried to help her recall memories from their childhood: "Do you remember when . . ." There was no response, no flicker of recognition. But as soon as Pat pronounced the ritual words preceding communion, "Behold the Lamb of God. . . . Blessed are those who are called to the supper of the Lamb," Mary replied without hesitation, "Lord, I am not worthy . . . only say the word and my soul shall be healed." In this moment these ritual words, prayed over a lifetime, held Mary when she could no longer hold on to much else.

---

[35] Story related by anthropologist Pia Moriarty, who taught English and literacy with Southeast Asian refugees in the late 1970s.

[36] Gustavo Gutiérrez, *We Drink from Our Own Wells* (Maryknoll, NY: Orbis Books, 2003).

So, let us become text-people as we explore the ritual words and actions of the gathering rite. Because I am placing my own Roman Catholic tradition in conversation with that of my Protestant sisters and brothers, I am looking especially for parallels. These parallels exist, as a comparison of various church orders shows. Here are some examples, starting with the Roman Rite:

Table 1

Gathering Rites Compared		
Roman Catholic	**Evangelical Lutheran**	**United Methodist**
Procession with song	Prelude music	Instrumental or vocal music as people gather
Sign of the Cross and Greeting	Sign of the Cross	Greeting
Presider's Introduction		Hymn of Praise
Penitential Act, options: A. "I confess" + Kyrie B. "Have mercy on us" + Kyrie C. Three invocations with Kyrie response to each	Confession and Forgiveness	Opening Prayer can include Prayer of Confession and Act of Pardon
or	or	
Sprinkling Rite	Thanksgiving for Baptism	
Gloria (except in Advent/Lent)	Gathering Song: one or more of the following: Hymns, Psalms, Kyrie, Gloria, Canticle of Praise	Acts of Praise, options: Glory to God, a Psalm or Scriptural Song, Gloria Patri, or Anthem
Collect	Prayer of the Day	

Though not included in this table, the gathering of the Episcopal Church comes closest to the Roman Rite, featuring a procession with song, the greeting, and then a penitential order or rite. The Kyrie and the Gloria are options here, as well as in the Lutheran and Presbyterian introductory rites. Since there is more than one way of saying the same thing, comparison of church orders reveals both similarities and variations. One begins with biblically based assembly song and a procession of ministers, followed by the sign of the cross and the greeting. Another begins with prelude music, a scriptural greeting or call to worship, followed by congregational song. In other words, the biblical *letter* of the introductory rite is specific to each church tradition. But amid these differences there is an underlying similarity in spirituality. Each in its own way calls worshipers into the shared story of the Gospel. Each is a call beyond one's individual workaday world into the living, dying, and rising of Jesus.

The Beginning of the Gathering

Brief as they are, as quickly as they go by, there is a depth dimension in these opening texts and actions of the gathering. Take communal song, for example. In continuity with the preliturgical prelude of "going to church" and relinquishing the "it's all up to me" posture, communal song shapes us into shared action and identity with others. This is another stage in the movement of self-transcendence that regathers and actualizes the local church anew. "Music's words in our mouths and melodies on our lips," Catherine Vincie writes, "make demands on us, calling us beyond our individual feelings to express communally the tone and sentiments of the feast or season."[37] Worshipers, like actors, begin to engage a shared script that takes them beyond themselves into larger meanings.

The sign of the cross, featured in Catholic and Lutheran gathering, provides another example. As we saw in chapter 5, ritual texts serve as our memory alphabet and as symbolic speech. In a small thing, the whole of the Gospel is embedded and evoked rather than explained in detail. Louis-Marie Chauvet says that this sign and its accompanying words "condense in themselves the whole of Christian identity."[38] Our lives are like pages that God has created in order to inscribe on them the Word "Christ" or, more exactly, "other Christs."

---

[37] Vincie, "The Mystagogical Implications," in *A Commentary on the Order of Mass of the Roman Missal*, ed. Edward Foley, 145 (Collegeville, MN: Liturgical Press, 2011).

[38] Chauvet, *The Sacraments*, 47; also, Louis-Marie Chauvet, *Symbol and Sacrament*, trans. Patrick Madigan and Madeleine Beaumont (Collegeville, MN: Liturgical Press, 1995), 221–22.

And so we inscribe his mystery on our bodies not only in baptism but at every celebration of the Eucharist. Signing our bodies means signing our lives, personal and communal: one's own human life, the communal life of the Body of Christ, the larger body of society, and the body of creation.

Beginning with this sign that incorporated our bodily selves into the mystery of Christ means that personal and liturgical prayer is prayed within the life of the triune God. Traditions lacking the sign of the cross evoke this trinitarian context in the greeting: "The grace of our Lord Jesus Christ, the love of God, and the communion of the Holy Spirit be with you all."[39] Both say we do not approach God from without but from within *the life of God moving within us*. We pray from within Christ, because we have been clothed with the risen One in baptism. We pray within the Spirit, for to be so clothed in Christ is to receive the Spirit. Our whole lives, including the liturgy, are *in* God, Creator of heaven and earth, who in every moment holds us in being and approaches us as self-bestowing love. Our whole lives are *in* this self-bestowal of God inscribed in the flesh of Christ's humanity, Jesus, who moved unconflictedly with the life of God moving within him "for the life of the world" (John 6:51). Liturgical prayer and spirituality is not a human approach toward God but always a response to God's gratuitous movement toward and in us.

A call to worship, a greeting, the sign of the cross, communal song—all of these are forms of self-transcendence and self-donation. They initiate the process of gathering us together into the story of God's way with us, a story shared from generation to generation. By voicing them, we begin to explicitly own and move with the life of God moving within us; we practice spirituality. These initial texts and actions bring us to the core of the gathering rite.

The Core of the Gathering

Between the initial texts and actions we have just been considering and some form of a closing prayer (Collect or Prayer of the Day or Prayer for Illumination to hear the Word) we meet the core of the rite. The similarity between Roman Catholic and Protestant traditions

---

[39] This greeting is shared by Roman Catholics and Presbyterians. A similar greeting in the Episcopal rite begins with: "Blessed be God: Father, Son and Holy Spirit." *The Book of Common Prayer* (New York: The Church Hymnal Corporation, 1979), 323, 351.

concerning this core is striking. It is the motion from penitence to praise. We move from acknowledgment of human failure to grateful praise for God's mercy and kindness. Despite surface differences in the letter of these rites, they sound a common spirit or spirituality. Liturgical gathering cannot repress or bypass the reality of human evil and suffering. It must engage it honestly because Jesus himself entered into our brokenness, bringing mercy, healing and transformation. The acknowledgment and integration of the negative is intrinsic to the paschal mystery. No one should be surprised that the gathering rite entails this acknowledgment.[40] There are several stages in the ritual movement from penitence to praise:

1. preparation for acknowledgment of sin

2. acknowledgment of sin

3. request for or thankful acceptance of God's gracious forgiveness

4. an act of praise, usually in song

As we explore these stages, the question is this: What psychological-spiritual ground are we meant to cover in this movement from penitence to praise?

Each church tradition has a prayer or invitation calling us to reflect on our sins, followed by a moment of silence. "Brothers and sisters, let us acknowledge our sins, and so prepare ourselves to celebrate the sacred mysteries," says the Roman Rite. After a prayer asking for God's mercy and the power of the Spirit, the Evangelical Lutheran Rite says, "Let us confess our sin in the presence of God and one another."[41] As one of their options for this moment, the Presbyterian and Episcopal churches cite this passage from 1 John 1:8-9: "If we say that we have no sin, we deceive ourselves, and the truth is not in us.

---

[40] Some early commentators on Vatican II's reformed liturgy bemoaned the placement of the penitential act during the gathering rite. It seemed to call a halt to joyful gathering in favor of private introspection concerning one's sins. Especially in light of our growing awareness of social sin, this is not so much a problem in the rite itself but in how it is enacted. The presider's introductory remarks can help worshipers appreciate the full spectrum of what is involved in calling to mind our sins.

[41] *Evangelical Lutheran Worship*, Pew Edition, 95.

But if we confess our sins, God, who is faithful and just, will forgive our sins and cleanse us from all unrighteousness."[42]

We respond in two ways, with a moment of silence and then a public prayer of confession. There is only a brief pause before launching into one or another formal confession prayer. No time, in other words, to recollect particular sins in the focused way that a Catholic would for the sacrament of penance or one might do in preparation for counseling. We may, of course, think of some recent event that is uppermost in our consciousness. But to this ritual moment we also bring our whole selves before the living God. And in bringing our whole selves we bring our everyday practice of spirituality. This ritual moment presumes reflective living, a truthful awareness of self and world, all the good, all the bad. This awareness is cultivated through prayer, meditation, practical works of service, mercy, and justice. We bring the ache of what we already know to this moment. What do we already know?

In this ritual moment I may think of personal sin, especially recurring failings or attachments that compromise my following of Christ and my relationships to others. I may think of social sins, unjust and harmful political and economic structures in which I am somehow complicit. Human regret may cast the net even wider. There are things that the human race—*my family*—has done that I have not personally done or condoned. One may well say, "Then I am not morally culpable, these are not my sins, and I need not acknowledge them." But if we have a heart of flesh rather than stone, we will feel their disvalue. The needle of one's moral compass points unswervingly to "this thing should not be." The Holocaust or apartheid, the mass killings under the Khmer Rouge in Cambodia, the current mistreatment of the Palestinians, human trafficking, the destruction of the rainforests and animal life (the list goes on and on)—these things should not be, and it is a blot on our humanity that they are. Though I may not be directly and personally culpable for these things, it is right that I feel shame for what my human family has done. It is right that, to the extent possible, I seek to redress such harms. And so, it is right that we lament them before the face of God. We lament how our human family culpably and repeatedly misses the mark.

---

[42] *Book of Common Worship*, 52; *The Book of Common Prayer*, 352.

In all these ways we become ready, we stand in truth rather than illusion and self-deception. We inhabit a broken world and are complicit in various ways in this brokenness. The journey toward gatheredness must acknowledge rather than repress human failure. This act of truth telling, however, is only the penitential moment in the overall movement from penitence to praise. What makes for this larger process? Again, what psychological-spiritual ground are we meant to cover in this movement? In all the traditions we have been discussing, a prayer of forgiveness follows confession of sin. The request for (Roman Catholic) or assurance of (Protestant) God's forgiveness seems to account for the movement to praise. But this does not take us far enough.

To go further, we must place one more ritual item in the mix. Both Roman Catholic and Lutheran orders of worship offer a rite recalling our baptism as an alternative to the penitential rite.[43] This suggests equivalence between penitential and baptismal symbolism. In the gathering rite, *either one* can carry us from penitence to praise. A penitential dimension does belong to baptismal symbolism. Water does a lot of things for us but one of them is to cleanse. One of the suggested texts for the sprinkling antiphon in the Roman Rite is from Ezekiel: "I will pour clean water upon you, and you will be made clean of all your impurities, and I shall give you a new spirit, says the Lord" (36:25-26). But baptismal symbolism says more than cleansing from sin. It is also anointing for discipleship. It places penitence within the larger context of the call. The forgiveness that seems to propel us from penitence to praise always comes with the call.

Two Symbolisms, One Underlying Spirituality

Chauvet has shown how a piece of stone may function symbolically, opening up the whole world of the Berlin Wall—formation and demise, captivity and freedom, dictatorship and democracy, and so on. When we ask what psychological-spiritual ground are we meant to traverse in the motion from penitence to praise, we are asking: What world is opened up by this piece of the gathering rite? Since either ritual option—confession/forgiveness or memorial of baptism—can carry us from penitence to praise, should not the same

[43] Actually, the blessing and sprinkling of water in the Roman Rite is not an alternative *to* but an alternative form *of* the penitential act.

world of meaning and spirituality underlie both, granting their different emphases? On the surface, it looks as though this one symbolic referent and spirituality is *penitence*. But the specific character of Christian sorrow for sin arises only along with an awareness of something more. A hint is given in the quotation above from Ezekiel—the cleansing from one's impurities is held in relation to "and I shall give you a new spirit."

To gain further light, consider the call of Peter (Luke 5:1-11), the lectionary reading on the Fifth Sunday in Ordinary Time, Year C. In the gospels, Peter's outsized ego often gets him into trouble. John Shea builds imaginatively on this story, recasting the scene of Peter and Jesus in the boat together, looking for a catch of fish. As Shea tells it, Peter is a fisherman of great renown. Other fishermen watch his every move, following wherever he goes, hoping to benefit from his expertise. Peter revels in this. But an all-night fishing expedition has turned up nothing. In the morning he and his coworkers are empty-handed. So, what happens to "Peter the Great" when Jesus, who is no fisherman, gets into his boat and says, "Put out into deep water and lower your nets for a catch" (Luke 5:4)? At first, nothing. They go here and there, but no fish are on offer. As they return to shore, Shea writes, it happens.

> All the fish in the sea of Galilee came to the surface. They leapt on one side of the boat and they leapt on the other side of the boat. They leapt behind the boat and they leapt in front of the boat. They formed a cordon around the boat, escorting it toward shore in full fanfare. Then in a mass suicide of fish, they began to leap into the boat. They landed in the lap of the laughing Lord. They smacked the astonished St. Peter in the face.

Shea displaces the concluding dialogue of this story to a tavern later in the day. Peter says to Jesus,

> Go away from me. You go away from me. I wanted the fish to be over them, not with them. I wanted the fish to rule them, not feed them. You go away from me. I am a sinful man.[44]

---

[44] John Shea, *An Experience Named Spirit* (Chicago: Thomas More Press, 1983), 213–14.

So far, so good. The other readings on this Sunday fall into line, preparing us for this story with similar acknowledgments of sin and unworthiness before God. The first reading features the call of Isaiah (6:1-2a, 3-8), who experiences the glory of the living God "with the train of his garment filling the temple." Seraphim cry out to one another, "Holy, holy, holy," but the prophet cries out, "Woe is me, I am doomed! For I am a man of unclean lips, living among a people of unclean lips; yet my eyes have seen the King, the LORD God of hosts." In the second reading (1 Cor 15:1-11), Paul similarly acknowledges his sin and unworthiness. "For I am the least of the apostles, not fit to be called an apostle, because I persecuted the church of God." By the time we get to Peter's "Depart from me, Lord, for I am a sinful man," it is the third time we have heard the acknowledgment of unworthiness.

Now, if this were all these stories conveyed, they would not be very revealing. Just the same old story about humans—nothing but sinners. When we complete each of them, however, we encounter a challenge to this human self-estimate. Despite their supposed unworthiness, all three "sinners" are granted a hierophany, the mysterious glory and power of God coming close and acting in their midst. Their acute sense of unworthiness is evoked specifically in relation to God's self-communication, not outside of it. For Isaiah, it comes through the vision of the Lord of hosts in the temple. For Paul, it is the vision and voice of the risen Christ. For Peter, the revelation of divine presence is mediated through Jesus in the great catch of fish. In each case the revelation provokes a crisis. This moment of truth demolishes strategies of self-deception and the pretense of the fully autonomous self. This false self is unveiled and left naked. What turns these accounts from flat statements about human sinfulness into profound narratives is the tension God's self-revelation creates, a tension waiting to be resolved in one way or another.

In Isaiah's case, the purification of his unclean lips with the burning ember is not enough. The tension remains and is sharpened by God's question, "Whom shall I send?" Resolution comes only with Isaiah's answer, "Here I am, send me." Similarly, God touches Paul through the voice and vision of the risen Christ: "Last of all, as to one born abnormally, he appeared to me." The appearance is not a resolution but rather initiates a crisis in Paul's self-understanding that awaits resolution. It comes only with Paul's conversion and mission as a preacher of the Gospel he formerly persecuted.

And the resolution of the Peter-Jesus story? Shea's imaginative retelling draws us into the tension at the story's center. We are witnessing the reconstruction of Peter's ego, and the first step is decentering. The great catch of fish has nothing to do with his prowess; all his efforts have failed. The catch comes as pure gift. The gratuitousness of God infinitely outstrips his puny powers. Having the leaping fish slap Peter in the face is the spiritual equivalent of Paul's being knocked down. Reading between the lines, Shea wrestles with this question: What allows persons to let their guard down and accept their failings? And further, to move from one's acknowledged *sin identity* to something new? For the recognition of failure can draw us in the opposite direction. The recovering alcoholic, after months, even years, of sobriety, falls off the wagon and reasons perversely: "Well, now that I've blown it, I might as well go whole hog and drink myself to death." It is like that unfortunate typo in an infamous edition of the Bible. It left out just two letters and has Jesus saying: "Go, sin more." Peter equates himself with his unworthiness as though it is his only possibility: "Depart from me, Lord, for I am a sinful man." He will stay with himself in his sinfulness. Like Lazarus in the tomb, he needs to be called forth from this lethal self-definition. And God's approach in Jesus, rather than putting him in his place, calls him forth. Shea writes,

> The first response to the inrush of divine love is the recognition of sinfulness. We have grounded ourselves wrongly, and that wrong grounding has brought pain into the world. There will be no possibility of a new grounding and a new life unless the past is confessed.[45]

We have reached a precarious moment because, according to Shea, "the sudden exposure that we are sinners is extremely painful." It requires us to move from defending and protecting our false ego to undergoing the paschal pattern: surrendering one's life in order to save it. Shea continues, "At this moment we need a love that loves us more than we love ourselves. . . . The act of surrendering is really a process of re-centering, a free acceptance of ourselves as constituted by a larger power."[46]

---

[45] Shea, *An Experience*, 216–17.
[46] Ibid.

What propels the move from "I am a person of sinful lips" to "here I am, send me"? Or the move from "leave me, Lord, I am a sinner" to "they left everything and followed him"? Interior to God's self-communication in all of these hierophanies is an affirmation: "I shall give you a new spirit," to recall Ezekiel's words (36:26). The power displayed is not of the "I am bigger than you are" kind. It is the power that Scripture names "loving-kindness," celebrated in the psalm of this Sunday: "When I called, you answered me; you built up strength within me . . . your kindness, O LORD, endures forever" (Ps 138:3, 8). It is the love that "looks beyond our faults and sees our need," as Greg Boyle says, citing the lyrics of an African American spiritual. He explains the dynamic as follows: "My own falsely self-assertive and harmful, unfree ego gets drawn into the expansive heart of God. It is precisely in the light of God's vastness and acceptance of me that I can accept the harm that I do for what it is."[47]

In our biblical stories, God's acceptance and affirmation is expressed in the call to partnership: "Whom shall I send?" and "Do not be afraid, from now on you will be catching people." "God's good wish," as Julian of Norwich says, "is to have us."[48] We meet this love beyond telling in the story of the Father who sees the prodigal child from afar and runs out to embrace and kiss him. The truest experience of penitence is not outside of but within what Shea calls "the inrush of divine love"—an inrush that is loving-kindness, affirmation, containing as it does the call to partnership with the Holy Mystery.[49] As we have seen from earlier chapters, this inrush is in one sense happening always and everywhere, because creation is of the order of love. But this love is mediated historically through persons, communities, events. Christ is the face of God's loving mercy. As members of his body, we are to be hierophanies of God's loving mercy to others. A story of such mediation comes out of the Sayings of the Desert Fathers. An old monk is the face of God's mercy for a hesitant sinner:

> An old man was asked by a certain soldier if God received a penitent man. And after heartening him with many words, he said to him at

---

[47] Gregory Boyle, *Tattoos on the Heart* (New York: Free Press, 2010), 44.

[48] Julian of Norwich, *Reflections of Divine Love*, trans. Elizabeth Spearing (New York: Penguin Books, 1998), 50.

[49] Shea, *An Experience*, 216–17.

last, "Tell me, beloved, if thy cloak were torn, wouldst throw it away?" He says, "Nay, but I would patch it and wear it." The old man said to him, "If thou wouldst spare thy garment, shall not God have mercy on His own image?"[50]

Even when this experience of God's loving approach leans more toward the subjective pole of consciousness, as in meditation or even mystical experience, seeming to bypass created mediums, it is still mediated by our own creaturely, embodied subjectivity. Though it can seem to come out of nowhere, as in W. H. Auden's account of feeling himself invaded by a power "certainly not mine," still, it was mediated to him in a creaturely time and place—as he sat with colleagues on a lawn one summer evening.

Spirituality is moving with the life of God moving within us. The motion from penitence to praise is the move from the old ego, ever wanting to assert its primacy, to the new self of the call. We surrender ourselves to the process of recentering, which entails dying to the old self. But this very surrender itself is borne by God's merciful movement toward and within us. No one has better expressed the vulnerability of entrusting oneself to God than Melissa Musick Nussbaum. She describes it in terms of the nakedness of the lover with the beloved. With our self-concealments demolished we are "to lie in nakedness, as one lies still under the soft, exploring touch of the beloved, and to reveal oneself, marked, flawed, scarred, misshapen—and begin to understand that the beloved alters not, when it alteration finds." She continues:

> It is the image Jesus gives us of the prodigal son: ill-clad, ill-fed, and having squandered all of his father's gifts, embraced in his father's arms, standing close under his father's gaze. The son cannot conceal the toll of the road—its odor, its dusting of grit and streaky sheen of sweat—nor can he produce what he does not have, the lost fortune. With neither the means nor the strength for concealment, the son had to choose: To come at all was to come stripped and naked. Yet the father does not withdraw or turn away. He sees and he loves.[51]

[50] Helen Waddell, *The Desert Fathers*, trans. Helen Waddell (New York: Vintage Books, 1998), 133–34.

[51] Melissa Musick Nussbaum, quoted in *A Reconciliation Sourcebook*, ed. Kathleen Hughes and Joseph A. Favazza (Chicago: Liturgy Training Publications, 1997), 143.

What this detailed exploration has uncovered is that penitence is not a human work in the face of an overpowering God but a divine-human work in the face of a divine call. Because Christian penitence is a case of responding to God who has first loved us, it moves from penitence evoked by Love to a return of love and praise. Its very character is determined by the gracious Love that provokes it. For Christian spirituality, interior to the awareness of failure is the recognition that all of this has been confronted by the mercy of God who "looks beyond our faults and sees our need."[52] It is precisely God's movement toward us as mercy and affirming love that creates the possibility of repentance and the abandonment of the illusory self.

The third form of the penitential act in the Roman Rite reveals this most clearly. All three forms have a Kyrie. In the first and second forms, the Kyrie follows the confession and absolution prayer. But the third form has a different structure. It features three invocations with a Kyrie response to each, and this comes *before* the absolution prayer. For example:

1. You were sent to heal the contrite of heart: Lord, have mercy.

2. You came to call sinners: Christ, have mercy.

3. You are seated at the right hand of the Father to intercede for us: Lord, have mercy.

> May almighty God have mercy on us,
> forgive us our sins,
> and bring us to everlasting life. Amen.

The reality of human failure is acknowledged in each invocation—"to heal," "call sinners," "intercede for us." But the accent is on how God meets our failure with mercy and the affirming call to partnership. And this comes even before the absolution prayer and Gloria. Within these penitential invocations there is a dynamism toward something beyond penitence. Addressing Christ, these invocations say in so many words: "Lord, you did this wonderful thing for us: Lord, have mercy. And you did this wonderful thing for us: Christ, have mercy." This form strikingly anticipates the preface of the eucharistic prayer, which recounts God's salvific deeds for us in Christ

---

[52] Boyle, *Tattoos*, 52.

and culminates in the praise of the Sanctus/Holy. "Lord, have mercy" is obviously a plea for mercy, but in the context of the invocations, it is also an acclamation of praise. In this way, this third option reveals the underlying dynamic of the Kyrie in all three options: the movement from penitence to praise. As the General Instruction says, it is not only a plea for mercy but an acclamation, an act of praising Christ.[53]

These stories of sin-recognition, provoked by God's call, are stories of transformation from an old life to a new one, of dying to the old self so that a new self can be born: "and I shall give you a new spirit" (Ezek 36:26). We come full circle if we ask: what sort of new life or spirit is this? John Shea's retelling of Peter's call ends with the observation that when the Divine Presence surrounds us, touching our *aha!* misshapenness with love, other-centered energies are released within us.[54] We begin to participate, however imperfectly, in the self-emptying love of Christ toward the One who sent him and toward human beings. We become *other Christs*. This is what makes reconciliation possible. This is the meaning of "Here I am, send me" and "they left everything and followed him."

In this way, the symbolism of the penitential rite coincides with that of the sprinkling. At heart, both evoke the same grace-enabled passage from the old life to the new, understood as a participation *YES* in the dying and rising of Jesus. The new self into which one is initiated is the *Christ-self*, as in Paul's "it is no longer I who live, but it is Christ who lives in me" (Gal 2:20; NRSV). By the same token, initiation means membership in the ecclesial body of Christ. This new "I" belongs to a "we." The Letter to the Romans speaks in the plural: "we have been buried with him by baptism into death, so that, just as Christ was raised from the dead by the glory of the Father, so we too might walk in newness of life" (6:4; NRSV). What lives at the heart of the movement from penitence to praise is our initiation into the self-emptying love, the paschal living, dying, and rising, of Jesus. To recall Boyle's words, held in this love, "I can accept the harm that I do for what it is."[55] Held in this love, we are freed for love. The other-centered energy released from within takes the ritual form of loving praise.

---

[53] GIRM, par. 52.
[54] Shea, *An Experience*, 218–21.
[55] Boyle, *Tattoos*, 44.

Praise

The psychological-spiritual motion from penitence to praise, already at play in the penitential or sprinkling rite, becomes full-blown in the Gloria. Similarly, across the range of Protestant liturgies already cited, the Kyrie, Gloria, Trisagion, or another hymn of praise follows the confession of guilt and assurance of pardon. We should not imagine that praising God is like Dorothy and her companions groveling in fear before the "great and powerful Oz," as in the movie version of *The Wizard of Oz*. Alternatively, we should not imagine that the God we glorify is the harmless, bumbling old man behind the curtain! Think instead of the shepherds in Luke's gospel (2:8-14), working people, filled with wondrous joy and glorifying God. Think of the overflowing love the prodigal son must feel for his father, who says: "Quickly, bring out a robe—the best one—and put it on him; put a ring on his finger and sandals on his feet . . . and let us eat and celebrate; for this son of mine was dead and is alive again; he was lost and is found" (Luke 15:22-24; NRSV). Think of the great love pouring forth from the woman who washes the feet of Jesus with her tears, dries them with her hair, kisses them, and anoints them with costly oil. Her sins, Jesus says, "which were many, have been forgiven; hence she has shown great love" (Luke 7:47; NRSV). The approach of God's loving-kindness makes possible a true acknowledgment of our personal and communal failings *and* releases other-centered energies from within. This liberation of love expresses itself existentially in love of God and love of neighbor. But at this moment in the liturgy, it is expressed ritually in the Gloria or other acts of praise. Still, even here, the love of God has a horizontal as well as vertical dimension: "Glory to God in the highest, and on earth peace."

à la CGS +

Resumé of Gathering Spirituality

We began this chapter by asking what it means to be truly gathered. Each moment of the rite speaks to this question from a particular angle. If there is a single line uniting all the moments of the rite, we can look once again to Alexander Schmemann for its expression: "We are in Christ and Christ is in us."[56] It is in Christ and his Spirit that

---

[56] Schmemann, *The Eucharist*, 23.

we are gathered to the mystery of God, our Abba, as adopted daughters and sons. Gathered to Christ and his Spirit, we move toward true gatheredness within ourselves, with other persons, communities, and all creation. This requires ongoing conversion and attunement to God's call, dying to the old self so that the new self can emerge more and more across our lives. In short, this means participation in the self-emptying love of Jesus. This is ritually expressed in the personal-communal move from penitence to praise through either penitential or baptismal symbolism. To live and move and have our being in Christ in this way is to be his sign and instrument. As his self-emptying love gathers all into God's healing mercy, our liturgical gathering must be *for* and *with* all, far beyond the walls of the church building or even our church communion. In the gathering rite we practice a spirituality of standing up amid all the divisions and harms of this world, signing for one and all the call to embody *communion with God* and *communion among human beings,* love of God and love of neighbor. A few years ago, I tried to express this spirituality in a song for gathering, "With All the Saints":

> With all the saints, with prophets and martyrs,
> with holy Mary and Joseph,
> with those who came before and those who will follow,
> we gather here today, one body in the Lord,
> a sign and sacrament of Christ.
>
> With all in need, the poor and forsaken,
> to whom the innkeeper shuts the door,
> with those who are the least, yet first in the kingdom,
> we gather here today, one body in the Lord,
> a sign and sacrament of Christ.
>
> With refugees, and victims of violence,
> with those made homeless by Herod's sword,
> with all the disappeared and those who still mourn them,
> we gather here today, one body in the Lord,
> a sign and sacrament of Christ.
>
> With all who live compassion and mercy,
> all who defend human dignity,
> with people of good will from every faith and nation,

we gather here today, one body in the Lord,
a sign and sacrament of Christ.

With all who dare to toil for that city
whose light shall shine from the mountaintop,
where all may dwell in peace and know life's full measure
we gather here today, one body in the Lord,
a sign and sacrament of Christ.

So may this flock, this church once more gathered,
faithfully follow its Shepherd's voice.
To be a living sign of the love of God and neighbor,
we gather here today, one body in the Lord,
a sign and sacrament of Christ.[57]

---

[57] "With All the Saints," Bob Hurd, © 2003, 2009. Published by OCP. All rights reserved. Used with permission.

Chapter 7

Finding Ourselves in the Word

A book is like a mirror: if an ape looks into it,
it won't be an apostle who looks back.
Georg Christoph Lichtenberg, 1742–1799

"Come, let us go up to the LORD's mountain . . . that he may instruct us in his ways, and we may walk in his paths." In the last chapter, this quote from Isaiah 2:1-5 served as an image for the spirituality of gathering. Climbing the mountain of God means climbing *AHA !* out of our ego insofar as it claims to be the center of reality. Dying to this illusory posture, we open inwardly and upwardly toward fuller reality and truth. Or, as Steve Smith, speaking from his Quaker tradition expresses it, "I must drop the strivings of my small self if I am to surrender to the presence of Christ within."[1] Time and again the liturgy calls us back to the *Christ-self* within, an identity we explicitly received in baptism. In this way we move toward true gatheredness with the self, others, creation, and the living God.

Dorothee Sölle expresses this gatheredness toward God and others eloquently, saying: "It is an exercise in seeing how God sees."[2] What do we see when we see how God sees? We see the story of God's way with us. And this brings us to the second part of the Isaiah quotation: we make the climb so that God may teach us to walk in holiness. We

---

[1] Steve Smith, *Eastern Light: Awakening to Presence in Zen, Quakerism and Christianity* (Duluth, MN: QUPublishing, Quaker Universalist Fellowship, 2015), 38.

[2] Dorothee Sölle, *The Silent Cry: Mysticism and Resistance* (Minneapolis: Fortress Press, 2001) 293.

learn this in all the dimensions of our lives but, ritually speaking, it happens in the Liturgy of the Word. Liturgical gathering is toward the Word, the Christ, the Person of the Word. Our task, then, is to explore the spirituality at play in this encounter. What does it mean, then, to find ourselves in the Word?

The Ecclesial Context of the Word

Speaking from his Jewish faith, Abraham Heschel writes, "To believe is to remember."[3] Christians can only really live their faith *forward* by remembering the Gospel. Across the liturgy, they enact this remembering through the word in the rites and the word in the readings. Ritual texts such as the sign of the cross are *abbreviated* remembering, the Liturgy of the Word is *elaborated* remembering. Assemblies unfold the story in great detail by proclaiming, hearing, and so rehearsing the Word of God. Rehearsal is for the sake of reenactment: we learn the Christ-script in order to embody it.[4]

By Word I mean both Christ who is the Word and the inspired Scriptures as human and time-conditioned words that nevertheless mediate the presence of God, the Risen Christ, and his Spirit to us. Because these inspired words are also human and time-conditioned, we need various reflective frameworks beyond our own immediate impressions to guide our understanding of them. Finding ourselves in the word entails the critical question: is our "take" on the Scriptures true or mistaken or some combination of the two?

The Buddha once told a parable about the right and wrong way to grasp a water snake. Grasped wrongly, the snake can hurt you. Grasped rightly, you catch it without harm. The parable illustrates the point that "grasped wrongly the Scriptures conduce to hurt and harm." Commenting on this story, Steven Voris writes: "While reading the scripture is good and life-giving, reading scripture inappropriately creates problems that can cause harm to the religious community."[5] Islamic fundamentalists misuse the Qur'an to justify their violence and will to power. Christian fundamentalists feel com-

---

[3] Abraham Joshua Heschel, *Man Is Not Alone: A Philosophy of Religion* (New York: Farrar, Straus and Giroux, 1976), 161.

[4] John Navone develops this notion in *Seeking God in Story* (Collegeville, MN: Liturgical Press, 1990), 89–100.

[5] Steven J. Voris, *Preaching Parables* (New York: Paulist Press, 2008), 43–45.

pelled by Scripture to show up at the funerals of gay and lesbian soldiers, telling the bereaved that God hates their lost ones, consigning them to hell. These are the extremes. But it is really an issue for everyone. Dare I say it: does it not sometimes happen that otherwise learned Scripture scholars force the Scriptures to fit a pet theory? In some respects (not all) the decades of competing and often contradictory theories of biblical scholars is not unlike what Chesterton once said of the history of philosophy: it is the history of brilliant error. Are we sufficiently aware of the unexamined assumptions we bring to our reading of God's Word? Do we, perhaps unconsciously, reduce the Scriptures only to that which confirms our own agendas and current ideologies? We must always bring some horizon of understanding to the Scriptures. Can we nevertheless allow this horizon to be led, stretched, and challenged by the Word?

Encountering the Word within an ecclesial community at worship safeguards us to some extent from wrongheaded and "lone ranger" interpretations. Multiple traditions guide us: first, the liturgy itself (*lex orandi, lex credendi*: as we pray, so we believe), but also church teaching, theology, biblical scholarship, and historical studies (what was happening at the time of Jesus and the formation of the New Testament?). Taken together, these guiding interpretive frameworks are always on the move—passing on the wisdom of the past but also putting forth shoots of new understanding. Important as these frameworks are, however, worshipers are not required to have doctorates in theology or biblical scholarship before they can encounter Christ in the Scriptures. In actual practice, it is our ongoing encounter with the Word, especially in the liturgy itself, from childhood up, that stirs the desire and shows the necessity of consulting these frameworks and traditions.

Becoming Text-People

In chapter 6 we read Abraham Heschel's comments about the need for text-people. What does that mean? According to John Dunne, becoming text-people is a process of passing over and coming back.[6] We pass over from our own lives into the world and time of the Scriptures and then come back again. In this *passing over* and *coming back*

---

[6] John Dunne, *Reading the Gospel* (Notre Dame, IN: University of Notre Dame Press, 2000), 3–19.

we are changed because the Word shapes our self-interpretation and therefore our identity. Through the Scriptures, but more fundamentally through the Person who is *the* Word, God interprets us to ourselves. But from our side, what spirituality is required for this to happen? What kind of spiritual practice is involved in finding ourselves in the Word?

The Emmaus episode provides a clue (Luke 24:13-35). In the guise of a stranger, the risen One accompanies the two on the road. Before he can speak to them and rekindle their desolate hearts, something else must happen. Though Jesus is the catalyst—grace is always first—this must happen *from their side*. He asks: "What are you discussing as you walk along?" So, they open their hearts to him. They tell their story, recounting how Jesus was handed over and executed, how the women went to the tomb, found it empty, and had a vision of angels "who announced that he was alive." Notice, they have all the pieces of the story but cannot grasp its true meaning. As far as they are concerned, their hoped-for redeemer is dead, his body is missing, and their identity as followers has been shattered. The measure of their trauma can be seen in the fact that these two are leaving Jerusalem, the center of their ministry. Recalling how Jesus sent out disciples in pairs to prepare towns and villages for his ministry, Eugene LaVerdiere says these two are not just ordinary disciples "but two presbyters, prophetic teachers, who were abandoning the way."[7]

Now on this road *away* from their disciple-identity, they open their hearts to the stranger, making room for him to accompany them. Only then does Jesus tell them *his* story, which is also the true meaning of theirs. By situating their story within his own, "beginning with Moses and all the prophets," he transforms their desolation into joy. But first he seeks *their seeking*, their ache, their trauma. They must lay it before him. Then he not only restores but deepens their identity as disciples. That darkest of things—death—turns out to be a meaningful part of the story rather than a rupture in it. "Was it not necessary" Jesus asks them, "that the Messiah should suffer these things and enter into his glory?"

Whatever words we use in prayer and worship, the essence from our side is this interior work of opening the heart to God. We bring

[7] Eugene LaVerdiere, *Dining in the Kingdom* (Chicago: Liturgy Training Publications, 1994), 157.

our story, with all its doubts and difficulties, to the risen One. Looking into the mirror of the Christ-story (the Gospel), we find our truest Christ-selves reflected back to us. Joy and clarity follow. "Were not our hearts burning [within us] while he spoke to us on the way and opened the scriptures to us?" But, as the epigraph of this chapter reads, "a book is like a mirror. If an ape looks into it, it won't be an apostle who looks back." Without this spiritual practice of opening the heart to God, making space for God's story and accompaniment in our lives, the scriptural Word is a dead letter to us. "It is not just a matter," John Shea wisely says, "of exposure to Christ. It is a matter of what we are able to let in, of what we can truly hear and integrate."[8]

As the spirituality of gathering brings about purification or liberation from the constricted, illusory self, opening to the Word deepens the process. The clarity it brings corresponds to the illuminative way of Western spirituality. These two belong to the well-known triad of spiritual stages: purification, illumination, union.[9] In what does this illumination consist? In order to see as God sees, we must give ourselves to the Word, letting the Person who is the Word re-create us. A friend of mine often jokes about Christ the interior decorator. Once you let the interior decorator into your home and she has a look around, she begins calling for the ejection of some treasured things! "That picture has to go; that couch is really pretty ugly, it needs replacing. You've got way too much stuff here, you need to down-size." Being re-created takes a lifetime but also has turning points. As we saw in chapter 6, a turning point happens to Peter's ego when he is called by Jesus.

The Introduction to the Lectionary has a name for the spiritual practice of opening to God—*meditation*.[10] It keeps resurfacing across the document. "The liturgy of the word must be celebrated in a way that fosters meditation." The entire assembly is to "listen to God's word and meditate upon it." The sung responsorial psalm aids the meditative process. If not sung, it should be voiced "in a manner conducive to meditation on the word of God." The silences between

---

[8] John Shea, *The Spiritual Wisdom of the Gospels for Christian Preachers and Teachers: Year B, Eating with the Bridegroom* (Collegeville, MN: Liturgical Press, 2005), 27.

[9] This is discussed earlier on pp. 33–34.

[10] *Lectionary for Mass* (Collegeville, MN: NCCB/Liturgical Press, 1998). Quotations are from pars. 28, 8, 21–22, 28, and 24, respectively.

readings allow the assembly to "take the word of God to heart and prepare a response to it in prayer." The homily too must "be truly the fruit of meditation." Clearly, meditation is the primary activity of the assembled church during the Liturgy of the Word. Catholics and Protestants using the lectionary share substantially the same structure:

First Reading, Silence

Psalm, Second Reading, Silence

Gospel Acclamation, Gospel

Homily, Silence

Creed or Affirmation of Faith, Intercessions

Sitting ritually signals stillness, the posture for meditation. Notice too that silences are integral to the rite. Shortchanging or eliminating these silences eliminates the assembly's meditative role. Proclamation becomes a solo performance for a passive audience. Whether listening as readings are proclaimed, or responding vocally in singing the psalm and gospel acclamation, or attending to the homily, the assembly is to be actively engaged in meditation. Or, as Dunne says, we are to pass over to the story in order to come back changed. How do we do that? How does the *finding of finding ourselves in the word* work?

Assembly Meditation: A Staged Process

The Liturgy of the Word is a staged process. The lectionary readings are structured to spark the interior work of opening mind and heart to the paschal story that shapes our identity. The more we understand this staging the more easily we can move with it. The dance steps of the tango are objectively given, and they can be described. But knowing the steps is not enough. One has to learn how to embody them in one's own movement. There is an objective pattern to the readings, and a subjective process for engaging them. First, let us explore the objective staging or patterning of the readings. This is marked by intertextuality, repetition, and variation. Then we will consider subjective appropriation by exploring *lectio divina* as a model for the assembly meditation.

Intertextuality

We experience the word intertextually, that is, across a series of readings. Why have multiple readings? Why not just a gospel passage? There are communities that hear only one reading proclaimed and preached on any given Sunday, dictated by the interests of the preacher. By contrast, churches using the Lectionary ask much more of worshipers and ministers. We do not simply set up camp in this or that reading but dwell in the *interrelation* of several readings, following the Emmaus pattern: "Then beginning with Moses and all the prophets, he interpreted to them what referred to him in all the scriptures" (Luke 24:27). "The Christian Bible," Chauvet writes, "is nothing else than a rereading of the Hebrew Bible in the light of the death and resurrection of Jesus Christ. . . . This explains why Christian revelation consists in the joining of both testaments."[11]

Intertextuality, further, means that we do not rely on the preacher for everything but instead collaborate with him or her in opening the Scriptures. In effect, each member of the assembly interprets the Scriptures even before the interpretation given in the homily. The first prepares for the second. Gathered *by* and *toward* the Person of the Word, we are like Eli in the temple: "Speak, LORD, for your servant is listening" (1 Sam 3:9). The local assembly—presider and people together—is this listening servant, poised to "taste and see" the goodness of the Word (Ps 34:8). Taking up this posture is a spiritual practice that anticipates the paschal mystery itself. Gregory Collins writes: "It calls for a kind of *kenosis*, an emptying out of one's own plans, desires, ideas so as to become free and open to God's Word."[12]

Forest-bathing, we are told, is a matter of entering the forest, breathing in the scents and oils emitted by trees, feeling the ground beneath one's feet, hearing birds, the babbling brook, branches swaying in the wind. Studies show it is good therapy. Blood pressure goes down, stress is reduced, the immune system is strengthened.[13] The

---

[11] Louis-Marie Chauvet, *Symbol and Sacrament: A Sacramental Reinterpretation of Christian Existence*, trans. Patrick Madigan and Madeleine Beaumont (Collegeville, MN: Liturgical Press, 1995), 195.

[12] Gregory Collins, *Meeting Christ in His Mysteries* (Collegeville, MN: Liturgical Press, 2010), 70.

[13] "Forest Bathing: A Retreat to Nature Can Boost Immunity and Mood," NPR's *Morning Edition*, July 17, 2017, www.npr.org.

rich intertextuality of the Word is like that. Still, this verdant forest of meaning requires a path—a way in and through. That is what we are seeking. Without such a path, the density may overwhelm us.

In the community where I live, we have a meeting room for ecumenical meditation and worship. On the wall there is a woodcut of a minister preaching. From a distance, it appears that his head is surrounded by a swarm of bees. Closer up, you realize that this swarm is coming out of his mouth. And each bee is just the word, *words.* Just a swarm of words. The artist's comment on preaching could also be said of the lectionary readings. Without learning to read intertextually, discerning the pattern that anticipates and culminates in the gospel, we are just confronted by a swarm of words. Luckily, a path into this forest is already there. We just have to discern it. While preaching may elucidate resonances among the readings, the Liturgy of the Word presumes assembly meditation *during* the readings and *before* the homily. The homily, then, is meant to build on and complete a meditative process already begun by the assembly.

Repetition and Variation

Intertextuality means passing through a *series* of readings in order to come back changed. But something more is needed if we are not to drown in a sea of words: *repetition* and *variation.* The first reading floats a word, phrase, or image. The psalm then mirrors and elaborates it. Finally, the image or idea comes to final restatement in the gospel.

Earlier we saw an example in the call of Peter on the Fifth Sunday in Ordinary Time, Year C (Luke 5:1-11). By the time we get to Peter's "Depart from me, Lord, for I am a sinful man," we have heard the acknowledgment of unworthiness first in Isaiah's "I am a man of unclean lips," and Paul's "I am the least of the apostles, not fit to be called an apostle, because I persecuted the church of God."[14] Psalm 138, links these stories, emphasizing God's loving kindness toward our unworthiness: "you built up strength within me . . . your kindness, O LORD, endures forever." All three confessions of unworthiness are provoked by a hierophany and conclude with an affirming call

---

[14] Though the second reading in Ordinary Time is not chosen to mirror the other readings, in this case it is thematically related. This does occasionally happen.

to partner with God and do great things. The verse of the gospel acclamation (Matt 4:19) reinforces the meditative process. It is not only
an acclamation ("Alleluia") but a proclamation (the verse), capturing
the gist of the story: "Come after me and I will make you fishers."
In all these ways *repetition* is at play.

Variation is at play because recurring words, images, and situations
also differ from each other. Their relation to each other is analogical—like but also different: Isaiah in the temple, Paul on the road to
Damascus, Peter by the seashore. Each call, each confession of unworthiness, and each transformation into serving God occurs in a
quite different context. By bringing these differences into play with
each other, intertextual reading provokes and deepens meditation.
We are encouraged to add our own story to the mix. How are we like
Isaiah, the psalmist, Paul, and Peter?

Repetition and variation are especially characteristic of biblical
literature. Exploring this phenomenon in the Jewish Bible, Robert
Alter speaks of "techniques of repetition" and the "web of reiteration"
by which biblical personages and events are presented: "The repetition
of single words or brief phrases often exhibits a frequency, a saliency,
and a thematic significance quite unlike what we may be accustomed
to from other narrative traditions."[15] Our context differs from his,
however. He is exploring repetition across a chain of stories in the
Jewish Scriptures. We are concerned with the "web of reiteration"
across a chain of Old and New Testament passages that make up the
Liturgy of the Word. The *finding* of finding ourselves in the Word
occurs by tracking repetition and variation across the readings.

To intertextuality, repetition, and variation we must add one more
element: semi-continuous reading. During Ordinary Time or the
nonfestal season, the second reading is not chosen to mirror the
others. Instead, over successive Sundays we hear selected passages
in sequence from one of the New Testament writings. We are exposed
to significant portions of Paul's letters to the Corinthians, Romans,
or Galatians and so on. Though not chosen to mirror the other readings, by happy accident they sometimes do. When this happens, there
is no reason not to take advantage of it, as in our example from the
call of Peter above. This gives us two forms of staging across the

---

[15] Robert Alter's from *The Art of Biblical Narrative* (New York: Basic Books, 2011),
141, 223.

liturgical year. During Ordinary Time, what I have just described is
the rule: first reading, psalm, and gospel are thematically related; the
second reading usually is not. During festal seasons (Advent/Christ-
mas/Epiphany and Lent/Easter/Pentecost), the second reading
combines with the others to resonate with the gospel.[16]

Intertextual reading of the Scriptures serves a deeper intertextual
event: the interplay of the readings with the "text" of our lives. The
Emmaus story illustrates this well. Given the trauma of Jesus' death,
the two disciples on the road could not help but misinterpret the text
of their lives: he's dead, his body is missing, the mission is over, time
to leave. But they find themselves anew in light of the story the un-
recognized Jesus tells them. Opening the Scriptures to them, he restores and deepens their identity as disciples, a process reaching
completion in the breaking of the bread and their return to ministry
in Jerusalem. Hearing and meditating on this story, we become the
two on the road, placing our own concerns before the risen One who
speaks to us here and now, renewing and deepening our discipleship,
and sending us forth today.

Given that the readings are structured to provoke meditation, what
kind of meditation are we to practice? What model of the meditative
act—personal and communal—does the Liturgy of the Word presume? We do not have to look far for it because the word "meditation" has a history in Christian tradition, rooted in the centuries-old
practice of *lectio divina*.

Lectio Divina

Lectio divina or prayerful reading is not simply a method for culling
information out of one or more texts. It is a process of self-donation
to the Word, a spirituality, a way of moving with the life of God moving within us. Repetition and variation are important elements within
it. Even if pondering only a single passage, the process naturally
evokes memory of related texts and situations, making such meditation intertextual as well. One can practice this form of meditation
on one's own. But we are interested in how the Liturgy of the Word
and the entire liturgy can be an experience of communal *lectio divina*.

---

[16] Easter season is a bit more complex. Correspondence of all three readings is not
as strong on every Sunday.

Let us first review the stages of *lectio divina* and then see how it applies to communal worship. In its classic form, it consists of four steps or stages: *lectio, meditatio, oratio,* and *contemplatio* (reading, meditating, praying, and contemplating).

Lectio—*a first look at a passage of Scripture.* This first step concerns not only what we do with the Scripture but what we do with ourselves. We become still, quiet, and gathered before the Word, assuming a posture of prayerful openness. Citing the Quaker insight that *the God who spoke still speaks,* Steve Smith writes: "If God is speaking to me, should I not be listening?"[17] We place the passage on which we will meditate before us, but we must also place ourselves in the Presence speaking to us through this passage.

Since God is speaking to us through Scripture, this is an "I-Thou" rather than an "I-it" relation. The part-whole mechanism referred to in chapter 5 is at work here because during this first pass something grabs our attention—a particular word, phrase, or image. This small thing, this part, anchors the whole story in our memory and unlocks its meaning for us. Take the parable of the sower and the seed (Matt 13:3-9, 18-39). I invite you to open your Bible to this passage. In a first pass you might identify with the ground on which the seed is sown. Conversely, you might identify more with the sower. This first focusing "sets up" the next stage of *meditatio* (meditation).

Meditatio—*chewing the cud of the Word.* Conversing with God, you ask, "Am I like rocky ground in which the seed cannot really take hold? Am I too distracted by worry or desire to let the seed bear fruit?" Or, if you are drawn to the figure of the sower, you might ask: "How I am doing as a sower? Do I find welcome for the seed I am sowing or disconcerting resistance?" Pursuit of such questions is *meditatio,* in the course of which you may return to the text repeatedly for light.

John Dunne illustrates how a teacher's mind and heart may be led along the way of *meditatio*:

> Passing over here is like all passing over, it is followed by coming back.
> If I pass over into the parable of the Sower, I pass over into the figure
> of the Sower who sows the seed. . . . I think of my own experience
> of teaching, how my students come to my words with many different

---

[17] Smith, *Eastern Light*, 38.

frames of mind, some more, some less receptive. Coming back to myself, I realize I am like the Sower. . . . At the same time I realize I have no control over the ground on which the seed falls, no control over the results of my teaching. I have to let go of the seed as I broadcast it, to let my listeners be as receptive or unreceptive as they are.[18]

What is God telling me in this Scripture? Perhaps, that there is wisdom in doing one's best but then letting go of the fear-based need to control the results: "and I become heart-free, letting go of the seed as I broadcast it, letting my listeners listen as they will."[19] We are able to become heart-free and let go because all this is held within our I-Thou relation to God. We entrust ourselves to the Mystery in which all things abide. Resting in the Mystery means becoming decentered toward God, living a duet with God rather than a solo act, as though we are god unto ourselves and must carry everything on our shoulders alone.

We can also imagine different subjective contexts for the same reflection: parents trying to share the faith with their growing children, who are ready to throw the church overboard. Or it might be the preacher who struggles to do well but encounters difficulties and doubts. Additionally, meditation on this passage may call to mind other Scriptures, such as Jeremiah's struggle with sowing God's Word:

> The word of the LORD has brought me
>   reproach and derision all day long.
> I say I will not mention him,
>   I will no longer speak in his name.
> But then it is as if fire is burning in my heart,
>   imprisoned in my bones;
> I grow weary holding back,
>   I cannot. (20:7-9)

This passage may in turn call up the more joyful sentiments of Psalm 119: "I will never forget your word" (v. 16) and "Your word is a lamp for my feet, a light for my path" (v. 105). There is also the beautiful passage from Isaiah 55:10-11:

---

[18] Dunne, *Reading*, 61.
[19] Ibid.

Yet just as from the heavens
   the rain and snow come down
And do not return there
   till they have watered the earth,
   making it fertile and fruitful,
Giving seed to the one who sows
   and bread to the one who eats,
So shall my word be
   that goes forth from my mouth;
It shall not return to me empty,
   but shall do what pleases me,
   achieving the end for which I sent it.

In light of this exercise, you may find your anxiety as a preacher, teacher, or parent graciously transformed by the realization that it is not about you but about the God who made, loves, and calls you. One still encounters challenges, but no longer from self-absorbed fear or desire concerning one's performance. You do the best you can, resting and trusting in God who has chosen you as an instrument of the Word. Pope John XXIII possessed this kind of equanimity. At the end of a hard day's work he would say, "It's your church, Lord. I'm going to bed."

There is in this process an element of rehearsal, rehearing, resaying the text, much like an actor practicing lines over and over in order to memorize them. M. Basil Pennington gives us another example of personal *meditatio* extended over a day: "How different would our day be if we took from our lectio a word like, 'Whatever you do to the least, you do to me,' and it kept sounding in our hearts all through the day? As we encounter each person, we hear again, 'Whatever you do to the least, you do to me'? It is Christ, no matter what guise he comes in."[20] Notice how *intertextuality*, *repetition*, and *variation* animate the process. So far, we have been chewing the cud of the Word, releasing the flood of flavors in the sower passage, "tasting and seeing," as Psalm 34 says. This brings us to the third stage, *oratio* (prayer).

Oratio—*conversing with the Word*. The Word, taken to mind and heart in *meditatio*, touches our emotive core and awakens a response. We speak a word back to the Word who has made us heart-free. The

---

[20] M. Basil Pennington, *Lectio Divina* (New York: Crossroad, 1998), 61–62.

incoming Word, on our lips and in our hearts, sparks outgoing energy from within us. We answer in words or just wordlessly, holding the self before God in lament, petition, joy, gratitude, or love. And this opens onto the final stage, *contemplatio*, or communion with the Mystery in which all things abide.

Contemplatio—communion beyond words. We are beyond words or requests or any particular insights. All this is now left behind for simply resting or being-with: "Be still, and know that I am God" (Ps 46:10; NRSV). In a pamphlet he prepared for the United Nations meditation room, Dag Hammarskjold wrote, "We all have within us a center of stillness surrounded by silence." Citing these words, John Dunne says that reading the gospel "leads us into that inner silence."[21] This silence of *contemplatio* or resting in the holy Mystery may be more or less intense, more or less dramatic. There is an everyday mysticism as well as those extraordinary experiences of a few mystics. Often it is just a momentary but significant release from the small constricted self toward union with the fullness of Being. Since communion with God is not having an object before us, but rather closeness to that which must always exceed our grasp, it is difficult to put into words. But my Quaker friend, Steve Smith, describes it well:

> My experience widens and deepens—and wonder creeps in at the margins. Like a fish that for the first time becomes aware of the ocean in which it swims, I awaken to unbounded intimacy, a benign and encompassing love, a searching light over all, a sense of bathing in and being permeated by blessedness. Momentarily I no longer exist; there is only the experience of being known. . . . I have no doubt that this aura of beatitude is the love of God, the blessed release, the "peace of God which surpasses all understanding."[22]

Why is this contemplative dimension important for liturgical spirituality, which seems so concerned with external actions, things, and symbols? Dunne writes: "When I am in my center of stillness surrounded by silence, I am able to see my way where I cannot when I am off center, caught up in desires and fears."[23] Notice how his notion of centeredness echoes what we said earlier about *gatheredness*. Reach-

---

[21] Dunne, *Reading*, vii.

[22] Smith, *Eastern Light*, 44.

[23] Dunne, *Reading*, 15.

ing one's "center of stillness surrounded by silence" deepens what begins in the gathering rite. We transcend or go deeper than the "it's all up to me" self, propelled by fears, desires, aggressiveness, and an inflated sense of autonomy. We enact the wisdom of the Sabbath, which says, "Stop." In other words: "Be still and know," or better, "Be still and *be known*." As we heard Steve Smith say, in contemplative union, "there is only the experience of being known." We recover our in-every-moment graced origin from God, in which the self is "as it were, coming from the hands of God and waking up to itself."[24] Gathered or centered in this truth, we can see our way more clearly. Through the Word in our hearts and on the pages of Scripture, we begin to see as God sees, not fleeing from the world but relating to it differently.

Contemplatio implies *compassio and actio.* To these four classic stages, something more must be added. The final stage of *contemplatio* is closeness or union with God. God is love. God wills the healing of harms and the flourishing of creatures. "The glory of God," St. Irenaeus said, "is the human person fully alive."[25] Being fully alive, flowing from communion with God, means living from the standpoint of God's compassion. The compassion of God moving within us impels us to act, to "go and do likewise," as Jesus says after washing the feet of the disciples (John 13:1-15). So, *contemplatio* implies two further stages—*compassio* and *actio* (compassion and action).[26] Dunne implies as much below when he says, "In the strength of the Presence, I am able to 'cast aside regret and fear,' I am able 'to do the deed at hand.'" He is quoting these phrases from Tolkien's *The Lord of the Rings*.[27] They call to mind 1 John 4:18: "love drives out fear." Similarly, Steve Smith concludes his description of "bathing in and being permeated by blessedness" with "I am freed for constructive engagement with the world, I give myself to the work before me."[28]

[24] Swami Abishiktananda (pen name of Benedictine Henri le Saux), quoted by Kallistos Ware, "How Do We Enter the Heart?," in *Paths to the Heart: Sufism and the Christian East*, ed. James S. Cutsinger (Bloomington, IN: World Wisdom Books, 2002), 4.

[25] St. Irenaeus, *Against Heresies*, 4.20.7, from *Ante-Nicene Fathers*, vol. 1, ed. Alexander Roberts; available online at The Gnostic Library: www.gnosis.org.

[26] Pennington, *Lectio Divina*, 87–90.

[27] Dunne, *Reading*, 31.

[28] Smith, *Eastern Light*, 44.

Contemplative union clears the way for action by bringing clarity of vision. The purification of being rightly gathered or centered is complemented by illumination. Freed from self-absorbed fears and desires, we see our way more clearly. In this clarity, says John Shea, we notice something we otherwise miss, especially when we are off-center. We begin to notice in every experience the "lure toward redemption, to maximizing value, to making something the best it can be." Discerning this, we pour ourselves into "the work of responding to and engaging in this possibility."[29] In this way the contemplative dimension grounds agapic love and ethical action. And agapic love in action likewise throws light back on our grounding in God's compassion. This is what we give ourselves to when we genuinely give ourselves to the word and the Person of the Word.

Contemplatio-compassio-actio is Christic. In view of God's holding us in being through the Word, and God's incarnate relation to us in the Word made flesh, this contemplative dimension is *Christic.* Christ's humanity, his human knowing, loving, and willing, is unsurpassably grounded in and expressive of the Word of God's compassion for the world. Thus, the contemplative moment of *lectio divina* as well as the agapic practice flowing from it is participation in Christ. We see through God's eyes become human eyes in the incarnate and risen One. So, the Mystery continues to speak to us through the Word made flesh, mediated by the words of Scripture: Whatever you do to the least, you have done to me (see Matt 25:31-46). By meditating on the Scriptures in one's center of stillness surrounded by silence, one encounters the Person of the Word, not only through the words on the page (through the objective pole of our consciousness), but as the root of one's own being (through the subjective pole of consciousness). Christ within me directs my meditation on the Christ of the Scriptures. The Christ of the Scriptures informs my experience of Christ within me. Dunne writes, "The Presence I can feel in the surrounding silence is 'the Word of life' and in the strength of the words, in the strength of the Presence, I am able to 'cast aside regret and fear,' I am able 'to do the deed at hand.'"[30]

---

[29] John Shea, *Eating with the Bridegroom: The Spiritual Wisdom of the Gospels for Christian Preachers and Teachers, Year B* (Collegeville, MN: Liturgical Press, 2005), 22.

[30] Dunne, *Reading*, 29.

In the history of spirituality Ignatius of Loyola brought this modification to the ancient practice of *lectio divina*. Its final stage, at least in this life, is not union with God *beyond the world* but union with God's will *for the world*, that is, participation in the self-emptying of Christ. Javier Melloni writes,

> In Ignatius the movement of union is one of incarnation, not elevation, or more accurately, the form of elevation for Ignatius is that of descent. . . . To perceive this kenosis as source of life, and way of union and divinization, is the key to Ignatius's whole project and mystagogy.[31]

Contemplative union is for the sake of casting aside fear and discerning the deed at hand: how am I called to be another Christ, to incarnate the love of God *in the world*? Contemplation and action are not opposites we must choose between; they are partners within a healthy spiritual life: "be doers of the word, and not merely hearers" (Jas 1:22; NRSV).

The Eucharistic Liturgy as Communal *Lectio Divina*

Our task now is to see how lectio divina is personally and communally enacted in the liturgy.

Meditation on the parable of the sower revealed intertexuality as well as repetition and variation. These elements are especially prominent in the Liturgy of the Word since it features multiple readings. But the entire liturgy, not only the Liturgy of the Word, can be enacted as communal lectio divina. Pastoral leadership—the presider, readers, and music ministers—can mark out a path for the assembly to walk. To see how this is possible, consider the striking parallel between the successive stages of lectio divina and the major ritual units of the liturgy. It may be charted as follows:

---

[31] See Javier Melloni, *The Exercises of St. Ignatius Loyola in the Western Tradition*, trans. Michael Ivens (Leominster, Herefordshire, UK: Gracewing, 2000). For a shorter version, see "The Specificity of the Ignatian Exercises," in *An Ignatian Spirituality Reader*, ed. George W. Traub (Chicago: Loyola Press, 2008), 130–35.

Lectio Divina Stages	Ritual Stages
Lectio	Gathering Rite
Gathered in and by the Word; focusing on images or phrases we will use to explore God's message to us	
Meditatio	Liturgy of the Word
Chewing the "cud" of the Word to release its full flavor	
Oratio	Eucharistic Prayer
Speaking a word of self-offering back to God who has given the Word that offered himself for us	
Contemplatio/Compassio/Actio	Communion/Sending
One with and sent by Christ, the compassion of God	

In this approach, the day's Scriptures shape the whole liturgy. The word in the readings is interwoven with the word in the rites throughout. From gathering to communion and sending, the assembly is led progressively into a deeper encounter with the Word. In communion/sending this interweaving of ritual word and scriptural word achieves the closest possible unity. Communing with Christ's presence in the Scriptures is fulfilled by communing with Christ's presence in the sacrament. The Christ of the Scriptures is the Christ of the sacrament.

To illustrate this approach, let us look to a particular Sunday. Having first explored its readings, I will then show how presiding, reading, and music ministry can collaborate to lead the assembly into a progressively deeper encounter with the Word in the readings.

A Case in Point: The Third Sunday of Lent, Year A— Jesus and the Samaritan Woman

When I ask students to find repetition and variation across a particular Sunday's readings, their first inclination is to "go abstract" too quickly. They look at the readings and immediately move toward some abstract statement about a theme. I urge them, instead, to dwell in the particular details of each reading. One then notices how specific words, images, situations, or patterns are *repeated* in *varying* forms across the series of readings. One discerns the "web of reiteration," to recall Robert Alter's phrase. Any further step toward generalization should grow out of and return to the concrete images of the texts. It is best to begin with the gospel, since it controls the choice of the other readings, then trace how the first reading, psalm, and second reading lead up to it. I invite readers to open up their Bible or missal and read the gospel (John 4:5-42). Since this is a complex story, it will help to break it down into parts.

1) Setting the Scene

Jesus sits down by Jacob's well in a town of Samaria. This opening is significant for two reasons. On his way back to Galilee, he has stopped in hostile territory. As the narrator tells us, "Jews use nothing in common with Samaritans." Samaritans were Jews who had intermarried with conquerors and were despised as collaborators. Two incidents illustrate this ongoing hostility. Raymond Brown writes, "About a hundred years before Christ the Jewish high priest had destroyed the Samaritan temple on Mount Gerizim."[32] And close to the time of Jesus' birth, a group of Samaritans desecrated the Jerusalem temple with the bones of a corpse.

Jacob's well is also significant. Here, Genesis recounts, Jacob meets and falls in love with Rachel (29:1-12). Sent by his father to find a wife, he comes upon a well in a field with some sheep gathered about it, "for flocks were watered from that well." But the stone covering the well could only be removed once all the flocks had arrived.

> As soon as Jacob saw Rachel, the daughter of his mother's brother Laban, and the sheep of Laban, he went up, rolled the stone away from the mouth of the well, and watered Laban's sheep. Then Jacob kissed Rachel and wept aloud.

This incident quickly leads to their betrothal. We are invited to see the parallel between Jacob-Rachel and Jesus-Samaritan Woman. A betrothal of a spiritual kind is happening in our gospel story. These two backstories—hostility between Jews and Samaritans, and the

---

[32] Raymond Brown gives a short synopsis in *The Gospels and Epistles of John: A Concise Commentary* (Collegeville, MN: Liturgical Press, 1988), 36.

betrothal of Jacob and Rachel—explain much of what follows that at first seems puzzling.

2) Give Me a Drink

Beginning with Jesus' request for a drink, the woman's distrust and hostility emerges: "How can you, a Jew, ask me, a Samaritan woman?" and "you do not even have a bucket and the well is deep; where then can you get this living water? Are you greater than our father Jacob, who gave us this well?" Historical enmity between Samaritans and Jews dogs this initial dialogue. We should hear a mocking tone in the woman's remarks. Her initial hostility is not simply personal but represents this collective history, as is so often the case with enmity between peoples down to our own time. A whole culture of racism, for example, lies behind the racist acts of a single person.

But Jesus' promise of living water makes her curious enough to continue the conversation. He says, "If you knew the gift of God and who is saying to you, 'Give me a drink,' you would have asked him and he would have given you living water." "Sir, give me this water," she says, even though "Jews use nothing in common with Samaritans." As the conversation unfolds, hostility dissipates, and old boundaries are crossed. Jesus does not cross them alone; the woman is collaborating with him on this venture toward something new.[33]

3) Go, Call Your Husband

Now a seemingly abrupt, puzzling change of topic occurs: from thirst/water imagery to marital imagery. When she says she has no husband, Jesus answers, in so many words: "No kidding, you've had five, and the one you have now is not your husband." This woman has husband issues! In response she says: "Sir, I can see you are a

---

[33] Barbara Reid cautions against reducing this to a story about a sinful woman whom Jesus forgives. While her interaction with Jesus reveals her problems, the central element is her transformation into discipleship. That is why this gospel is part of the cycle of readings for those who are candidates for initiation. Barbara E. Reid, *Abiding Word: Sunday Reflections for Year A* (Collegeville, MN: Liturgical Press, 2013), 26.

prophet." Jesus, like a prophet, shows true insight into her situation. The Samaritan woman, whether as a person or as a symbol of her people, needs liberation from being *overly betrothed* or *wrongly betrothed*.[34] Whether her husbands have died or have divorced her, it seems her thirst for a true husband has gone unmet. Meeting Jesus, she begins to undergo a spiritual betrothal, because her thirsting spirit receives life from him. It explains why later the returning disciples are scandalized. Jesus should not be speaking with this woman, just the two of them, alone by the well, never mind that she is a Samaritan and he is a Jew.

4) A Question about Worship

Thinking that Jesus is a prophet, she poses a question, and the dialogue abruptly shifts yet again from marital relations to worship: "Our ancestors worshiped on this mountain; but you people say that the place to worship is in Jerusalem." The backstory of hostility between Samaritans and Jews is again invoked. Jesus converts this question about the right place to the question of what true worship really is: "neither on this mountain nor in Jerusalem . . . true worshipers will worship the Father in Spirit and truth; and indeed the Father seeks such people to worship him. God is Spirit, and those who worship him must worship in Spirit and truth."

We have apparently come a long way from thirsting for living water and marital imagery. But in fact, there is an underlying unity. To worship God in Spirit and truth is to fulfill the covenant by giving one's heart to God rather than to idols. Scripture portrays this covenant in marital imagery: "For your husband is your Maker. . . . My love shall never fall away from you" (Isa 54:5, 10). Speaking of Israel, Hosea announces "On that day—oracle of the Lord—You shall call me 'My husband.'" (2:18) and "I will betroth you to me forever: I will betroth you to me with justice and with judgment, with loyalty and with compassion" (2:21). Just a few paragraphs before our well story, John the Baptist describes Jesus as the bridegroom of the people (3:29-30). "The true Israel has been solemnly betrothed to God,"

---

[34] Thomas L. Broadie, *The Gospel According to John: A Literary and Theological Commentary* (New York: Oxford University Press, 1993), 218.

writes Raymond Brown, and now Jesus is coming to claim his bride."[35] Receiving living water from Jesus, being spiritually betrothed to him, worshiping God in Spirit and in truth—these are different images for abiding in God and God abiding in us through the mediation of Jesus and his Spirit.

As this section closes, the Samaritan woman says she knows that the Messiah, the Christ, is coming and "he will tell us everything." With wonderful Johannine irony, Jesus, who has just *told her everything* she had done concerning husbands, says, "I am he, the one who is speaking with you." The woman's naming of Jesus has progressed from simply "a Jew," to "Lord" or "Sir," to "a prophet," and finally to anticipation of the Messiah-Christ. A few sentences later she asks her townspeople, "Could he possibly be the Messiah?"

5) The Disciples Return; the Woman Brings the Townspeople to Jesus

The disciples, returning with food, are amazed and scandalized to find Jesus interacting with the Samaritan woman. The narrator tells us what they think but do not say aloud: "What are you looking for? . . . Why are you talking with her?" Here again, there is a hint of the impropriety of Jews and Samaritans interacting, especially a Jewish man with a Samaritan woman at a well (a traditional archetype for betrothal). Jesus is crossing boundaries, forcing others beyond their comfort zones. Leaving her water jar, the woman goes into town and urges the people to come out and see the one who "told me everything I have done. Could he possibly be the Messiah?"

When the disciples urge Jesus to eat something, he says "My food is to do the will of the one who sent me and to finish his work." This is a food the disciples do not know, because they are thinking of physical rather than spiritual food, just as earlier the woman was thinking in terms of physical water rather than the spiritual, life-giving drink that Jesus gives. Jesus is always stretching people beyond their limited viewpoints.

Referring to the work he must finish, Jesus then speaks of the harvest and "gathering crops for eternal life." In part, this speaks to

[35] Brown, *The Gospels and Epistles*, 35.

two previous moments in the text. The disciples had been thinking "Why speak to her? What are you looking for?" And earlier Jesus spoke of the Father seeking true worshipers. Jesus seeks people for the kingdom, and this seeking is not limited to Jews but goes out to everyone, including this Samaritan woman and her people. It transcends old boundaries and enmities. His dialogue with the woman sows a seed that, through her witness, reaches the townspeople. The returning disciples, johnnies-come-lately to the scene, are sent to reap what God has long prepared and Jesus, with the collaboration of the Samaritan woman, has already sown: "I sent you to reap what you have not worked for; others have done the work, and you are sharing the fruits of their work."

6) Conclusion: This Is Truly the Savior of the World

What Jesus has sown in the heart of this woman has begun to bear fruit. She brings the whole town out to hear him. Jesus abides with them for two days and they begin to believe in him. Having first heard the woman's testimony, they say, "We no longer believe because of your word; for we have heard for ourselves, and we know that this is truly the savior of the world."

From this review of the gospel, it is possible to see how the preceding readings are *staged* to prepare us for it and support meditation. I invite readers to have these additional readings open before them.

The first reading, from Exodus 17:3-7, parallels and anticipates the gospel as follows:

- people thirsting for water / woman's desire for "living water"

- thirsting in the desert / desert of the woman's life: many husbands but thirsting for real love

- people's grumbling hostility toward Moses / woman's initial hostility toward Jesus

- water flowing from the struck rock / Jesus is the rock from whom living water flows

- people's doubt: "Is the Lord in our midst or not?" / Jesus is God's presence in our midst

Psalm 95:1-2, 6-7, 8-9 is a flashback to the Exodus reading and points toward the gospel:

- "hail the rock who saves us" recalls "struck rock" / Jesus the rock from whom water flows

- "harden not your hearts" recalls distrust and hostility toward Moses and God in the desert / woman's initial hardness of heart toward Jesus

- "your ancestors put me to the test," "they tried me," recalls Exodus doubt ("Is the Lord in our midst or not?") / points to woman's "testing of Jesus" and Jesus as God's Christ in our midst

- expresses worship of God: "let us bow down in worship" / Gospel question of true worship of God

The second reading, Romans 5:1-2, 5-8, looks backward and forward as well:

- peace with God, hope, and "grace in which we stand" contrasted to loss of faith, hopelessness and turmoil in which the Exodus people stand

- "love of God poured into our hearts" echoes water imagery of Exodus / points to the living water Jesus gives, welling up to eternal life

The verse of the gospel acclamation (John 4:42, 15) shows how previous themes are recapitulated in the gospel:

- resolution of doubt, hostility, spiritual thirst into self-donation and faith: "Lord, you are truly the Savior of the world; give me living water, that I may never thirst again."

We have immersed ourselves in this Scripture but also received further insights from biblical commentary and scholarship. *Lectio divina* is not an alternative to modern scholarship but its partner. Holding these "I-it" insights within our "I-Thou" openness to God speaking to us here and now, they become elements within our prayer and meditation. The wise homilist will not try to cover all this ground. Better to focus on a few connections. Preaching may settle on the recurring water images culminating in Jesus, the living water. Or it may reflect on how we receive God's visitation, which may come in surprising ways that challenge our prejudices. Do we welcome it or harden our hearts? What enables us to move from the hardened heart to a responsive one? The homilist may develop the betrothal theme, stressing how the God of Love calls us into a deep and abiding partnership from which agapic love may flow toward others.

Since this story is chosen especially for those approaching Christian initiation, the homilist may highlight the woman's journey toward faith, expressed in the changing titles she uses to address Jesus across the story, from a Jew, to Sir (or Lord), to a prophet, to the Christ-Messiah. She becomes a witness to Christ, bringing others to him. She models the "job description" of the church as well as those to be initiated at the Easter Vigil: bearing witness to Christ in their lives and drawing others to him. In whatever direction the homily goes, however, it must first be "truly the fruit of meditation"[36] to recall the Introduction to the Lectionary. Such meditation is deepened by study. Engaging in the same process, lectors understand, perhaps for the first time, how they are to proclaim their reading. They know how it is related to the other Scriptures and points toward the gospel. Music ministers have an array of themes and images to inform their choice or composition of song. All have a role in leading the assembly into communal *lectio divina*.

Enactment of Communal *Lectio Divina*

How might enactment of communal *lectio divina* take place on this particular Sunday? Though the following illustration follows the pattern of the Roman Catholic liturgy, I invite members of other church traditions to consider how their own pattern of worship may be similarly shaped by the word of the day. For the most part, Protestant traditions allow worship leaders great leeway in nuancing their rites.

The Gathering Rite as Lectio

Gathered in and by the Word; focusing on images or phrases we will use to explore God's message to us. There are three moments across the rite that can invite the assembly into *lectio* or a first pass at the Word: the

---

[36] *Lectionary*, par. 24.

gathering song, the presider's introduction, and the third form of the Penitential Act with Invocations. All three can feature texts that anticipate the gospel story. Collaboration between the presider and music ministers is especially important here. The presider may reiterate a phrase or image from the song in opening remarks and later in the homily itself.

As a gathering song, "Drink Living Water/Tomen Agua Viva" by Colleen Fulmer and Rufino Zaragoza, anticipates the gospel scene but also names additional situations of human need and woundedness.

> Come, you hungry, come, you thirsty; drink living water, come unto me.
> Come, you weary, bring your burdens; drink living water, come unto me.
> Come, you poor ones, come, you lowly; drink living water, come unto me.
> Come, rejected, come, abandoned; drink living water, come unto me.[37]

The well-known hymn "I Heard the Voice of Jesus" evokes the thirst/water imagery threading across the readings to the gospel.[38] If one wants to situate the gospel story within the broader sweep of Lenten rituals and gospel stories, Alan Hommerding's "From Ashes to the Living Font," set to the ST. FLAVIAN hymn tune, allows one to do so. Verses 1, 2, and 4 speak more generally about the season, but for verse 3, one inserts a text specific to the Sunday gospel. For the Woman at the Well Sunday the text is:

> For thirsting hearts let waters flow, our fainting hearts revive;
> and at the well your waters give our everlasting life.[39]

Music ministers of each church tradition may find others examples in their own repertoire.

---

[37] "Drink Living Water," Colleen Fulmer and Rufino Zaragoza, OFM, © 1990. Published by OCP. All rights reserved. Used with permission. This song's verses have Spanish versions so that it can be done all in English, all in Spanish, or bilingually.

[38] Text: CMD; Horatius Bonar, 1809–1889, alt. Music: Trad. English melody; *English Country Songs*, 1893; adapt. by Ralph Vaughn Williams, 1872–1958.

[39] "From Ashes to the Living Font," Alan Hommerding, © 1994. World Library Publications, wlpmusic.com. All rights reserved. Used with permission.

After the song and greeting, the presider carries forward the song's "first pass" at the readings with introductory words leading to the next component of the rite, the Penitential Act (Confession and Assurance of Forgiveness in the Protestant tradition). Making use of the rite's options, consider the effect of hearing/praying something like the following across the gathering rite:

Presider's Introduction
Sitting down by the well of our lives, Jesus offers us life-giving drink but also challenges us to change. Do we welcome this visitation with genuine openness? Are we not sometimes hampered by fear, mistrust, even hardness of heart?

Penitential Act with Invocations
Mindful of this, brothers and sisters, let us acknowledge our sins and so prepare ourselves to celebrate the sacred mysteries.

Invocations sung by cantor or other minister
1. Lord Jesus, you change hardened hearts and teach us to worship in Spirit and truth:
Kyrie, eleison. *All:* Kyrie, eleison.

2. Lord Jesus, you are the Messiah of God, you give us living water:
Christe, eleison. *All:* Christe, eleison.

3. Lord Jesus, you make us your witnesses by the Spirit poured into our hearts:
Kyrie, eleison. *All:* Kyrie, eleison.

The rite concludes with the Collect or Opening Prayer. The assembly is set on the path of communal *lectio divina* through words, phrases, and imagery borrowed from the upcoming readings. This begins the focusing process that leads to *meditatio*.

Liturgy of the Word as Meditatio

Chewing the cud of the word to release its full flavor. The Liturgy of the Word is communal *meditatio*. Repetition and variation across the readings support the assembly in chewing the cud of the word. The responsorial psalm, "If today you hear his voice, harden not your hearts," explicitly links the desert grumbling of the first reading to the Samaritan woman's initial hostility toward Jesus in the gospel. The verse of the gospel acclamation provides further guidance by providing a scriptural encapsulation of the gospel: "Lord, you are truly the Savior of the world; give me living water, that I may never thirst again."

The meditative process undertaken by the assembly now culminates in the public *meditatio* of the preacher or homilist. At each stage a leading minister—lector, cantor, homilist—evokes the communal action of receiving and exploring the Word. Having passed through this Word we reaffirm our faith by praying the creed or affirmation of faith. The intercessions that follow should not be mini-homilies. But they can be cast in light of the day's Word. On this Sunday, for example, a petition might be worded as follows: "That, impelled by the Spirit of Love, we may bring healing to the divisions and hatreds that wound our families, our communities, and the world, we pray to the Lord."

The Eucharistic Prayer as Oratio

Speaking a word self-offering back to God who has given the Word that offered himself for us. How does the eucharistic prayer correspond to the *oratio* stage of *lectio divina*? The specific motion of *oratio* is the heart's response to the Word received. The response is to give, not some thing, but one's very self to God. "For it is loyalty that I desire, not sacrifice, and knowledge of God rather than burnt offerings," Hosea 6:6 says. But there is no self-donation to God without self-donation to the neighbor. The self-donation God wants, says the prophet Micah, is "to do justice, and to love kindness, and to walk humbly with your God" (6:6-8; NRSV). This self-offering is mediated by Christ who emptied himself in love of God and love of neighbor (everyone): "my body, which is given for you . . . this cup that is poured out for you" (Luke 22:19-20; NRSV). At the core of all the words that make up the eucharistic prayer is Christ's self-donation to God and humankind and our participation in it.

As communal *oratio*, the eucharistic prayer does not merely come after the Word but is a response to it. We are meant to pray it in light of the Word. "The same Christ who takes on flesh in the Eucharist does so according to different 'forms' in which he has spoken earlier in the Scriptures," writes Louis-Marie Chauvet. Referring to the table of the Word and the table of the Eucharist, he continues:

The liturgical and theological movement which proceeds from the first table to the second signifies concretely that the "this is my body" should be pronounced against the background of the Scriptures proclaimed on such-and-such a Sunday of Lent or during Easter time or on the feast of All Saints.[40]

This relation is always implicit and often, especially during festal seasons, made explicit. On the Sunday of Jesus and the Samaritan woman, the story spills over into the eucharistic prayer. After generic opening words, the preface says:

> For when he asked the Samaritan woman for water to drink,
> he had already created the gift of faith within her and so ardently
> did he thirst for her faith, that he kindled in her the fire of divine love.

The Communion Rite and the Sending as Contemplatio-Compassio-Actio

One with and sent by Christ, the compassion of God. We are finally brought to wordless intimacy with Christ the Word—communion. The Word is now our food and drink. Not only something for communal understanding but something shared as a communal meal. This mystery of communion beyond words, or *contemplatio*, is, paradoxically, shaped by many words: the spoken and sung words of the rite as well as the words of the communion song. This song may elaborate the word in the rite—the meaning of sharing in the Body and Blood of Christ. Or, it may echo the gospel and other readings. Songs such as "Give Us Living Water" return us to the word in the readings. While a song may repeat the gospel story, it may also link the story to other scriptural perspectives (intertextuality). "Give Us Living Water" adds verses from Psalm 34 to its evocation of the story. The way the Samaritan woman moves with the life of God moving within her can be interpreted now in terms of "Taste and see that the Lord is good," and "They are happy who seek refuge in the Lord."[41]

[40] Chauvet, *Symbol and Sacrament*, 222.

[41] "Give Us Living Water," from *Psallite*, © 2005, The Collegeville Composers Group. All rights reserved. Published and administered by the Liturgical Press, Collegeville, MN. Used with permission. Psalm text: The Grail (England), © 1963, 1986, 1993, 2000, The Grail Publications, Inc., agent. All rights reserved. Used with permission.

Still, all these words end in silence, not as a rebuff to words, but as their natural end point. Word and silence are partners. Words come out of silence and return into it. Because Christ is the Word *of God*, nearness to him is nearness to *the* Mystery, something both revealed and concealed, something that is Word but also wordless—the name above all names—the Word above all words!

The parallel between the liturgy and *lectio divina* can be taken further. What comes of intimacy with Christ? *Compassio.* Those who commune with Christ, the very compassion of God poured out on a suffering world, become compassionate with him. What comes of this compassion? *Actio* or action.[42] Consuming the Eucharist means entering into Christ's self-emptying action for others. Ritually speaking, the sending or dismissal is the natural outcome of the communion rite. That is why I have conflated the two in this presentation. To commune with Christ is to be sent forth as another Christ to others. This theme will be taken up in detail in our final chapter.

On this Sunday, a dismissal song that speaks of mission would not only express generally what it means to commune with Christ (the word in the rite) but also echo the heart of the gospel story: the Samaritan woman leaves her water jar behind to bring her townspeople out to Jesus. Ruth Duck's "Healing River of the Spirit" serves this purpose beautifully. Verse 2 exemplifies her blending of both the person and the community being sent forth to act for the kingdom:

> Wellspring of the Healing Spirit, Stream that flows to bring release,
> As we gain our selves, our senses, May our lives reflect your peace.
> Grateful for the flood that heals us, May your Church enact your grace.
> As we meet both friend and stranger, May we see our Savior's face.[43]

The Gospel as a Script for Reenactment

The spiritual practice of *lectio divina*, enacted personally and communally, offers a compelling method and model for finding ourselves

---

[42] Pennington, *Lectio Divina*, 87–90. Compassion and action as outcomes of communion correspond to the traditional notion of the "fruits" of the Eucharist.

[43] "Healing River of the Spirit," Ruth Duck, 1994; © 1996 The Pilgrim Press. All rights reserved. Used with permission. Another fine example is "God Has Chosen Me," Bernadette Farrell, © 1990. Published by OCP. All rights reserved.

in the word. John Navone provides a complementary image for this process—the gospel as a script for reenactment.[44] The actor/text analogy coincides especially with our understanding of the final stage of *contemplatio* or union with God, which implies being shaped for action by the compassion of God in Christ. What is heard in the celebration of the liturgy must be lived. This imitation of Christ is very like what an actor does. By putting on the character, one plays and thereby communicates the presence and actions of that character in one's own time and place. Reenacting Christ in this sense cannot be literal mechanical repetition. It requires what William Spohn calls "analogical reflection," in which "the imagination enters deeply into the particular images and stories of scripture and envisions possibilities in our own context."[45] That kind of reflection is already at work in the features of intertextuality, repetition, and variation: an image, action, or behavior is repeated but *variously* across several readings. How do we, then, repeat the call of the Gospel in our own time and place? For example, how do we reenact the washing of the feet? There is, of course, the ritual reenactment of Holy Thursday. But this *ritual* performance is to shape us for *existential* performance. Spohn writes:

> If the disciples had taken Jesus literally, Christians would be washing feet every Sunday. They knew better than to copy him. He had given them an example, a demonstration, that graphically pointed to a distinctive way of loving service. They had to figure out from this sign how they could become a corresponding sign to the world. In the new commandment Jesus tells Christians to use their imaginations, to think analogically in moving from "as I have loved you" to "so you ought to love one another."[46]

For such reenactment to happen, the actors must first learn their lines. In the Liturgy of the Word we learn the Christ-lines so that we can play the Christ-character. John Navone writes, "Unless the Gospel story redefines a person's character, he or she cannot follow the way of life proper to the disciple."[47] But fulfilling the word by doing the

---

[44] Navone, *Seeking*, 89–100.

[45] William Spohn, *Go and Do Likewise* (New York: Continuum, 2007), 50.

[46] Ibid., 52.

[47] Navone, *Seeking*, 279.

word is not only a question of individual ethics. It requires that the church, both universally and in local assemblies act communally as a social player, speaking truth to power. It follows that the spirituality of the assembly's encounter with Christ the Word is unfulfilled if it is proposed only in terms of individual sanctification. Not only must the social dimension of the Gospel be preached, but pastoral leadership should provide the local assembly with opportunities for acting communally as Christ's Body in the neighborhood, city, nation, and world. Such enactments beyond the liturgy nourish and deepen our appropriation of the word within the liturgy. Hearing and meditating on the story of the Good Samaritan may move us deeply. But if a local church has organized itself to give practical support to victims of violence, this activity will profoundly change how it experiences this story and its related readings from the Fifteenth Sunday in Ordinary Time, Year C. Navone summarizes the whole process as follows:

> Christians believe that the risen Christ and his Holy Spirit are actively present in the hearts and minds of the faithful, assisting them to grasp the meaning and value of the written biblical revelation. The Risen Christ and his Holy Spirit direct the hearts and minds of the faithful, in a role analogous to that of the director of a play, in the prayerful process of representing the Christ-meaning and the Christ-value to the world.[48]

In a play, the actor receives and enacts a new name. Lawrence Olivier becomes Richard III, Dame Judy Dench becomes Elizabeth I. In the play of Christian life and spirituality we likewise receive and enact a new name. There are, of course, saint's names. But the saint is really another Christ, an icon of Christ. As we heard the poet Hopkins say earlier in chapter 5,

> Christ plays in ten thousand places,
> Lovely in limbs, and lovely in eyes not his.[49]

May it be so for us! We might all pray with the old spiritual:

---

[48] Navone, *Seeking*, 92.

[49] Hopkins, "As Kingfishers Catch Fire." Available online at www.poetryfounda tion.org.

I tol' Jesus it would be all right if He changed mah name.

Jesus tol' me I would have to live humble if he changed mah name.

Jesus tol' me that the world would be 'gainst me if he changed my name.

But I tol' Jesus it would be all right if he changed mah name.[50]

---

[50] African American spiritual.

Chapter 8

Approaching the Eucharistic Prayer

What shall I return to the LORD
for all his bounty to me?
I will lift up the cup of salvation
and call on the name of the LORD.

Psalm 116:12-13 (NRSV)

This chapter addresses several preliminaries to the eucharistic prayer itself. First, we reflect on the presentation of the gifts, which anticipates the spirituality of the eucharistic prayer. Second, an initial overview of the prayer's spirituality is given. Finally, this overview leads us into three questions, two of which are answered here. The third is addressed in the next chapter.

The Presentation of the Gifts

We come to the eucharistic prayer by way of the presentation of the gifts. Though words "gifts" and "offering" are used in the Roman Rite, what Catholics once called the "offertory" is not the true offering. The true ritual offering by which we "lift up the cup" and make a return for God's goodness is within the eucharistic prayer. But here we anticipate the spirituality that marks the eucharistic prayer: welcoming the gift of God and making a return.

Both this theme and the form of the presentation prayers are indebted to Jewish table blessing (*berakah*). These prayers echo a fundamental ethical dimension in the spirituality of our Jewish brothers and sisters. It is a spirituality, Abraham Heschel says, animated by awareness that to exist is to have something asked of us: "We are asked to wonder, to revere, to think and to live in a way that is compatible with the grandeur and mystery of living."[1] Whether Descartes meant it this way or not, his dictum, "I think, therefore I am," is emblematic of modernity's wrongheaded attempt to make humans the center and measure of everything. Heschel turns this on its head: "I am commanded—therefore I am."[2] To mend the world and promote human well-being—everything that Christians call the social gospel or social justice or eco-justice—this profound Jewish spirituality shapes the Christian spirituality of the presentation of the gifts and the eucharistic prayer that follows it.

Bread, wine, and provision for the poor are brought forward from the assembly. The provision for the poor is essential to the rite's meaning, not an occasional extra. As the bread and wine are placed on the altar, two prayers are said in the Roman Catholic rite. Among several options, the Evangelical Lutheran rite has a similar prayer at this moment.[3]

Table 2

Roman Catholic	Evangelical Lutheran
Over the Bread Blessed are you, Lord God of all creation, for through your goodness we have received the bread we offer you: fruit of the earth and work of human hands, it will become for us the bread of life. *Blessed be God for ever.*	**After or as the Gifts Are Presented** Blessed are you, O God. maker of all things. Through your goodness you have blessed us with these gifts: our selves, our time and our possessions. Use us, and what we have gathered,
Over the Cup Blessed are you, Lord God of all creation, for through your goodness we have received the wine we offer you: fruit of the vine and work of human hands, it will become our spiritual drink. *Blessed be God for ever.*	in feeding the world with your love, through the one who gave himself for us, Jesus Christ, our Savior and Lord. *Amen*

[1] Abraham J. Heschel, *God in Search of Man* (New York: Farrar, Straus and Giroux, 1976), 113.

[2] Abraham J. Heschel, *Who Is Man* (Stanford, CA: Stanford University Press, 1965), 111.

[3] *Evangelical Lutheran Worship*, Pew Edition (Minneapolis, MN: Augsburg Fortress, 2006), 107.

Both traditions acknowledge the gift character of creation. We think we are bringing our gifts, but they are first God's gifts to us ("through your goodness we have received"). Spiritually speaking, this expresses the turn from *humans as the center* to experiencing our createdness (see chap. 1). With all other creatures we receive our being as *gift* from the Mystery in which all things abide. So, we are not initiating the gifting process but rather "making a return" (Ps 116).

Second, this ritual presentation of gifts implies an ethic. But the Catholic and Protestant versions express it differently. It is most explicit in the Lutheran prayer: "Use us, and what we have gathered in feeding the world." Its focus is less on the bread and wine, more on the ecclesial body that will be transformed for service by the Eucharist: "our selves, our time and our possessions." The other two options in the Lutheran order of worship do mention "food from the earth" (option 1) and "bread from the earth and fruit from the vine" (option 2). But here again concern is primarily with how participants will act on what they have received: "Turn our hearts toward those who hunger in any way, that all may know your care" (option 1), and "Nourish us with these gifts, that we might be for the world signs of your gracious presence" (option 2).[4]

By contrast, the Catholic prayers focus on the gifts of bread and wine that will become the sacramental presence of Christ. It is only later, after the institution narrative or consecration, that the Catholic liturgy especially emphasizes the ecclesial body—what the church as the body of Christ must be for the world. But an ethical dimension is not lacking in the Catholic presentation prayers. In the Lutheran version, it is God who "brings forth bread from the earth and fruit from the vine." The Catholic prayers explicitly connect the gifts of bread and wine with human labor. And this brings the ethical dimension into view.

Consider the words "fruit of the earth and work of human hands." Bread and wine are not purely natural but nature transformed by human labor. They carry, as Jean Corbon says, "the imprint of our hands."[5] So the bread and wine brought forth represent both the gift of creation and our working relationship with the earth, in biblical

---

[4] Ibid.

[5] Quoted by Goffredo Boselli in *The Spiritual Meaning of the Liturgy* (Collegeville, MN: Liturgical Press, 2014), 99.

terms, our stewardship. It is this stewardship, this working relationship to the earth, that will become the eucharistic presence of Christ.
How goes our stewardship these days? If our stewardship harms
nature and the poor—is that what we wish to bring to the Lord's
table? And once these gifts become the presence of Christ, who gave
his life not for a few but for all, are we not challenged to strive for a
more just and responsible economic order? In *Laudato Si'* Pope Francis
quotes John Paul II to highlight the link between care for creation
and care for human beings: "God gave the earth to the whole human
race for the sustenance of all its members, *without excluding or favoring
anyone. . . .* It is not in accord with God's plan that these gifts be
used in such a way that its benefits favor only a few."[6]

Goffredo Boselli writes profoundly of this brief rite in a chapter
titled "Mystagogy of the Presentation of the Gifts."[7] The ritual gesture
of offering God the fruit of the earth and work of human hands echoes
the offering of firstfruits in Deuteronomy 26:1-11. Several things are
involved at once in the symbolism of this ancient offering.

First, in harvesting, something is to be left unharvested for the
Levite and the resident alien, neither of whom could own land and
who therefore depended on others for food. Second, offering the
firstfruits to God obviously does not fill any need in God. Rather, it
keeps us in truth: we do not own creation. It is God's gift to all, as
John Paul II said above. So offering the firstfruits, Boselli writes,
"relativizes possession and puts some distance between the believer
and the fruit of the land and of work."[8] This is not an argument
against private property. Rather, what we "own" is on loan from God
and brings with it responsibilities to the common good and especially
the most vulnerable. Finally, once the firstfruits are ritually offered
they are to be shared, especially with the poor in view: "Then you,
together with the Levites and the aliens who reside among you, shall
celebrate with all the bounty that the LORD your God has given to
you and to your house" (Deut 26:11; NRSV). So, *provisions for the poor*

---

[6] *On Care for Our Common Home: Laudato Si'*, Encyclical Letter of the Holy Father
Francis (Washington, DC: United States Conference of Catholic Bishops/Vatican City:
Liberia Editrice Vaticana, 2015), par. 93.

[7] Boselli, *The Spiritual Meaning*, 79–101.

[8] Ibid., 83.

are not an occasional extra but something central to presenting the gifts of bread and wine.

Embedded in this brief rite is a series of calls to self-transcendence. Acknowledging the Creator, we also acknowledge our createdness ("Blessed are you, Lord God of all creation"). We are freed from the illusion of absolute autonomy. We are reminded that no one can simply own creation, much less hoard it: "for through your goodness we have received." Our use of it carries responsibilities to others, especially the most vulnerable. What comes forward in the gifts is our economic relation to creation and all of humanity: "fruit of the earth and work of human hands." All this is the ethical depth dimension of these prayers. Both Catholic and Protestant forms prepare us for the ethics and spirituality of the eucharistic prayer.

If our economic order is flawed, if it involves some sinning against the environment and the poor, should we be celebrating at all? Should we not, as Jesus says in Matthew 5:23-24, leave our gift at the altar and first be reconciled with our neighbor and creation and only then make our offering? Were we to interpret this saying literally, we would never celebrate the Eucharist! We would never obey the command, "Do this in memory of me" (Luke 22:19). We cannot wait until the world is perfect before offering our lives to God. It is like Wendell Berry's poem, "The Mad Farmer's Love Song":

> O when the world's at peace
> and every man is free
> then will I go down unto my love.
> O and I may go down
> several times before that.[9]

We have to "go down unto" that gracious Love that wants to realize the reign through us, even before the world is at peace and every woman and man is free. It is just this "going down," following the kenotic way of Jesus that enables us to bend the arc of history more and more toward justice and compassion.

What we bring in the presentation of the gifts, our lives and our work symbolized in the bread and wine, is in fact our imperfection,

---

[9] Wendell Berry, "The Mad Farmer's Love Song," in *Collected Poems: 1957–1982* (San Francisco: North Point Press, 1985), 162.

but with longing and hope in God's grace, already enacted for us in the One who bore our griefs. Bringing gifts of a flawed economic order to the table we bring not our perfection but our lack, our ache, for the kingdom to come. It is with this same lack or ache that we engage in the eucharistic prayer. "What we offer at the threshold of the anaphora," Jean Corbon wrote, "is not gifts but an incompleteness, an appeal (the epiclesis is a groaning), the anxious expectation of creation that carries the imprint of our hands but not yet the imprint of the light."[10]

A First Look:
The Spirituality of the Eucharistic Prayer

Moving with the life of God moving within us is the notion of spirituality that has animated these pages. This *moving with* is Christic. In his humanity borne by divinity, Christ empties himself in a spiritual motion responsive to God moving within him. Doing the will of the One who sent him, freely and lovingly, he enacts God's compassion toward the whole creation, especially human beings in their brokenness. Thus, our own spirituality is identification with Christ in the sense of a *being-like* that flows from *being-in*. "Do this in memory of me." In other words, do the whole thing, the whole life journey, with our minds stayed on Jesus. Have the mind of Jesus among you (see Phil 2:5). Jesus says, "Abide in me as I abide in you" (John 15:4; NRSV).

Abiding in this sense is also *in the Spirit* or pneumatological. It is by the Spirit dwelling in our hearts that we abide in Christ. This is what Colossians means by "Christ in you, the hope of glory" and "your life is hidden with Christ in God" (1:27; 3:3; NRSV). But abiding in and imitating is not mechanical, automatic, or magical. This imitation, borne by the indwelling grace of Christ and the Spirit, is a free and conscious response. It calls on all the intelligence and imagination we can muster. To paraphrase William Spohn, we have to figure out from the sign—Christ, the sacrament of God's compassion—how we

---

[10] Jean Corbon, *The Wellspring of Worship*, trans. Matthew J. O'Connell (New York: Paulist Press, 1988), 160. Quoted by Boselli in *The Spiritual Meaning*, 99. What I have written here is only a partial summary of Boselli's remarkable analysis of the presentation rite, 79–101.

are to become a corresponding sign to the world in our own day.[11] This is what the opening paragraph of the Dogmatic Constitution on the Church (*Lumen Gentium*) means by calling the church a sign and sacrament of Christ (1).

When there is failure to abide, it is often because consciously or unconsciously other influences are functionally more primary than the Gospel. On the web one can find images of a gun-toting Christ, advocate of the NRA, or a Christ with the face of Che Guevara. Clearly, one's political affiliation is top dog in these examples. Christ is made to serve rather than challenge human ideologies. But the Word, to which we return time and again, challenges us to identify with Christ and his teaching above all else. It is only because, as Alexander Schmemann says, "Christ is in us and we are in Christ" that Christian persons and communities stand a chance of being the signs they are meant to be. The liturgy and, in a specific way, the eucharistic prayer draw us into the central action whereby we abide in Christ and sign him to the world: self-offering. And self-offering is but another word for self-emptying.

Psalm 116 asks: what return shall we make for God's bounty to us? "I will lift the cup of salvation," says the psalmist (v. 13), and a few lines later adds:

> I am your servant; the child of your serving girl.
>   You have loosed my bonds.
> I will offer to you a thanksgiving sacrifice
>   and call on the name of the LORD.
> I will pay my vows to the LORD
>   in the presence of all his people,
> in the courts of the house of the LORD. (vv. 16-19; NRSV)

Viewed through Christian eyes, the servant, indeed the suffering servant, is Jesus, child of Mary. His advent as servant flows from God and servant Mary's yes ("your serving girl"). This momentous yes is the return she makes to God who "has done great things" for her (Luke 1:46-55; NRSV). The sacrifice of thanksgiving is Christ's self-offering in his life and death, a self-emptying love affirmed by God in the resurrection ("you have loosed my bonds"). This is the essential

---

[11] William Spohn, *Go and Do Likewise* (New York: Continuum, 2007), 50–52.

content of the eucharistic prayer. This is the Christic motion of the prayer we trace through, with, and in Christ. "Do this in memory of me." These words do not simply mean repeating the ritual but living what the ritual symbolizes and renders present: the self-emptying love of Christ. In him, we become the servant, humanly born of woman, offering the thanksgiving sacrifice ritually and existentially. This is how we make a return, how we "pay our vows" to God. But in the spirit of Psalm 116, it is a responsive gift of love courageously and gladly given.

This pattern corresponds to what we found in chapter 7, concerning the parallel between the stages of *lectio divina* and the liturgy. The third stage of *lectio divina* is *oratio*: speaking a word of self-offering back to God who has given the Word made flesh that offered himself for us. The ritual-liturgical form of this is the eucharistic prayer. We make this return in many ways across our lives, not only within, but beyond the liturgy. But in liturgical prayer we explicitly *say* our love of God who has first loved us. We explicitly "say ourselves," to recall Yves Congar's phrase,[12] in relation to the paschal mystery.

There is always the temptation to think of sacramental ritual as secondary to reality, something floating above our lives that is not strictly necessary. But are not our most real and self-actualized experiences those in which we give ourselves by explicitly "saying ourselves" to an *other*—a friend, a lover, a spouse, a community, a moral cause, a spiritual path? When I explicitly say my love to my beloved, this is not icing on the cake—this is the cake, even if I am not literally voicing it constantly. Karl Rahner once said that he prayed not because he believed but rather "I believe because I pray."[13]

Citing Psalm 116 above, I initially described the spirituality of the prayer as "welcoming the gift of God and making a return." This is shorthand, in fact, for how Louis-Marie Chauvet understands this prayer. Before looking at his approach in some detail in chapter 9, it will be helpful to explore two questions: What kind of script is it? Who enacts it? A final question—what is its structure?—will be treated in the next chapter.

---

[12] Yves Congar, *The Word and the Spirit* (San Francisco: Harper & Row, 1986), 10.

[13] *Encounters with Karl Rahner*, ed. and trans. Andreas Batlogg and Melvin E. Michalski (Milwaukee, WI: Marquette University Press, 2009), 263.

Two Questions:
What Kind of Script Is It? Who Prays It?

First, what kind of script is this? Earlier, I introduced the distinction between the word in the readings and the word in the rite. The eucharistic prayer is a case of the word in the rite. It communicates the paschal mystery in a highly abbreviated form compared to the detailed elaboration of the Scriptures. Chauvet makes a similar distinction under the heading "Word-Scripture and Word-Sacrament."[14] Borrowing a term from chemistry, he says every sacrament is a "precipitate" or crystallization of the Scriptures. This is how we must understand the eucharistic prayer, culminating in the sacrament of Holy Communion. It is rooted in the Scriptures, summarizing, paraphrasing, and quoting them throughout. So, Word-Scripture, enacted first in the Liturgy of the Word, pervades, informs, and is crystallized in Word-Sacrament—the bread and wine made holy and received by the church. Meditating on the Scriptures is "tasting and seeing," that is, chewing the cud of the word. Consuming the sacramental presence is a further stage in chewing the book, eating the scroll of the Word, as the prophets were once commanded to do.[15] Every sacramental rite is thus a mediation or sacrament *of the Word*. Chauvet appeals to the Emmaus story: *"From the table of the Scriptures to the table of the sacrament* the dynamic is traditional and irreversible. . . . From the time of Emmaus, one sees the distinctively sacramental moment preceded by the scriptural moment."[16] The same risen One, present to the two on the road, citing and interpreting the Scriptures, becomes present and known to them in the breaking of the bread.

As we move into the eucharistic prayer we are not really leaving the Liturgy of the Word behind. Rather, we take it with us into this next stage. The famous formula of Augustine says when the Word is pronounced over the elements a sacrament comes to be.[17] On the one hand, this means the ritual formula spoken over the elements, such as the words used with the water for baptism ("I baptize you in the name of the Father, and of the Son, and of the Holy Spirit"). These words are scriptural, drawn from Matthew 28:19. But in a broader

---

[14] Louis-Marie Chauvet, *Symbol and Sacrament*, trans. Patrick Madigan and Madeleine Beaumont (Collegeville, MN: Liturgical Press, 1995), 220–21.

[15] Ibid., 222–23.

[16] Ibid., 220–21.

[17] Augustine, *Tractates on the Gospel of John*, Tractate 80.3.

sense the whole Liturgy of the Word *informs* the Liturgy of the Eucharist. Summarizing Rahner on this point, David Power writes:

> The word of the sacrament embraces the proclamation of the gospel, the offer of grace that is expressed in scripture and preaching. It is this that is connected with the sacramental elements and rites. . . . The word already has a sacramental character when it is proclaimed as God's offer of grace within the church. When united with the elements and ritual actions, it constitutes these as offer and communication to those who are ritually touched.[18]

Rahner too, along with Chauvet, can say that every sacrament is a crystallization of the Scriptures. So, the word in the readings flows into the word in the rite. But who enacts this prayer, this word in the rite? An answer is provided by the dialogue that begins and the doxology that ends the prayer.

The Beginning: "Let Us Give Thanks"

"Marley was dead, to begin with. There is no doubt about that. He was as dead as a doornail." So begins Dickens's *A Christmas Carol*. Everything that happens to Scrooge begins from his partner's death. "In the beginning was the Word." So begins the Gospel of John, echoing the first words of Genesis. Everything that follows concerns this Word. Beginnings are important. They set a narrative in motion and often introduce its primary characters. Since I began this book with Thornton Wilder's *Our Town*, consider how it begins. Speaking to the audience, the Stage Manager, a character in the story, gives the title and author, then says:

> In it you will see you will see Miss C . . .; Miss D . . .; Miss E . . .; and Mr. F . . .; Mr. G . . .; and Mr. H . . .; and many others.[19]

This odd manner of beginning does not name the play's characters but the actual people who will assume these characters and make

---

[18] David N. Power, *The Eucharistic Mystery: Revitalizing the Tradition* (New York: Crossroad, 1995), 273.

[19] *Our Town*, in *Thornton Wilder: Collected Plays and Writings on the Theater* (New York: The Library of America, 2007), 149.

the play happen. Miss C, Mr. D, Miss E—these are just placeholders for whoever is actually involved in the play in this or that locality. The blanks are to be filled in with their actual names. This fits the ethos of the play well. Wilder wants everyone to experience *Our Town* as *their* town. In a local production, all the parts will be played by people they know, their neighbors and acquaintances, members of *their* town. This is just what the opening dialogue that begins the eucharistic prayer does. It says who is responsible for it, who will enact the prayer.

> The Lord be with you. And with your spirit.
> Lift up your hearts. We lift them up to the Lord.
> Let us give thanks to the Lord our God. It is right and just.

The key line: "Let *us* give thanks to the Lord our God." The key word: *us*. But who is this "us"? It is neither the priest alone nor the congregation alone, nor even the sum of the two together, but the underlying unity to which both belong—the church. The gathered church or local assembly prays this prayer. "It is the whole *community*," says the *Catechism of the Catholic Church*, "the Body of Christ united with its Head, that celebrates."[20] Yes, it is a *presidential* prayer, with significant portions spoken by the priest alone. But this very word—presidential—indicates a relation, a *doing by one member* in service to a *doing by all members of the gathered church*. "One presides; all celebrate," Chauvet writes.[21] This is borne out by the back-and-forth motion, in which the priest and people take turns speaking or singing various parts of the prayer. And insofar as the priest speaks alone, it is always in the name of the assembly, it is the "we" of "Make holy, therefore, these gifts we pray . . . so that they may become for us . . ." and "we offer you, Lord, the Bread of Life . . . giving thanks that you have held us worthy." As Chauvet says, the same "we" is apparent in Paul: "The cup of blessing that we bless, is it not a participation in the blood of Christ? The bread that we break, is it not a sharing in the body of Christ?" (1 Cor 10:16).[22]

---

[20] *Catechism of the Catholic Church* (New York: Doubleday, 1997), par. 1140.

[21] Louis-Marie Chauvet, *The Sacraments*, trans. Madeleine Beaumont (Collegeville, MN: Liturgical Press, 2001), xxiii.

[22] Chauvet, *The Sacraments*, 33.

Clearly, then, the word "assembly" is not a synonym for the congregation over against its priest. It is a synonym for the church to which both the presider and the congregation belong. This church is universal and local. Universal because in belonging to Christ, we belong to the baptized everywhere, not just other members of our local parish or congregation. In the Catholic tradition, church leadership—pope, bishops, ordained clergy—exists to serve and safeguard this unity of local churches. On the other hand, the most concrete manifestation of the church is in actual liturgical celebrations. They are by definition local. That is why the Dogmatic Constitution on the Church (*Lumen Gentium*) says it is "in and from these that the one and unique catholic church exists" (23). That statement is a stunner and goes against our usual habit of thought. So, one is first baptized, made a member of the church. The additional call to ordination, then, does not remove one from this assembly (universal and local) but gives one a new, sacramentally conferred role within it.

Presiding over the communal prayer of the church is like conducting a symphony. Both conductor and players belong to the one orchestra that makes the music. All are actively engaged, though one presides over their effort. Chauvet writes, "Not only is it erroneous to say that 'such and such a priest celebrates' (what the priest does is preside 'in the name of Christ'), but it is insufficient to think that the community celebrates only by uniting itself to what the priest does. In fact, this community acts; it acts *as a body*, as a constituted body, as body of Christ, even though the roles and functions, the priest's in the first place, are distributed within it in different ways."[23]

One of the great accomplishments of the Second Vatican Council has been the restoration of the local assembly/church as agent of the liturgy, an ecclesiology that had largely been lost during the Middle Ages. The decline of the liturgy toward an exclusively clerical act began even earlier. St. John Chrysostom provides a glimpse of its beginnings in a remark concerning the eucharistic prayer:

> The eucharistic prayer is common; the priest does not give thanks alone, but the people with him, for he begins it only after having received the accord of the faithful. . . . If I say that, it is so that we learn

---

[23] Ibid.

that we are all a single body. Therefore, let us not rely on the priests for everything, but let us, too, care for the Church.[24]

That Chrysostom has to emphasize this shows that change is already underway. He reminds his people that the action is *common* because it is the action of the church of which they are members along with their priest. In fact, we know that in place of this most ancient understanding, the liturgy of the medieval era devolved into an exclusively clerical action performed *on behalf of* but no longer *with* the gathered people.

In whatever way Protestant traditions understand ministerial leadership, they face a similar issue. In actual practice, is prayer/ preaching leadership, whether by a single minister or shared among a number of them, a performance aimed at inspiring and edifying an audience-congregation? Or is it a matter of evoking and energizing an action that properly belongs to the whole assembly? Catholics and Protestants alike do not have to look far to see how easily the culturally dominant entertainment model insinuates itself in worship, replacing communal agency with the performer/audience model. The advantage of ritually structured worship is that as a repeatable and predictable script it more easily becomes an action of the whole gathered body. The locus of celebration is not this or that leader but the ritual that belongs to everyone. When worship rests solely in what a charismatic or not so charismatic preacher can provide, perhaps with the help of musicians, the center of gravity shifts from the whole gathered people to a few individuals and what they choose to present.

Why is all this important for the spirituality of the eucharistic prayer? In John's gospel, Jesus says the grain of wheat must fall to the ground and die in order to bear much fruit. That is the heart of the paschal mystery and the central plot of the eucharistic prayer. But there is more. This grain is not Jesus alone. This grain is you and me, every Christian, and every ecclesial community. In the same passage Jesus says, "Whoever serves me must follow me, and where I am, there also will my servant be" (John 12:24-26). If Jesus is the grain of wheat that falls to the ground and dies—for the life of the

---

[24] Quoted by Herve-Marie Legrand in "The Presidency of the Eucharist According to the Ancient Tradition," in *Living Bread, Saving Cup*, ed. R. Kevin Seasoltz (Collegeville, MN: Liturgical Press, 1982), 218.

world—then we must follow him there. The eucharistic prayer is nothing else than ritually following Jesus, going where he goes, joining him in "making a return." So we are not only patients of Christ's activity, but sharers in it.

The Ending:
"Through Him, with Him, and in Him"

If beginnings are important, so are endings. Often mystery stories end by revealing *who done it*. In a quite different way, the ending of the eucharistic prayer also tells us *who done it*:

> Through him, and with him, and in him,
> O God, almighty Father,
> in the unity of the Holy Spirit,
> all glory and honor is yours,
> for ever and ever.

Our first task was to determine who the "us" of "Let us give thanks" is. It is the church, actualized in the local assembly, presided over by the priest and animated by additional ministries. But the doxology that ends the prayer shows us something else. It is only through, with, and in Christ that it is possible to pray this prayer. In doing so, we are not looking to Christ as a past and far-off ethical model to imitate. We are *in* the risen One: "abide in me as I abide in you" (John 15:4; NRSV). And because Jesus is the original enactor of this return-gift, giving himself out of love for the One who sent him and for humankind, the Eucharist is first of all not the action of the community but the action of Christ. It is Christ's priestly act. It is our priestly act by participation: through, with, and in Christ, as the doxology says.

Further, we must not forget the significance of the phrase "the one who sent me" (John 8:29; Matt 10:40) as well as Paul's saying that God was in Christ, reconciling the world to God (2 Cor 5:19). Christ's priestly act is the gift of God, a *from-God-toward-us* action. Chauvet writes, "The operating subject of the sacraments is always God (through Christ and in the Spirit)."[25] But insofar as Christ is the Word

---

[25] Chauvet, *The Sacraments*, xxiv.

made flesh, the very *humanity* of God, this priestly act is also a *from-humanity-toward-God* response. Human reality, created, sustained, and graced by God, is transformed and sanctified to co-enact God's will in this world. Therefore, Chauvet completes the previous citation, saying, "thus sanctified, human daily life becomes liturgy or spiritual offering to God's glory."[26] In this sense, the eucharistic prayer is the most explicit sacramental expression of a Christian spirituality that is lived in the whole of our lives—moving with the life of God moving within us, mediated by Christ and the Spirit.

John Dunne describes well this participatory nature of Christian spirituality. It is a question of entering into the relation of Jesus with God. This is especially true when the local assembly enacts the eucharistic prayer. "I am entering into the very relation of Jesus with God and so he is *present* in me, 'I live, yet not I, but Christ in me.'" Dunne continues, quoting a line from the poet Rilke: "Entering into this 'I and thou' with God, I am entering into a stance of prayer and bringing 'all that is unsolved in my heart' to God in prayer."[27]

The relation we enter into is not just doing the ritual but, through it, what the ritual renders sacramentally present. We must not forget this symbolic/sacramental character of the Eucharist. The bread, the wine, the words spoken over them from the Last Supper—these are symbols through and in which something else is rendered truly present. This something else is a presence that is also an action, Jesus and all that he undertook and endured in "making a return" to the One who sent him, culminating in his dying and rising. The supper and its symbols point to the cross and, through it, to glorification. The term "paschal mystery" names the whole reality.

This sheds further light on the words previously cited from Colossians 3:3: "your life is hidden with Christ in God" (NRSV). Our life—with all that is *unsolved* in our hearts—is with Christ whose heart was fully and unconflictedly *resolved* toward God. Commenting on the phrase "and the Word was with God" from John's Prologue, biblical scholar Francis J. Moloney writes, "The preposition *pros* means more than the static 'with.' It has the sense of motion toward the person

---

[26] Ibid., xxv.

[27] John Dunne, *On Reading the Gospel* (Notre Dame, IN: University of Notre Dame Press, 2000), 17.

or thing that follows."[28] Because Jesus is the Word made flesh, this motion toward the Father—the One who sent him—pervades his humanity and all that he humanly does.[29] His resolution to go to Jerusalem when "the days drew near for his being taken up" is indeed toward Jerusalem. Literally, it says, "he hardened his face to go" (Luke 9:51).[30] But it is simultaneously resolution toward God, an act of obedience and love. This is the "once for all" character of Christ's moving with the life of God moving within him. This is the resolution to which we bring "all that is unsolved in our hearts" in Christian spirituality.

We have experiences of such *participatory* resolution. From age to age, and often against great odds, people have brought all that was unsolved in their hearts to the Christic motion of self-offering, with faith, hope, and love. In recent years, such resolution brought Martin Luther King and many other civil rights workers across the bridge in Selma. It carried Dorothy, Ita, Maura, and Jean to martyrdom in El Salvador, along with Oscar Romero and countless others. It brought Dietrich Bonhoeffer to the scaffold in Nazi Germany. These are not always stories of physical martyrdom. Resolution animated the churches of South Africa in their ultimately successful struggle to end apartheid. It sustained Dorothy Day in her leadership of the Catholic Worker Movement. Organizations such as Heifer International are resolved to help people all over the world to escape from hunger and poverty. In recent years we have witnessed Amish and African American communities forgiving gunmen who took the lives of their children and adult members. Such resolution, understood as participation in God's compassion, animates Fr. Gregory Boyle and his colleagues in their work with former gang members. To live Christian spirituality is to bring all that is unsolved in our hearts to the God-resolved heart of Christ. As Pope Francis prayed in his Easter

---

[28] Francis Moloney, *The Gospel of John*, ed. Daniel J. Harrington, Sacra Pagina Series (Collegeville, MN: Liturgical Press, 1998), 35.

[29] As discussed in chapter 4, this always being turned toward God in the depths of Jesus' humanity does not preclude him from growing in his awareness of sonship and of knowing and willing in a genuinely human way. It does not assume some ongoing, direct vision of God that would sidestep his humanity.

[30] Luke Timothy Johnson, *The Gospel of Luke*, ed. Daniel J. Harrington, Sacra Pagina Series (Collegeville, MN: Liturgical Press, 1991), 162n51.

Vigil homily, "May we allow the beating of his heart to quicken our faintness of heart."[31]

The Catholic Church also believes that such a spiritual movement may happen among all people of good will, whether or not they formulate it in terms of Christianity or some other religious belief. The Pastoral Constitution on the Church in the Modern World (*Gaudium et Spes*) says, "since Christ died for everyone . . . we must hold that the holy Spirit offers to all the possibility of being made partners, in a way known to God, in the paschal mystery" (22). At all times, but especially when we as church pray the eucharistic prayer, we are mystically "hidden with Christ in God." His living, dying, and rising and our participation in it is the existential reality of the prayer. And this reality, this spirituality, is reflected in the very structure of the prayer. To that structure we now turn.

---

[31] Homily of His Holiness Pope Francis, Vatican Basilica, Holy Saturday, 15 April 2017.

Chapter 9

The Eucharistic Prayer

This movement of self-offering and identification with Christ is
precisely what is at the heart of worship, as expressed both in
ritual acts and in the daily living of the Christian faith.

Paul Philibert [1]

The previous chapter explored two questions. What kind of text
is the eucharistic prayer? It is a case of the word in the rite in contrast
to the word in the readings. Who enacts the prayer? The assembly
or local church, a unity underlying the distinction between presider
and congregation. But the assembly is celebrant only *in Christ*, who
is the primary celebrant. Only by standing in the self-offering of
Christ does the church make this prayer. Consider now a third question: What is the structure of the eucharistic prayer?

A Structure Expressing a Spirituality

My friend, Janet Vandevender, is a gifted weaver. She makes wonderful things and wins ribbons at the county fair. Among these are
beautiful shawls. Just the sight of the finished shawl with its various
colors and patterns evokes appreciation and wonder. How does she
do that? When she explains how, showing me her loom, the multi-
colored yarns she has chosen, how the threads are aligned and woven
together, what is meant by the "warp" and the "weft," and so on,

[1] From Paul Philibert's introduction to Yves Congar, *At the Heart of Christian Worship: Liturgical Essays of Yves Congar*, ed. and trans. Paul Philibert (Collegeville, MN:
Liturgical Press, 2010), vii.

I appreciate the shawl in a whole new way. These structuring elements are not neutral carriers but shape and express the beauty of the finished garment. Likewise, the structure of the eucharistic prayer is not neutral; it expresses the shape of Christian spirituality, a particular way of moving with the life of God moving within us. It is Christic because it expresses the way Jesus responds to the divine presence and initiative at the heart of his being. His response begets a narrative, a ritual, and an ethics for participation and thus founds Christian spirituality. Drawing on Psalm 116, I initially described this movement as welcoming the gift of God and making a return (chap. 8). So we are about to explore the warp and weft of the eucharistic prayer, not only to appreciate it more fully, but to enact it more profoundly.

Our focus will be the new eucharistic prayers that emerged in the wake of the Second Vatican Council. Among these are six for adults and three for children. With some differences, the same basic structure underlies the prayers current in various Protestant traditions. In addition to these new texts, the reform of Vatican II retained and only slightly modified the centuries-old Roman Canon, now called Eucharistic Payer I. It had supplanted all others of the Western church in the early Middle Ages, remaining the only eucharistic prayer until the Reformation of the sixteenth century. It remained the only Roman Catholic prayer until the Second Vatican Council. Because only slightly revised, it preserves and expresses the medieval ethos of the church rather than the liturgical and theological outlook of Vatican II. Its structure differs markedly from the new prayers. In actual practice, as one commentator puts it, "the prayer in effect has dropped out of the assembly's consciousness."[2] Accustomed to the new prayers, presiders and people alike have difficulty following and praying Eucharistic Prayer I on the few occasions when it is recommended.

---

[2] Mark E. Wedig, "The Mystagogical Implications," in *A Commentary on the Order of Mass of the Roman Missal*, ed. Edward Foley (Collegeville, MN: Liturgical Press, 2011), 294–95. While this venerable prayer has its own elegance and beauty, it also has theological and pastoral limitations that many scholars have noted. Penitential in tone, it focuses heavily on the elements of offering and supplication while underplaying memorial and thanksgiving. Unlike the new prayers and the various ancient texts on which they are based, the Roman Canon lacks any reference to the role of the Holy Spirit.

For these reasons we will focus on the new prayers in what follows, not limiting ourselves to any single text, but considering examples from a number of them. These will include examples from Protestant versions and those of the Eastern churches to show the parallels across traditions. As we do so, differences going back to the Reformation will surface. These differences have been the subject of profound theological study and ecumenical dialogue. Our purpose is not to explore them in all their complexity but rather to see if, despite these differences, the shared structure bespeaks a shared spirituality.

Our situation is like a family reunion. Family gatherings not only strengthen bonds but also surface old wounds and divisions. We could avoid all this by just staying apart, but by coming close we accept the need to confront and heal these wounds. We live in a time of coming close. And, as in family gatherings, the Christian family can experience breakthroughs and reconciliations, even if not every difference is resolved. A first step is to emphasize what we share in common and let go of misleading stereotypes.

Ecumenical Convergence

Many Catholics, for example, are unaware how widespread eucharistic celebration is among Protestant churches. To mention only a few in this country, the Episcopal, Lutheran, Methodist, and Presbyterian churches, the United Church of Christ, and Disciples of Christ combine a service of the Word and Holy Communion (Liturgy of the Word, Liturgy of the Eucharist). Some always celebrate the service of the Word and the Sacrament together; others add the Eucharist or Holy Communion to the service of the Word less often. Many Protestant churches are beginning to celebrate the Eucharist more often, if not yet every Sunday.

All these churches have new settings of the eucharistic prayer or the Great Thanksgiving, inspired in part by the renewal of the Second Vatican Council. Kenan Osborne writes, "The liturgical renewal as found in the *Lutheran Book of Worship* and the *Book of Common Prayer*, and the approved eucharistic prayers of the Roman Catholic Church, were worked out in deliberate mutuality."[3] James White observes

---

[3] Kenan Osborne, *The Christian Sacraments of Initiation* (New York: Paulist Press, 1987), 208.

that the "results of liturgical revision are so similar that in many cases it is often hard to tell which tradition has produced a new eucharistic rite if the title page is lost."[4] When several North American Protestant denominations wanted to create a prayer they could use in common, they based it on Eucharistic Prayer IV of the Roman Rite.[5] Similarly, this shared structure is substantially the same as the anaphoras of St. John Chrysostom and St. Basil, used by Eastern rite churches. In all these efforts and across denominational lines, scholars have been guided by historical scholarship into ancient forms of the prayer.[6]

It is also not true that Catholics alone believe in true communion with the risen Christ through the Eucharist. There are differences in understanding *how* this happens. And there are differences in whether the belief *that* Christ is truly received requires believers to subscribe to a particular theory of *how* this takes place (transubstantiation? consubstantiation? whatever?).[7] Some traditions explicitly affirm Christ's presence and explicitly step back from trying to explain how.

Anglicans, Episcopalians, Lutherans, and Methodists are closest to the Roman Catholic position that the bread and wine are truly made holy and that in partaking of them worshipers partake of Christ. But they affirm this without accepting the theory of transubstantiation. Here, for example, is the joint statement of the First Anglican–Roman Catholic International Commission on Christ's presence in the Eucharist: "The Lord's words at the last supper, 'Take and eat; this is my body,' do not allow us to dissociate the gift of

---

[4] James F. White, *Introduction to Christian Worship*, rev. ed. (Nashville: Abingdon Press, 1990), 237.

[5] See H. Boone Porter's discussion of this in "Episcopal Anaphoral Prayers," in *New Eucharistic Prayers: An Ecumenical Study of Their Development and Structure*, ed. Frank C. Senn (New Jersey: Paulist Press, 1987), 69–70.

[6] For more, see the following: Senn, *New Eucharistic Prayers*; *Baptism and Eucharist: Ecumenical Convergence in Celebration*, ed. Max Thurian and Geoffrey Wainwright (WCC Publications, Geneva, in collaboration with Eerdmans Publishing, Grand Rapids, Michigan: 1983); *Baptism, Eucharist and Ministry: Faith and Order Paper No. 111* (Geneva: World Council of Churches, 1982). For a general overview of the development of the Eucharist, including convergence in recovering patterns for contemporary prayers, see White, *Introduction to Christian Worship*, 219–53.

[7] Historically, such theories arose from an authentic concern to safeguard the church's faith that Christ is truly present in the Eucharist. But *that* Christ is present and received was commonly held for centuries without requiring believers to subscribe to a theory of *how* this is so, whether transubstantiation or any other theory.

presence and the act of sacramental eating. The elements are not mere signs; Christ's body and blood become really present and are really given."[8] In the pithy words of the hymn text attributed to Anglican poet John Donne, "He was the Word that spake it, he took the bread and brake it, and what the Word did make it, I do believe and take it."[9] Emblematic of a growing ecumenical consensus in the understanding of the Eucharist is the following statement summarizing decades-long work of the Lutheran–Roman Catholic Commission on Unity:

> Lutherans and Catholics together can affirm the real presence of Jesus Christ in the Lord's Supper: "In the Sacrament of the Lord's Supper, Jesus Christ true God and true man, is present wholly and entirely, in his Body and Blood, under the signs of bread and wine" (Eucharist, 16).[10]

Again, we have a shared belief *that* Christ is truly received in the Eucharist without a shared theory of *how* this is best explained and safeguarded. On the level of *how*, Catholic teaching holds that the most apt explanation is transubstantiation. Lutherans hold that just as Christ is both truly human and truly divine, the bread and wine made holy are both truly bread and wine *and* truly the sacramental presence of Christ.

Following Calvin, Presbyterians believe that in the Lord's Supper worshipers are lifted up ("lift up your hearts") through the Holy Spirit to real communion with the Risen Christ. They differ from the churches discussed above in holding that, though the bread and wine are necessary signifiers of this event, given by Christ himself, they are not the locus of Christ's presence.[11] Still, for Calvin there is real

---

[8] See n. 9 of the First Anglican–Roman Catholic International Commission: Eucharistic Doctrine (1971); available online at iarccum.org.

[9] Cited in the entry "Real Presence," in *An Episcopal Dictionary of the Church*, ed. Don S. Armentrout and Robert Boak Slocum (New York: Church Publishing, 2000); available online at episcopalchurch.org.

[10] *From Conflict to Communion: Lutheran-Catholic Common Commemoration of the Reformation in 2017* (Leipzig: Evangelische Verlagsanstalt GmbH and Bonifatius GmbH Druck-Buch-Verlag Paderborn, 2016), par. 154.

[11] On various theories of eucharistic presence, a general overview may be found in White, *Introduction to Christian Worship*, 243–50.

communion, and he can say that Christ "feeds his people with his own body, the communion of which he bestows upon them by the power of his Spirit."[12] The current Great Thanksgiving Prayer A of the Presbyterian Church says, "As this bread is Christ's body for us, send us out to be the body of Christ in the world."[13] These differences are not unimportant, but equally or more important is the shared belief that worshipers truly commune with the risen Christ, however this is explained.

Finally, many Western Catholics and Protestants are unaware of our liturgical indebtedness to the Eastern churches. The new eucharistic prayers, Catholic and Protestant alike, represent a move toward the shape of the prayer in the East. Their structure is indebted to the anaphoras (or eucharistic prayers) of St. John Chrysostom and St. Basil and other ancient Eastern prayers.[14]

For all these reasons, we will explore the prayer as though we are at a Christian family reunion. Since my immediate family is Roman Catholic, I will begin from the new Roman Catholic eucharistic prayers, placing them in conversation with various Protestant and Eastern versions. I take seriously the Decree on Ecumenism (*Unitatis Redintegratio*) of the Second Vatican Council, which exhorts Catholic Christians to "avoid expressions, judgments and actions which are not truthful and fair in representing the situation of the members of the separated Christian communities" (4). The same document urges Catholics "to acquire a more adequate understanding of the respective doctrines of the separated communities, their history, their spiritual and liturgical life, their religious psychology and cultural background" (9). Let us take this to heart as we study this prayer.

---

[12] *Calvin: Institutes of the Christian Religion*, 4.17.18, ed. John T. McNeill, trans. Ford Lewis Battles, *The Library of Christian Classics*, vol. 21 (Philadelphia: Westminster Press, 1960), 1380–81.

[13] *Book of Common Worship* (Louisville, KY: Westminster John Knox Press, 1993), 72.

[14] The prayer of St. Basil can be viewed online at www.abbamoses.com; to view the prayer of St. John Chrysostom, see www.mci.archpitt.org.

The Structure of the Eucharistic Prayer

Louis-Marie Chauvet's Tripartite Approach

The structure common to the new eucharistic prayers of the Roman Catholic Rite can be laid out in three blocks of material: (1) the Opening Dialogue through the Sanctus (in most versions continuing beyond it), (2) Epiclesis 1 through the Anamnesis, (3) Epiclesis 2 to the Final Doxology and Amen. This division reflects the approach of Louis Marie-Chauvet, whose analysis we will follow. He derives this template from Eucharistic Prayer II, but it applies to all the prayers. The following table compares this structure with Protestant versions of the prayer, noting differences. Because of the wide variety of Protestant forms I have had to generalize and oversimplify to some extent.

Table 3

Roman Rite Prayers	Protestant Prayers

Opening Dialogue
Preface-Thanksgiving
Sanctus/Holy
    Preface material often continues after
    the Sanctus
	Opening Dialogue
	Preface-Thanksgiving
	Sanctus/Holy
	    Preface material often continues after
	    the Sanctus

Epiclesis 1 (over the gifts: sacramental
    body)
Institution Narrative
Mystery of Faith Acclamation
Anamnesis
    We remember and we offer
	----------------------- 	
	
	Institution Narrative
	Mystery of Faith Acclamation
	Anamnesis*
	**Variations on the offering element,
	including:*
	    a. remembering but no offering
	    b. remembering Jesus/offering ourselves
	    *c. offering ourselves in union with Christ's
	        offering for us*

Epiclesis 2 (over the assembly: ecclesial
    body)
Intercessions
 	
    a. for church on earth (unity and service)
    b. for the dead
    c. eschatological prayer
Doxology & Amen
	Combined Epiclesis (over gifts and
	    assembly)
	Intercessions*
	**Often highly condensed, almost one with the
	Epiclesis*
	    a. for church on earth (unity and service)
	    b. sometimes but often not present
	    c. eschatological prayer
	Doxology & Amen

Chauvet explores the eucharistic prayer as a narrative.[15] He begins as we did in the previous chapter by considering its beginning and ending. He poses the questions: What makes the narrative move? What propels it? A narrative begins, he writes, from "a negative situation of lack and stops (at least if the text of the discourse is coherent) when this lack is filled."[16] The opening dialogue announces the *lack* to be filled: "Let us give thanks to the Lord our God." Giving thanks or glory to God is what needs to be fulfilled. The closing doxology announces the resolution of this need. "Our text stops, in fact, when the program is accomplished, as shown by the final prayer of praise (doxology), 'Through him, with him, in him . . . all glory and honor is yours.' "[17] This ending says we have accomplished what we have set out to do. All the material in between expresses how this is done.

To modern ears, speaking of giving glory to God in this way is likely to conjure up unhelpful images and connotations. The true meaning of worship, of giving glory, is a return of love for God's love, with all the deeds of mercy and justice that are implied. It has an ethical dimension because it includes giving ourselves to all that God wills for our sisters and brothers, as well as the whole of creation. It is significant, then, that Chauvet adds the word "grace" to "glory."[18] The need announced by the opening dialogue, he says, is to give "grace/glory" to God. What does this mean?

Christian spirituality and worship is not only welcoming God's gracious approach but being gracious toward God and others in return. On the one hand, God's free and gratuitous gift comes first. On the other hand, "grace requires not only this initial gratuitousness on which everything else depends but also the *graciousness of the whole circuit.* . . . The wholeness of grace is never so well attested as when one takes into account the freedom of the human return-gift it

---

[15] Chauvet's analysis appears in two versions, one of which is slightly abbreviated compared to the other. His most extended presentation is in *Symbol and Sacrament: A Sacramental Reinterpretation of Christian Existence,* trans. Patrick Madigan and Madeleine Beaumont (Collegeville, MN: Liturgical Press, 1995), 286–89. The other is in *The Sacraments: The Word of God at the Mercy of the Body,* trans. Madeleine Beaumont (Collegeville, MN: Liturgical Press, 2001), 129–52.

[16] Chauvet, *The Sacraments,* 129.

[17] Ibid., 130.

[18] Ibid.

solicits."[19] That means not only receiving God's grace but being gracious in return. It means not only receiving and revering Christ but following him, giving ourselves as other Christs.

It may at first sound strange to speak of our being gracious toward God. But consider all those places where Scripture speaks of God desiring our hearts and acts of love such as mercy. Quoting Hosea, Jesus says: "Go and learn the meaning of the words, 'I desire mercy, not sacrifice'" (Matt 9:13). Reiterating Jewish teaching that the greatest commandments are to love God and neighbor, Jesus expands the category of neighbor to include everyone, especially the most vulnerable. He changes the question "who *is* my neighbor" to "who *was* I neighbor to" (Luke 10:25-37). On Ash Wednesday we hear the words, "return to me with your whole heart. . . . Rend your hearts, not your garments" (Joel 2:12-13). When Isaiah describes the fast God desires, it consists in acts of agapic love: releasing those bound unjustly, sharing bread with the hungry, sheltering the oppressed and the homeless, clothing the naked (Isa 58:6-7). God desires and enables this gracious love from us. It is a matter of moving with the more-than-human love of God moving within us. This dynamic of God's grace eliciting human graciousness is enacted above all in the Christ. This circuit of grace is the itinerary we travel in praying the eucharistic prayer. It explains the title Chauvet has given to his chapter on the eucharistic prayer: "Symbolic Exchange Between Humanity and God."[20]

The qualifier "symbolic" requires some initial explanation. Chauvet distinguishes between market exchange and symbolic exchange. In market exchange I give you twelve dollars in exchange for a bottle of wine. Exchange involves a calculable value focused on the worth of the goods traded: *this* is equal in value to *that* and may therefore be exchanged for *that*. But symbolic exchange is of an entirely different order. The things exchanged are *symbols* that mediate a mutual self-donation that is beyond price, not calculable in a market sense. Wedding rings do have a market value—alas, jewelers do not give them away! But in the wedding ritual they symbolize the gift of the partners to each other. Chauvet writes, "*The true objects being*

---

[19] Chauvet, *Symbol and Sacrament*, 108–9.
[20] Chauvet, *The Sacraments*, 129.

exchanged are the subjects themselves."[21] It would be absurd to measure their mutual love by the value of the rings exchanged. In this sense sacraments, especially the Eucharist, are signs/symbols "beyond price" that mediate the gracious exchange between God and humanity. We call it grace, but it is not a thing, though it is mediated by ritual-symbolic things such as water, oil, bread, wine, and word. It is a relationship in which deep calls unto deep. Through Christ and the Spirit, the deep of God's self-communication calls forth the deep of our gracious return of self to God and neighbor.

The eucharistic prayer expresses the gift of God and human response, enacted and mediated by Christ who is both. To pray it, Chauvet writes, is to follow "the way of conversion which Christians are called to walk throughout their lives."[22] Between the bookends of the Opening Dialogue and Final Doxology, he explores this itinerary of conversion in three stages which he names narrative programs 1, 2, and 3.

Narrative Program 1: The Preface through the Sanctus

The Preface of Eucharistic Prayer II, ending with the Sanctus, narrates in highly abbreviated form what the Scriptures say in detail—the history of God's way with us culminating in the Christ:

> It is truly right and just, our duty and our salvation,
> always and everywhere to give you thanks, Father most holy,
> through your beloved Son, Jesus Christ,
> your Word through whom you made all things,
> whom you sent as our Savior and Redeemer,
> incarnate by the Holy Spirit and born of the Virgin.
> Fulfilling your will and gaining for you a holy people,
> he stretched out his hands as he endured his Passion,
> so as to break the bonds of death and manifest the resurrection.
> And so with the Angels and all the Saints
> we declare your glory, as with one voice we acclaim.[23]

---

[21] Chauvet, *Symbol and Sacrament*, 106; emphasis in original.

[22] Ibid.

[23] Some Catholic versions have a built-in preface, for which another may be substituted in line with a season or feast. The integral structure of Eucharistic Prayer IV requires that only its given preface be used. Eucharistic Prayer III has no given preface; a generic, seasonal, or festal preface must always be chosen for it.

Most preface prayers, however, continue after the Sanctus, providing more detail. Eucharistic Prayer IV recounts salvation history at length, speaking of creation and the fall, covenants and the prophets, the coming of Christ, his ministry, death, resurrection, and the sending of the Holy Spirit. This is the more usual pattern in both Catholic and Protestant versions.

In chapter 7 above, "Finding Ourselves in the Word," we saw that the preface may be even more narrowly focused on a seasonal theme or a particular story from the Sunday gospel. Here, for example, is the Evangelical Lutheran Preface for Easter:

> It is indeed right, our duty and our joy,
> that we should at all times and in all places
> give thanks and praise to you, almighty and merciful God,
> for the glorious resurrection of our Savior Jesus Christ,
> the true Paschal Lamb who gave himself to take away our sin;
> who in dying has destroyed death,
> and in rising has brought us to eternal life.
> And so, with Mary Magdalene and Peter and all the witnesses of the
>   resurrection, with earth and sea and all their creatures,
> and with angels and archangels, cherubim and seraphim,
> we praise your name and join their unending hymn.[24]

In all these variations, Chauvet discerns an underlying pattern: "what God has done for humankind according to the Scriptures."[25] It follows that,

> even when thanksgiving has the mystery of Christ for its sole object, in the background the Old Testament is always presupposed. On the other hand, the thanksgiving always culminates in the mystery of Christ, so that even if only one aspect of Jesus' work is mentioned, this aspect is relevant only inasmuch as it is understood as one of many facets of the whole paschal mystery.[26]

Another facet of the mystery of Christ is the gift of creation. Explicitly connecting Christ to creation, Eucharistic Prayer II speaks of "your Word through whom you made all things." Based on the same

---

[24] *Evangelical Lutheran Worship*, Leaders Desk edition (Minneapolis, MN: Augsburg Press, 2006).

[25] Chauvet, *The Sacraments*, 131.

[26] Ibid.

ancient text that inspired this prayer, the Presbyterian Great Thanksgiving Prayer G says: "He is your Word, inseparable from you, through whom you made all things and in whom you take delight."[27] Christ's kenosis embraces the entire cosmos. As Pope Francis says, the risen One holds creation to himself and is directing it toward fullness: "The very flowers of the field and the birds of the air are now imbued with his radiant presence."[28] Just before the concluding doxology, Eucharistic Prayer IV echoes Romans 8:21, by including all of creation in final glory: "There, with the whole of creation, freed from the corruption of sin and death, may we glorify you through Christ our Lord, through whom you bestow on the world all that is good."

What is the significance of this first stage? In continuity with the Liturgy of the Word, we remember/rehearse the foundational events that give us our present identity. We do this with praise because these foundational events are the gift of God. But God's ultimate deed and gift is Jesus, the Christ, who actualizes in his person God's self-communication and human response. The preface presents what God *gives*, "the gift of the Son, Jesus, that is, of his historical body (born of the Virgin Mary, dead on the cross) and of his glorious body (risen)."[29] Telling the story of God's gift evokes our response of praise and thanks. What is uppermost, then, is keeping memory with thanksgiving.[30]

Narrative Program 2: Epiclesis 1 through the Anamnesis

In the preface, we make a beginning in giving grace/glory to God. Since the text continues, this project is not yet complete. Chauvet says, "To give thanks in a properly Christian way demands other

---

[27] *Book of Common Worship*, 150. The ancient text in question, from the *Apostolic Tradition*, is customarily, though probably wrongly, attributed to Hippolytus.

[28] *On Care for Our Common Home: Laudato Si'*, Encyclical Letter of the Holy Father Francis (Washington, DC: United States Conference of Catholic Bishops/Vatican City: Liberia Editrice Vaticana, 2015), 100.

[29] Chauvet, *The Sacraments*, 131.

[30] One of the criticisms of Eucharistic Prayer I (the Roman Canon) is its lack of memorial and thanksgiving. Though this element comes out in whichever preface is chosen, once it is over, the rest of the prayer is a plea that God accept the offering the church makes and give blessings in exchange.

conditions, especially the reception of the gift, which up to now has been spoken of exclusively in the past tense. This is done by the second program."[31] This second program or block of material is more complex, so it will be useful to list it once again:

First Epiclesis (over the gifts: sacramental body)

Institution Narrative

Mystery of Faith Acclamation

Anamnesis

Between *welcoming* and *making a return* is *receiving*. In the preface, Christ is given to the church by remembering the historical past according to the Scriptures. But now Christ will be given to the church in the present under a new mode, "the mode of food and drink. . . . He is given in the present and no longer in the past."[32] Reception in the present, however, is narrated progressively, beginning *within* the eucharistic prayer and coming to completion in the communion rite. Within the prayer, these stages are the first epiclesis, the institution narrative, and the anamnesis. These stages show that Christ is given in sacrament to the church even before reception in the communion rite.

First Epiclesis. The epiclesis asks God to send the Spirit upon the gifts *to make them holy* and upon the people *to make them holy*. It takes two different forms in ancient and modern prayers. In most ancient texts, Eastern anaphoras, and current Protestant versions, both of these occur as one epiclesis after the institution narrative and anamnesis. Here are two examples, first, the Byzantine Catholic Anaphora of St. John Chrysostom;[33] second, Eucharistic Prayer D from Holy Eucharist II of the Episcopal *Book of Common Prayer*.

---

[31] Chauvet, *The Sacraments*, 131.

[32] Ibid., 132.

[33] This epiclesis as well as the whole anaphora of St. John Chrysostom of the Byzantine Catholic Church, in union with Rome, is substantially the same as that of the Eastern Orthodox Church.

Byzantine Catholic
Send down your Holy Spirit upon us and upon these gifts lying before us, and make this bread the precious body of your Christ, and that which is in this chalice the precious blood of your Christ, changing them by your Holy Spirit, that those who partake of them . . .[34]

Episcopal
Lord, we pray that in your goodness and mercy your Holy Spirit may descend upon us, and upon these gifts, sanctifying them to be holy gifts for your holy people, the bread of life and the cup of salvation, the Body and Blood of your Son Jesus Christ.[35]

In all new Roman Rite prayers, the epiclesis is split. This form is also found in ancient texts, but less often.[36] The request for the Spirit upon the gifts occurs before the institution narrative (the consecration); the request upon the people occurs later, after the anamnesis and mystery of faith acclamation. Since Chauvet is speaking from the Roman Catholic tradition, we are at this point meeting the epiclesis in the split form. In the unfolding narrative, epiclesis 1 represents the first stage of Christ becoming sacramentally present to the gathered church. The Eucharistic Prayer for Reconciliation I prays, "we entreat you: sanctify these gifts by the outpouring of your Spirit, that they may become the Body and Blood of your Son, whose command we fulfill when we celebrate these mysteries."

Because these prayers now explicitly credit the Spirit with bringing about the sacramental presence of Christ, they expand our understanding of consecration. How do we put these two together? The narrative form means that the different dimensions of this one action are recounted sequentially—first this, then that—and so on. That is why we can speak of *stages* of reception. But this narrative requirement should not lead us to think that the Spirit makes the gifts holy first, then Christ does so again through the words of institution or vice versa. This would mean two consecrations, two acts in which

---

[34] Available online at www.mci.archpitt.org.

[35] *Book of Common Prayer*, 375.

[36] Paul F. Bradshaw and Maxwell Johnson, *The Eucharistic Liturgies: Their Evolution and Interpretation* (Collegeville, MN: Liturgical Press, 2012), 75–110, 121–23. Across these pages the authors provide a survey of ancient prayers displaying both "split" and "joined" forms of the epiclesis.

the gifts are made holy. And whichever one comes first would make the second redundant. Nor can we rightly think that the Spirit's role is other than consecratory, as though it were only some kind of preparation for consecrating or making holy. The *Catechism of the Catholic Church* explicitly says, "in each celebration there is an outpouring of the Holy Spirit that makes the unique mystery present," and cites St. John Damascene in support of this view: "You ask how the bread becomes the Body of Christ, and the wine . . . the Blood of Christ. I shall tell you: the Holy Spirit comes upon them and accomplishes what surpasses every word and thought."[37]

The only reasonable way to understand this is that Christ and the Spirit, both gifts of the Father, are integral to consecrating or making holy the gifts of bread and wine. By reintroducing the Spirit's role, absent from the pre–Vatican II Roman Canon, these new prayers express the trinitarian nature of Christ's self-giving. In the graced inwardness and activity of Jesus' humanity not only the Logos but "the movement of the Spirit was present," as Congar writes.[38] Christ's act of giving himself existentially and in sacrament is also the work of the Spirit, and both are the gift of the Father. As the paschal mystery is trinitarian so too is its liturgical enactment. Whatever form the epiclesis takes—whether split or combined—its significance for spirituality is the same. Receiving the sacramental presence of Christ makes us his body in the Pauline sense. Being made the Body of Christ means embodying his kenotic love in our lives. Personally and communally, we move with the life of God moving within us, borne by the Spirit through whom the love of God is poured into our hearts (Rom 5:5).

The Institution Narrative. In the logic of the unfolding narrative, the second stage in reception is the institution narrative. It tells us that Christ not only gave himself for us *historically* but gives himself to us *sacramentally* in a ritual that he commanded us to do in memory of him.[39] Chauvet highlights a remarkable transition in this narrative. It begins, like the preface, by telling a story of the past ("At the time he was betrayed . . . he took bread . . . and gave it to his disciples").

---

[37] *Catechism of the Catholic Church* (New York: Doubleday, 1997), pars. 1104 and 1106.

[38] Yves Congar, *The Word and the Spirit*, trans. David Smith (San Francisco: Harper & Row Publishers, 1986), 86.

[39] Chauvet, *Symbol and Sacrament*, 270.

The church recounts the Christ *of the historical past* as the foundation of its identity. But then the risen One speaks to the church *in the present*, summoning it to fulfill its identity: "Take this, all of you, and eat. . . . Take this, all of you, and drink. . . . Do this in memory of me." Again, there is a linguistic shift *from* the church summoning past events as witness of its identity *to* Christ summoning the church here and now as witness to his identity. Chauvet writes, *"by citing Jesus at the Last Supper, the church sees itself in fact as cited by him, its Lord, cited to act."*[40] A few sentences later, he concludes, "The church is the church only in the measure in which it recognizes itself as dependent on Jesus, its only Lord. . . . The church holds its identity by constantly receiving itself from him."[41] The mystery of faith assembly acclamation highlights this "presentness" of Christ. It is one of the few moments when the assembly addresses him instead of the Father: "We proclaim your Death, O Lord, and profess your Resurrection until you come again." At the same time, it anticipates the anamnesis that follows it. Some form of this acclamation exists in many Protestant versions of the prayer.[42]

The Anamnesis. The third stage in the progression of reception within the eucharistic prayer is the anamnesis. This brief moment in the overall flow of the prayer is fraught with significance. The key notions in all Roman Catholic versions are *we remember* and *we offer*. Since they occur as a single statement, they must be understood in relation to each other. The remembering (or "celebrating the memorial") element is uppermost and retells all that God has done for us in Christ, thus echoing the gift character of salvation spelled out in the preface. Eucharistic Prayer III gives clear expression to this subordination of offering to thanking:

> Therefore, O Lord, as we celebrate the memorial
> of the saving Passion of your Son,
> his wondrous Resurrection

[40] Chauvet, *The Sacraments*, 134; emphasis in original.

[41] Ibid., 134–35.

[42] This is the first of three options for the acclamation in the Roman Rite. In the previous English translation there were four. But actually "Christ has died" and "Dying you destroyed our death" were alternate translations of the same Latin original. "Christ has died" was the only one not addressed to Christ directly. This translation is *about* rather than *to* Christ. Ironically, it became the most popular one and is still featured in some Protestant versions.

> and Ascension into heaven,
> and as we look forward to his second coming,
> we offer you in thanksgiving
> this holy and living sacrifice.

There is only one offering—the "once for all" self-offering of Christ recounted in the preface and institution narrative. Only by standing in the self-offering of Christ does the church offer this thanksgiving prayer. It is not an initiative starting with us and moving toward God, but a response to God's initiative toward us in Christ: "we offer you *in thanksgiving*." That is why the anamnesis of Reconciliation II ends with "we offer what you have bestowed on us." The "we offer" is intrinsically related and subordinate to remembering with thanksgiving. Offering is a mode of thanking. Offering, in other words, is always offering back.

Offering Is Offering Back. This relationship deserves extended reflection because the oblation or offering element has been a point of contention between Catholics and Protestants since the Reformation. According to the Lutheran liturgist, Frank C. Senn, "No other issue has divided Western Christianity since the 16th century as much as the concept of Eucharistic oblation."[43] As one commentator has put it: "How is the self-offering of Christians related to the self-offering of Christ, and how is that to be sacramentally expressed?"[44] When the offering element is cut loose from its moorings in memorial and thanksgiving, there is danger, as David Power writes, of "putting the church's own offering on a par with Christ's self-offering."[45] This is precisely how the reformers saw the medieval form of the Mass: an attempt to add something more to the self-offering of Christ, as if the "sacrifice of the Mass" was different from his, an offering made alongside that of Christ. By the same token, the Mass gave Luther and others the impression that humans were initiating an action or work toward God instead of thankfully receiving and responding to God's

---

[43] See the entry, "Eucharistic Liturgy, Names for the," in *The New Dictionary of Sacramental Worship*, ed. Peter E. Fink (Collegeville, MN: Liturgical Press, 1990), 450.

[44] From Mark Santer's foreword in Kenneth Stevenson, *Eucharist and Offering* (New York: Pueblo, 1986), vii.

[45] David N. Power, "The Anamnesis: Remembering, We Offer, " in Senn, *New Eucharistic Prayers*, 166; in this chapter Power explores the issue of offering extensively in relation to ancient and current liturgical texts.

action for us in Christ. Though this was never official Catholic doctrine, some theological opinions of the time, but especially widespread distortions in practice, certainly gave the reformers grounds for this impression. The practice of paying for Masses so that various benefits might be obtained reduced Christ's self-offering to a kind of object the church could use to barter with God.[46]

Replying to the reformers, the Council of Trent rejected any notion that the Mass adds something to or makes up for something lacking in Christ's self-offering. Summarizing Trent's teaching, Kenan Osborne writes, "The Church, the priest, the Mass itself adds absolutely nothing to this once-and-for-all propitiatory act of Jesus. . . . The same sacrifice is not reoffered, but only re-presented, in an unbloody manner."[47] But Trent's clarification, coming after the outbreak of so much hostility and ill will, came too late.

Ecumenical study and dialogue in recent decades has revealed that, despite remaining differences, no great gulf separates Catholics and Protestants on this issue today. Still, this history explains why Protestant versions of the anamnesis generally speak of the community offering itself as a sacrifice of thanksgiving and praise but shy away from speaking of the church offering Christ's self-offering to God. At a very basic level, one can certainly understand this reticence: it is Christ who in his living and dying offered himself to God. Any offering the church makes can only be participation in this one offering. The anamnesis in the United Methodist *Book of Worship* renders the relationship of the church's offering to Christ's offering as follows: "And so, in remembrance of these your mighty acts in Jesus Christ, we offer ourselves in praise and thanksgiving as a holy and living sacrifice, in union with Christ's offering for us."[48]

---

[46] Chauvet describes the growth of private Masses in the High Middle Ages, offered to obtain specific benefits for a client or to ransom a dead person from purgatory. "This multiplication of 'ransom Masses' entailed a multiplication of the *ordination of 'Mass priests'* and thus an inflation of the sacerdotal corps carrying out the roles of *intermediary* and *intercessor*." But Christian priests are not intermediaries or intercessors. Properly understood, they are signs of the one mediation and intercession of Christ. See *Symbol and Sacrament*, 310.

[47] Osborne, *The Christian Sacraments of Initiation*, 218.

[48] *The United Methodist Book of Worship* (Nashville, TN: United Methodist Publishing House, 1992), 38.

On the other hand, there is also an understandable logic to the Catholic sense of offering. First, if Christ is the agent of the prayer, then the church offers Christ only in the sense that Christ unites the church to himself in his self-offering, as the *Catechism of the Catholic Church* says: "This sacrifice of praise is possible only through Christ: he unites the faithful to his person, to his praise, and to his intercession."[49] We offer only through, with, and in Christ. So, when we describe this act from the side of our participation, what the church offers is his offering. His self-offering in life and death is *the event* of the Christian story. His is the *holy and living sacrifice*, remembered and offered in the prayer. Ours becomes a holy and living sacrifice of praise only in a secondary sense "in union with Christ's offering for us," as the Methodist prayer says. Eucharistic Prayer IV reflects this Catholic sense of priority. Only after the anamnesis, in the second epiclesis over the assembly, does it pray that we "may become a living sacrifice in Christ to the praise of your glory." In light of this, there is, perhaps, only a hair's breadth of difference between the Methodist prayer and the notion of offering in the current Catholic prayers. Can we today, with mutual understanding and charity, see the truth of both sensibilities? And that these different ways of expressing our participation in Christ's self-offering are not contradictory but mutually enriching?

In any case, this is why the new Catholic prayers explicitly carry forward the centuries-old tradition of saying that the church offers Christ's self-offering. The new prayers, however, never portray the offering as a standalone or primary element. Nor do they represent it as a human initiative toward God.[50] It is a moment within memorial and thanksgiving for God's gift so that offering is *offering back*, a mode of rendering thanks for God's initiative toward us.

---

[49] *Catechism*, par. 1361.

[50] One of the criticisms of the Roman Canon, now Eucharistic Prayer I, is that it verges on making offering the primary and standalone action of the prayer, along with supplication. For example, Wedig writes: "A discourse of sacrifice predominates throughout EP I . . . To *approve* and *accept* the sacrifice offered is the essence of the prayer." See Wedig, "The Mystagogical Implications," 296. Similarly, Mazza writes: "It is difficult to use this Eucharistic Prayer precisely because it is simply a lengthy plea, or intercession, for the offering of the sacrifice." See Enrico Mazza, *The Celebration of the Eucharist*, trans. Matthew J. O'Connell (Collegeville, MN: Liturgical Press), 270, n. 31.

Offering Back as Dispossession. This brings us to what is most interesting in Chauvet's understanding of the anamnesis. Catholics as
well as some Protestant traditions understand that even before communion, through the power of the Spirit and the words of institution,
Christ gives himself in sacrament to the church. Everything in this
second block of material, then, aims toward reception, though it will
reach completion only later in communion. So, what does the church
do with this gift it has now received? Before partaking of it, we offer
it back to God. Chauvet writes,

> We have here a paradox: this *reception* is effected by means of *oblation.*
> As in Deuteronomy 26:1-11, *the Christian mode of appropriation is through
> disappropriation:* the mode of "taking" is by "giving"—"giving thanks."
> . . . It is in rendering to God God's own grace, Christ Jesus given in
> sacrament, that the Church receives it.[51]

Offering is offering back, a form of thanking, of giving grace/glory
to God. The firstfruits offering in Deuteronomy 26 illustrates the opposite of human self-assertion toward God. It is a matter of decentering human autonomy in favor of thankful acknowledgment of God's
gifts, gifts that entail responsibility to care for others, especially the
most vulnerable. Similarly, in the offering element of the anamnesis,
the assembly gracefully offers to God what God has given. Chauvet
elaborates this understanding by combining the offering of the firstfruits with the manna from heaven episode of Exodus 16. The gift of
manna is a figure of grace, of covenantal fidelity—God to Israel, Israel
to God. Though thing-like, the manna in this story cannot be grasped
and hoarded like an object: "One receives it day by day without being
able to store it up."[52] One receives it only in the mode of continually
letting it be *gift* rather than one's self-assured possession.

> Like the manna in the desert, we do not receive the grace of God like
> a graspable "object"; only those receive it who open their hands anew
> each day. This is why *oblation* is constitutive of reception. Just as Israel
> receives its land only when it offers it back through the first-fruits that
> symbolize it . . . so too Christians do not appropriate God's gift except

---

[51] Chauvet, *Symbol and Sacrament,* 276.
[52] Ibid., 223.

in dispossessing themselves of it through the oblation of giving thanks.[53]

Receiving by letting go, by offering back, is a matter of "recognizing that of ourselves we have nothing to offer and that we can offer nothing to God that does not come from God as a gift."[54] In the words of Reconciliation II: "we offer you what you have bestowed on us."

More than mere wordplay, Chauvet's paradox of receiving by giving back touches on something quite spiritually profound. What is at first perplexing in this notion is that the "giving back" is not a subsequent response to receiving the gift; it is an *inner moment* of receiving it: "the mode of taking is by giving back," and *"oblation* is constitutive of reception." How to better understand this?

Human relationships at their best provide an analogy. If love be true, lovers receive and hold each other precisely by offering back, and that in two senses. The lover offers the beloved back by letting her or him go, recognizing the other *as other, as gift,* and not as a mere function or extension of oneself. This is not a secondary response after "possession" of the beloved; it is *interior* to holding the other so that *possession* is by *dispossession.* Subsequently, the lover may do things and offer gifts to show appreciation of the beloved, but this is secondary to *receiving as offering back.* Receiving by offering back is the interior content and quality of the relation.

Second, this offering back or letting be is not empty indifference. It is a motion filled with self-donation, that is, other-centered, self-emptying love. Love is reception in the mode of giving back. Within this dynamic, lovers partake of each other with great mutual joy! Where love is not receiving as offering back, relationships devolve into various distortions such as narcissism, domination, and abuse.

Holding by offering back is not limited to romantic love; it may transform all human relationships. If love be true, parents hold/possess their children by continually giving them back to themselves, releasing them to be their own. But far from indifference or neglect, this is a motion filled with love and self-donation. Bad parenting happens when there is failure to *hold by letting go,* and the child lives only to fulfill parental demands. Such a child will have great difficulty

---

[53] Ibid., 279.
[54] Ibid., 312.

developing healthy ego-strength. He or she will tend to be what Walter Brueggemann calls a "docile reactor" in all future relationships.[55] Similarly, in true friendship, one receives and holds the other *as* a gift, which means holding the friend in the mode of offering back with love and esteem. Are these examples of merely human loves? Are they not rather illustrations of how human loves become more-than-human love by the gracious, agapic love of God?

The liberating power of God's compassion seems to involve just this kind of dynamic. We saw it earlier in Gregory Boyle's work with former gang members. Kinship or community happens when people receive each other in the mode of offering back, filled with agapic love. We saw it in Jesus' answer to Peter's "Depart from me, for I am a sinner." The only gift Peter thinks he can offer Jesus is to shrink into his own unworthiness. Jesus receives Peter by an *offering back* filled with loving affirmation: "Do not be afraid. From now on you will be catching people" (Luke 5:10; NRSV). Earlier still, in chapter 1, we saw this dynamic in the Creator-creature relationship. God is closer to us than we are to ourselves. This closeness holds by letting be, offering creatures back to themselves in the very act of creating and sustaining them. Finally, we saw this in the Christ, whose humanity is given back to itself in its full integrity not despite but because of its very belonging to God (chap. 4).

At heart, the Eucharist is about Christ's self-offering and our participation in it. If this is so, then Catholics and Protestants are closer to each other than controversies of the past suggest. What is the significance of this for spirituality, for *moving with the life of God moving within us*? An inner moment of receiving God's gift—the Christ—is offering the self and the gift back to God with love and thanksgiving. Looking at it the other way around, Christ takes us with him in his self-offering "once for all," but going with him—that is a free act of self-giving on our part. The spiritual movement of reception by dispossession is enacted above all by the Christ. He possesses his human reality by dispossession to his divinity (Christology). He enacts himself, says Chauvet, by giving himself away (soteriology), by "love for God and humankind to the point of accepting death in martyrdom."[56] Our spiritual movement of dispossession, of receiving by giving back,

---

[55] Walter Brueggemann, "The Costly Loss of Lament," in *The Psalms and the Life of Faith*, ed. Patrick D. Miller (Minneapolis: Augsburg Fortress, 1995), 104.

[56] Chauvet, *The Sacraments*, 136.

is borne by Christ's movement of dispossession. It is participation in his kenosis or self-emptying. Always receiving our created and loved selves, including our loves and friendships, our plans and possessions, as well as the gift of creation, by offering back—that is the lifelong spiritual practice of Christians, ritually signified in the *we offer* of the anamnesis. This is the gracious symbolic exchange between God and humanity enacted in the eucharistic prayer.

Narrative Program 3: Epiclesis 2 through the Intercessions

Welcoming the gift of God and making a return—we now come to the "making a return" stage of this sequence. The discussion above may give the impression that the offering element of the anamnesis accomplishes the return-gift. But Chauvet has described offering primarily as a mode of reception—receiving by offering back. The fullness of offering back, Chauvet's return-gift, can only be completed beyond ritual in the liturgy of our lives. Here, then, is the third block of material:

> Second Epiclesis (over the assembly: ecclesial body)
> Intercessions
>   a. for church on earth
>   b. for the dead
>   c. eschatological prayer

Second Epiclesis. Reception of the gift evokes a return-gift, which is ultimately the gift of self and community, but precisely as *other Christs*, as members of Christ's Body. Such is the theme in this third block of material, beginning with the second epiclesis. Chauvet writes: "There is still something needed: that 'we' become ecclesially what we are going to receive eucharistically. This is the task of the last program."[57] So, this third section begins by requesting God to send the Spirit upon the assembly that we might genuinely be one as the Body of Christ. In the words of Eucharistic Prayer II: "Humbly we pray that, partaking of the Body and Blood of Christ, we may be gathered into one by the Holy Spirit." This unity is not for its own sake but for the sake of service. Reconciliation I prays for the Spirit's descent upon the people so that we "may be gathered into one Body

---

[57] Ibid., 132.

in Christ, who heals every division." Those final words emphasize that receiving Christ in the Spirit commits us to reconciling activity beyond the liturgy. Becoming a living sacrifice in Christ means entering into his spirituality of self-emptying love of God and neighbor. This is the meaning of becoming ecclesially what we will receive sacramentally.

Consider the symmetry between the first and second epiclesis: one over the gifts that they may become the Body and Blood of Christ, one over the people that they may become ever more truly the Body of Christ in this world. St. John Chrysostom says, "For what is the bread? It is the body of Christ. And what do those who receive it become? The Body of Christ—not many bodies but one body."[58] This is commentary on Paul: "Because there is one bread, we who are many are one body, for we all partake of the one bread" (1 Cor 10:17; NRSV). When the Spirit is requested on both gifts and people after the institution narrative and anamnesis—the usual Protestant form, and that of the ancient and current Eastern texts—the same symmetry is illustrated. In Holy Eucharist II of the Episcopal Church, the anamnesis ends with a sentence leading into the epiclesis:

> Recalling his death, resurrection, and ascension, we offer you these gifts.
>
> Sanctify them by your Holy Spirit to be for your people the Body and Blood of your Son, the holy food and drink of new and unending life in him. Sanctify us also that we may faithfully receive this holy Sacrament, and serve you in unity, constancy and peace; and at the last day bring us with all your saints into the joy of your eternal kingdom.[59]

Partaking of Christ's sacramental presence, the church is to become an agent of his presence beyond the liturgy. The Great Thanksgiving Prayer A of the Presbyterian Church features the combined epiclesis after the anamnesis and ends with, "As this bread is Christ's body for us, send us out to be the body of Christ in the world."[60] If the gift

---

[58] Quoted in Encyclical Letter *Ecclesia de Eucharistica* of His Holiness Pope John II, given in Rome, at St. Peter's, on 17 April, Holy Thursday, in the year 2003, par. 23; available online at www.vatican.va.

[59] *The Book of Common Prayer* (New York: Church Hymnal Corporation, 1979), 363.

[60] *Book of Common Worship*, 72.

of God in Christ and the Spirit makes us one Body, this Body has things to say and do in the world. It follows that, though our return-gift is signaled in the liturgy, it cannot be fully actualized there. "What is at stake," Chauvet says, "is everything that pertains to justice, sharing, reconciliation, forgiveness, all at the collective level of economic, political, and cultural relations between nations and races as well as at the level of interpersonal relationships."[61]

The content of this ethical practice is "mutual love as a response to the love of God which precedes it, that is, 'living-in-grace.'"[62] The *love of God which precedes it* has been recounted with thanks and praise in the preface. This same *love of God* becomes sacramentally present here and now in the eucharistic prayer, culminating in communion. Reception of the gift calls forth our return-gift, love of God embodied in love of neighbor. This gracious circuit or symbolic exchange summons us to an ethics of superabundant, Christic love, the paschal pattern of going the extra mile, making the reign of God tangibly (if not perfectly) present, even to the point of risking life and limb. Chauvet writes, "The reception of grace as grace (and not as something else which would be more or less magical) never goes without a task; it implies the ethical return-gift of justice and mercy."[63]

What makes this ethics Christian and eucharistic? In what way is the entire eucharistic celebration—Word and Sacrament together—foundational for this spirituality? Not, Chauvet says, because of its degree of generosity. All kinds of people, Christian or not, religious or not, can be ethically generous. Anyone can be caught up in the ethics of agapic love because the grace of God seeks everyone whether they are aware of it or not.[64] What makes it Christian is the explicit acknowledgment that it originates from the Holy Mystery rather than our own autonomy and initiative. We profess it as enabled by the gift/life of God moving within us in Christ and the Spirit and as our *return* for the gift received. The liturgy is "the place where this priority of the love of God freely bestowed is attested," Chauvet says.[65]

---

[61] Chauvet, *The Sacraments*, 138.

[62] Ibid., 137.

[63] Ibid., 138.

[64] The centrality of compassion across the world's religions and spiritual traditions, though inflected differently in each context, also gives witness to what Lonergan called the "force-field" of agapic love in human history. (See above, p. 47.)

[65] Chauvet, *The Sacraments*, 41.

Christian ethics, concretely lived, gives witness to the Gospel of Jesus. We become "a living Gospel proclaiming God's grace-gift of holiness," as Joyce Ann Zimmerman says.[66] Or as John's gospel has it: "By this everyone will know that you are my disciples, if you have love for one another" (13:35; NRSV).

The Intercessions. The intercessions that follow the second epiclesis (in Protestant versions, the combined epiclesis) elaborate it, spelling out in detail what it means to become ecclesially what we will receive sacramentally. They may be long or short and treat various themes in different versions of the prayer. Surveying Catholic and Protestant texts reveals that a number of verbs and expressions are used. We ask God to strengthen, renew, and enlighten the church and bring it to fullness of charity and communion. We ask God to open our eyes to the needs of others, to make the church a sign of communion, hope, and peace, and so on. A significant recurring verb is *remember*. We have been remembering God's deeds, culminating in the gift and deed of Christ. Now we ask God to remember us: the church, those gathered for the celebration, all who have died, not only church members but, as Eucharistic Prayer IV says, all "whose faith you alone have known." As Brian Wren's hymn "God Remembers" has it:

> God remembers us: all we were, all we are,
> lives within our Lover's care.
> Time may dull our minds and death will take us all,
> but in eternal Love ev'ry life is now:
> our life is hid with Christ in God.[67]

To be remembered by God is to be continually held in being and in love, a love that carries us to an absolute future in God. This love carries and evokes our return-gift of moving with the life of God moving within us, mediated by Christ and the Spirit. But does God have to be asked to remember us and our needs? If we stopped asking, would God forget? What really is the nature of intercessory

---

[66] Joyce Ann Zimmerman, "The Mystagogical Implications," in *A Commentary on the Order of Mass of the Roman Missal*, ed. Edward Foley (Collegeville, MN: Liturgical Press, 2011), 385.

[67] "God Remembers," Text: Brian Wren, © 1993 Hope Publishing. Used with permission.

prayer and the intercessions specific to the eucharistic prayer? What is the spirituality at work here?

Two aspects of intercessory prayer are worth noting. First, to intercede is *to act on behalf of*. Second, this action is always in the form of a request to God. It is centered not in ourselves but in our reliance upon God. All we can be and do on the path of agapic love is borne by God's self-gift, God's self-communication and action for us in Christ and the Spirit.

We easily understand the outward ways in which we intercede for others: immediate aid to persons in dire need, visiting and accompanying the imprisoned, the care of parents for children and of children for parents, supporting refugees, defending human rights, and so on. But concerning the inner action of prayer the questions naturally arise: Does intercessory prayer really accomplish anything? Does praying for justice bring it about? Does praying for the hungry feed them? To ask whether intercessory prayer really changes things outwardly is, I think, the wrong question. Prayer is not a substitute for practical action on behalf of others. It is disturbing to hear prayers of the faithful (at the end of the Liturgy of the Word) couched in terms urging God to take care of those in distress. God wants us to do that! That's our job. When asked if intercessory prayer really changes anything, a wise friend of mine said he wasn't sure but he knew it changed him. Our outer actions express what is in our hearts. There is not only outer action in line with God's will but "a willing spirit," as Psalm 51 says, a heart of compassion out of which practical action flows. The great sin in the Scriptures is hardheartedness. In place of stony hearts, God would give us hearts of flesh and feeling, hearts filled with empathy for others.

Intercession is the posture of Christ, inwardly and outwardly. To abide in Christ—"remain in my love" (John 15:9)—is to stand with him in his relation of willing and enacting what God wills for humankind. Intercession, then, is a form of agapic love, a *to God for others love*, or, as Rahner says, "Prayer can only be true prayer where it is open and ready to embrace the other within that movement in which the whole person gives himself to God."[68] Quakers express this beautifully as holding someone in the Light.

---

[68] Karl Rahner, "The Apostolate of Prayer," in *Theological Investigations*, vol. 3 (New York: Seabury Press, 1974), 215.

Intercession may also take the form of acting on behalf of oneself. We override immediate desires, impulses, and fears to act for our own good. We transcend what may be subjectively satisfying for what is genuinely good for us. It is an exercise in self-transcendence, dying to the narrow, or even illusory self so that the greater, truer self can live. If we understand this self-transcendence as *moving with the life of God moving within us*, then we are loving ourselves in and with the love of God. We are moving in a Christic way in relation to ourselves.

These two forms of prayer as *acting on behalf of* animate the intercessions of the eucharistic prayer. Often the first intercession is church focused. This is not narcissism but a call to self-transcendence. We are more than just our individual selves. Having our being in the Christ, we are sisters and brothers to each other and to all for whom he died and rose. It is in this very communion, this *ecclesia*, that we mediate the presence of Christ to others. We are only credible witnesses of God's compassion for humanity in Jesus to the extent that we remain in him and love one another as he has loved us. When we fail in this love, we become obstacles. Therefore, this intercession that we truly be church is a confession of need. For, as Chauvet has said, we do not make ourselves church; we continually receive ourselves *as church* from the Christ.

Second, in our character *as church* we intercede for the world. To abide in Christ in his relation to God is also to intercede with him for the world. Some versions of the prayer express this more explicitly than others. This beautiful intercession comes from the Roman Catholic Eucharistic Prayer for Various Needs—Jesus Went About Doing Good:

> Open our eyes
> to the needs of our brothers and sisters;
> inspire in us words and actions
> to comfort those who labor and are burdened.
> Make us serve them truly,
> after the example of Christ and at his command.
> And may your Church stand as a living witness
> to truth and freedom,
> to peace and justice,
> that all people may be raised up to a new hope.

Protestant versions generally express the intercessions more succinctly. In a quite wonderful way, the Great Thanksgiving B of the Presbyterian *Book of Common Worship* locates the church's intercessions within Christ's self-offering love for all:

> Help us, O God, to love as Christ loved.
> Knowing our weakness,
> may we stand with all who stumble.
> Sharing in his suffering,
> may we remember all who suffer.
> Held in his love,
> may we embrace all whom the world denies.
> Rejoicing in his forgiveness,
> may we forgive all who sin against us.
> Give us strength to serve you faithfully
> until the promised day of resurrection,
> when with the redeemed of all ages
> we will feast at your table in glory.[69]

An Eschatological Impetus. The last four lines of the Presbyterian intercessions sound the eschatological impetus of the prayer, present in some form or other in all Catholic and most Protestant texts. The church as the Body of Christ, signing and enacting God's reign, is a work in progress. So the epiclesis and the intercessions lean toward the future, ultimately what Rahner called our absolute future in God.[70] This future is meant for all. So, on this already/not yet pilgrimage, we do not forget the dead who have gone before us but hold them in the Light. In one sense, the reign is already accomplished in our midst through the paschal life, death, and resurrection of Jesus. But now, impelled by Spirit, it grows toward completion. For this reason, the intercessions in all Roman Rite versions culminate in supplication for final fulfillment. Reconciliation I sounds the eschatological impetus of the prayer as follows:

---

[69] *Book of Common Worship*, 129.

[70] Rahner addresses this notion in various writings, including "Marxist Utopia and the Christian Future of Man," in *Theological Investigations*, vol. 6, trans. Karl-H and Boniface Kruger (New York: Seabury Press, 1974), 59–68; "The Question of the Future," in *Theological Investigations*, vol. 12 , trans. David Bourke (New York: Seabury Press, 1974), 181–217; *Foundations of Christian Faith*, trans. William V. Dych (New York: Crossroad, 1982), 444–47 and 457–59.

Help us to work together
for the coming of your kingdom,
until the hour when we stand before you,
Saints among Saints in the halls of heaven,
with the blessed Virgin Mary, Mother of God,
the Blessed Apostles and all the Saints,
and with our deceased brothers and sisters,
whom we commend to your mercy.

Then, freed at last from the wound of corruption
and made fully into a new creation,
we shall sing to you with gladness
the thanksgiving of Christ,
who lives for all eternity.

Taken together, the second epiclesis and the intercessions express how the reception of God's gracious gift of the Christ both historically and now in sacrament calls forth our return-gift of service to God, humankind, and creation. We may feel that this or that eucharistic prayer is more successful in making these connections clear. Prayer for our unity as church, "living-in-grace with one's sisters and brothers,"[71] is always central, so that we may be for others what we are meant to be. In this way, as Chauvet writes, "the assembly, which is his present body of humanity, is the active sacramental mediation of his action, in particular of his praise of the Father and his supplication for his sisters and brothers."[72]

The Eucharistic Prayer and Christian Identity

For Chauvet, the eucharistic prayer ritually expresses and nurtures "the way of conversion which Christians are called to walk throughout their lives."[73] Its tripartite stages reveal three dimensions of Christian identity and spirituality: Scripture, sacrament, and ethics.[74] These three dimensions are displayed across the entire liturgy. Once gathered, we are shaped by the Scriptures (Liturgy of the Word), we re-

---

[71] Chauvet, *The Sacraments*, 145.

[72] Ibid., 33.

[73] Ibid., 133.

[74] In what follows, I am summarizing what Chauvet treats in detail in *Symbol and Sacrament*, 161–89, 278–81; see also *The Sacraments*, 19–42, 143–47.

ceive the sacrament (Liturgy of the Eucharist), and we are sent forth to embody an ethics of service (sending rite). But these three moments are also concentrated into the tripartite stages of the eucharistic prayer.

The preface thankfully recounts the scriptural story of salvation from the *past*. Because it crystallizes the Christian reading of the Scriptures, "beginning with Moses and all the prophets" and culminating in Christ (Luke 24:27), Chauvet calls this the moment of *Scripture* within the eucharistic prayer. From epiclesis 1 over the gifts through the institution narrative and anamnesis, the Christ of the past biblical record gives himself sacramentally in the *present* for the church to receive. This is the moment of *sacrament*. Finally, epiclesis 2 through the intercessions ritually expresses how the scriptural and sacramental gift of Christ obligates followers to make the return-gift of "the ethical conduct by which Christians testify to the gospel by their actions."[75]

The interrelation of Scripture, sacrament, and ethics in forming Christian identity must be understood dynamically rather than statically. Chauvet himself initially describes these three as a tripod on which Christian identity sits: "To be healthy, faith requires that Christians find their own balance on this tripod." But then he shifts to the imagery of motion: "In a domain which must remain in motion like faith or life, the right balance is, as in walking or bicycling, always unstable . . . it is normal that at times everyone relies more on one of these three poles. At least, the image of the tripod is a help to understanding that if the whole weight of Christian identity rests on only one pole, the center of gravity is displaced and a fall is unavoidable."[76]

One heads toward a fall when one of these dimensions is overvalued to the detriment of the other two. Church history illustrates the potential for imbalance. Chauvet sees in Roman Catholicism the tendency, at least in the past, to overvalue sacrament to the detriment of Scripture and ethics. This imbalance came to the fore in the medieval church, thus sowing the seeds of the Reformation. Overvaluation of Scripture to the detriment of sacrament and ethics is the tendency in some forms of Protestantism.

[75] Chauvet, *The Sacraments*, 31.
[76] Ibid., 41.

Overvaluation of ethics is perhaps the most popular current tendency. There is obviously a sense in which one cannot be too ethical! But if Christians dispense with the foundational sources of their identity—the gift of God attested in Scripture and sacrament—how could such an ethics, admirable as it might be in itself, still be Christian? As Chauvet said above, it is Christian not by its generosity but by its reference to the love of God in Christ as its foundation and energy. How could it avoid becoming just another merely human work always in danger of veering into ideology? "To declare bluntly," Chauvet writes, "that what is important 'is not the Mass, it's others,' is to exhibit a singular incomprehension of the Christian mystery."[77] Protestants could say the same, substituting the word *worship* for *the Mass*.

An Emerging, Common Spirituality?

The fruit of historical studies, ecumenism, and liturgical reform has been a convergence in both worship and spirituality. Churches have been righting their own histories of imbalance and overreaction as well as growing in mutual understanding. There is much more work to do. The commonalities and difference we have found between Catholic and Protestant versions of the eucharistic prayer merit further theological exploration and discussion beyond the parameters of this book. Granting all this, sharing as they do a common structure, might these Catholic and Protestant eucharistic prayers share and support a common spirituality? More precisely, do we find this pattern across the different versions of the prayer: recounting God's gift of salvation in Christ with thanks and praise, acknowledging Christ's presence in sacrament here and now, and making a return, signaled in various ways ritually but verified through agapic love in action beyond the liturgy? In my estimation the answer is yes. Perhaps this is a case of spirituality running ahead of confessional differences. Similarly, Christians often find they can join together in common works of love, peacemaking, and justice even while remaining in different traditions.[78] May it be so!

---

[77] Ibid., 42.

[78] Making common cause in works of compassion is really our Christian duty in today's world, not only with other Christians, but with other faiths and spiritual traditions.

Chapter 10

Communion/Sending: Receiving and Living the Self-Emptying Christ

Sharing the body and blood of Christ causes nothing less than our passing over into what we receive, and then in spirit and flesh we carry him everywhere, the one in whom we were dead, buried, and rose again.

St. Leo the Great, Sermon 63, 7[1]

The thesis of this final chapter is that Christ, the one who gives himself away in love, is what we receive in communion and what we are sent forth to embody in our lives. To really commune with the risen Christ is to receive a presence which is an action, "my body *given for you*, my blood *poured out for you*." What we receive, then, is the self-emptying Christ. Paradoxically, we consume self-emptying and our cup runneth over with this fullness that is self-donation. That is how we move with the life of God moving within us *Christianly*. That is the spirituality embedded and expressed in the communion and sending rites.

To Commune Is to Be Sent

Christian worship, Catholic and Protestant, East and West, follows communion with an additional rite, some form of final blessing and

---

[1] Quoted in Jeremy Driscoll, *What Happens at Mass* (Chicago: Archdiocese of Chicago/Gracewing, 2005), 93.

sending. Why consider the spirituality of these two rites as though they are one? Because below the surface of their distinction lies a unity: to commune with the risen One is to be sent. The Emmaus couple, communing with Jesus in the bread of the word and the bread of the table, is sent back to the Jerusalem community, the launching point for mission. Given back to themselves and the community they must now give themselves as witnesses of the risen Christ. They are sent back to be sent forth.

Twice before in these pages, this close connection between receiving Christ and being sent has surfaced. First, chapter 7, "Finding Ourselves in the Word," proposed a suggestive correspondence between the classic stages of *lectio divina* and the ritual stages of the liturgy. The fourth stage, *contemplatio*, corresponds to the liturgy's ritual stage of communion. Following a contemporary rethinking of *lectio divina*, we paired this fourth stage with two additional descriptors, *compassio* and *actio*. To experience union with God in Christ and the Spirit (*contemplatio*) is to be shaped by God's compassion for action (*compassio-actio*). Compassion means to suffer with; it is an other-centered motion of heart and spirit that issues in action. But such love is kenotic, a matter of spending oneself in service to others, and even caring for oneself as though one were an *other*. Seeing myself through the eyes of God's compassion, I love myself rightly. The origin of this more-than-human love of others and self is not in ourselves but from God in whom we abide. God is love and those who abide in love abide in God and God in them (1 John 4:16). To commune with Christ, the compassion of God, is to be sent.

This explains why the moment, *contemplatio* or union, is crucially necessary to the complex, *contemplatio-compassio-actio*. The temptation to see union with God as self-indulgence compared to compassion and action is great. "What really matters," the activist says, "is our love and action for others. This is what really changes the world, not your rituals, which, after all, are *only* symbolic." For a one-sidedly activist spirituality, the question is: *What* is sending us? Psalm 119 says, "Your word is a lamp for my feet, a light for my path" (105). Take away union with this word and what is left? By what light do we travel? Our own—that bundle of desires, fears, regrets, and limited knowledge that comprise the human ego? One cannot give a more-than-human compassion unless one is touched and shaped by it. Touching and being shaped by it is *contemplatio*. It is the font from which compassion and action flow. Contemplative union or communion is the discipline of holding ourselves to a will greater than our own so that our actions may be truly agapic. A character in *Our Town* says, "A star's mighty good company,"[2] stars being symbols of openness toward the Mystery as greater than ourselves. Robert Frost similarly urges us to "Choose Something Like a Star":

> It asks of us a certain height,
> So when at times the mob is swayed
> To carry praise or blame too far,
> We may choose something like a star
> To stay our minds on and be staid.[3]

If *contemplatio* anchors activism in God's compassion, *actio* keeps *contemplatio* honest. The question for a one-sidedly contemplative spirituality is: Where is the *sending*? Where is the going out to the *other* that is the very meaning of communion with Jesus who emptied himself for the world? The contemplative monk Thomas Merton felt this question keenly. An experience he reports in *Conjectures of a Guilty Bystander* is instructive:

> In Louisville, at the corner of Fourth and Walnut, in the center of the shopping district, I was suddenly overwhelmed with the realization that I loved all those people, that they were mine and I theirs, that we could not be alien to one another even though we were total strangers. It was like waking from a dream of separateness, of spurious self-isolation in a special world, the world of renunciation and supposed holiness. This whole illusion of a separate holy existence is a dream.[4]

This does not lead Merton to question his contemplative vocation. But he sees that this solitude must always, paradoxically, be held and practiced in relation to others: "My solitude, however, is not my own, for I see now how much it belongs to them—and that I have a responsibility for it in their regard, not just my own."[5] The test and

---

[2] Thornton Wilder, *Our Town*, in *Thornton Wilder: Collected Plays and Writings on the Theater* (New York: The Library of America, 2007), 208.

[3] Robert Frost, "Choose Something Like a Star," available online at www.cead serve1.nku.edu. Every effort was made to fulfill permissions requirements of copyright holders. The publisher is willing to rectify any omissions in future editions.

[4] Thomas Merton, *Conjectures of a Guilty Bystander* (New York: Penguin/Random House, 2014), 153–54.

[5] Ibid., 155.

measure of contemplative activism is the self-emptying of Jesus, going out to God and others in loving self-donation.

Chapters 8 and 9 on the eucharistic prayer provided a second example of the close connection between communing and sending. There we discerned a spirituality of thankfully welcoming God's gift of the Christ and making a return. This return-gift, signaled ritually in the epiclesis over the people, shows that we receive the Body of Christ sacramentally so that we can be his Body given "for the life of the world" (John 6:51; NRSV). But this means being sent. Bearing witness certainly means announcing the Gospel, but such announcement is credible only when verified in how we live. And the measure of credibility is the extent to which our personal and communal spirituality flows from and reflects the self-emptying of Christ. Clearly, then, we must now go more deeply into this spirituality of self-emptying.

Philippians 2:5-11

Christian spirituality as participation in the kenosis or the self-emptying of Jesus is most explicitly proposed in Paul's letter to the Philippians. But, as we shall see, what it means is spoken of in other ways all across the Scriptures. Christ "emptied himself," says Philippians 2:5-11:

> Let the same mind be in you that was in Christ Jesus,
>   who, though he was in the form of God,
>   did not regard equality with God as something to be exploited,
>   but emptied himself,
>   taking the form of a slave,
>   being born in human likeness.
>   And being found in human form,
>   he humbled himself
>   and became obedient to the point of death—
>   even death on a cross.
>   Therefore God also highly exalted him
>   and gave him the name
>   that is above every name,
>   so that at the name of Jesus
>   every knee should bend,
>   in heaven and on earth and under the earth,

> and every tongue should confess
> > that Jesus Christ is Lord,
> > to the glory of God the Father. (NRSV)

For spirituality, the important thing is how Paul introduces this hymn: "Let the same mind be in you that was in Christ Jesus." In short, Jesus' spirituality is to become ours. How does the self-emptying of Jesus, received in communion, become a reality in us? Notice, first, that the emptying of self unto death is not the whole story. We are tempted to think *immediately and only* of the cross, and then, perhaps, of some very questionable atonement theories of later times. Like bad varnish, these theories obscure and misrepresent the beauty, breadth, and depth of the original picture. We *do* have to think of the cross in this passage, but we have to think it as part of a larger story. That larger story includes the passage as a whole, the letter in which it occurs, and the whole of the New Testament. The full context shows that kenosis embraces at the least four dimensions: a way of living, a way of building and performing the Body of Christ,[6] and a way of dying. Behind and before these three is a fourth—the self-emptying of God. The kenosis of Jesus discloses precisely this God.

The Way of God

The opening lines of the Philippians hymn have traditionally been understood to express or at least imply what later theology calls the incarnation. Christ Jesus,

> > though he was in the form of God,
> > did not regard equality with God
> > as something to be exploited,
> > but emptied himself,
> > > taking the form of a slave,
> > > being born in human likeness.
> > And being found in human form,
> > > he humbled himself.

---

[6] The expression *performing* the Body of Christ comes from William Cavanaugh. His understanding of this will be addressed in some detail below.

In this interpretation, the first act of self-emptying is God's, or what John's gospel names the Logos of God that became flesh and was "born in human likeness." This first act of self-emptying is followed by the kenotic journey of the Word made flesh: "And being found in human form, he humbled himself."[7] Christ is "the image of the invisible God" (Col 1:15; NRSV), Emmanuel, God-with-us. Jesus says, whoever sees me, sees the One who sent me (see John 12:45). So, the kenosis of Jesus images the kenosis of God. Michael Downey writes, "God is the God of self-emptying, the one whose very life is Love pouring itself forth."[8]

God *is* love, Scripture says, not that God *has* love as a secondary attribute. No, God *is* love. Christian tradition describes the trinitarian life of God as *perichoresis*, literally a dancing around each other in love. The roots of this word are instructive. *Peri* means around, and *chorein* means to give way or make room (dance). The motion of God's trinitarian life is a motion of a mutual giving way to each other, an indwelling of each in each in love. But to give way to the other, to give up one's place for the other is kenosis. And it is not mere *withdrawal from* but a way of *being with* the other, a form of communion and shared life.

When the triune God acts outwardly, both establishing and sustaining creation, all the while remaining different from and yet closer to it than it is to itself, this is a free act of love. The way of God, both in creating and incarnating is the way of self-emptying, not self-aggrandizement. It is worth recalling words we heard earlier from Pope Francis: "The universe did not emerge as a result of arbitrary omnipotence, a show of force or a desire for self-assertion. Creation

---

[7] An alternate school of interpretation holds that the whole hymn is about Jesus' earthly life. Raymond E. Brown describes both approaches in *An Introduction to the New Testament* (New York: Doubleday, 1997), 491–92. Aloys Grillmeier, discusses Pauline Christology, including the Philippians passage, in *Christ in Christian Tradition*, trans. John Bowden (Atlanta: John Knox Press, 1975), 15–26. He acknowledges the alternate view but defends the traditional interpretation. Though the hymn is primarily about the self-emptying character of Jesus' earthly life, death, and his exaltation, "the pre-existence of Christ is included or at least presupposed in its approach" and, he concludes, "it would be false to refuse the later theology of the church the right to reflect upon the being of Christ with the help of this hymn" (22).

[8] Michael Downey, *The Depth of God's Reach: A Spirituality of Christ's Descent* (New York: Orbis Books, 2018), 25.

is of the order of love. God's love is the fundamental moving force in all created things."[9] "By virtue of God's unselfish love," Jürgen Moltmann writes, "God permeates all creatures and makes them alive. . . . The unselfish empathy of God awakens the sympathy of all creatures for each other. *Perichoresis* is also a mystery of creation."[10]

As we saw in chapter 4, lovingly creating beings who are not God takes place in view of a higher possibility: the creation of a creature who in its otherness from God also belongs to God so intimately as to be God's own humanity. All creation is held by Eternal Word because, as John's Prologue says, everything comes to be and is through this Word. But Bernadette Farrell's remarkable song "God Beyond All Names" completes the picture, saying, "all creation lives to hold you."[11] Creation lives to hold the Incarnate Word. The creaturely, human reality of Jesus comes to be and continues to be in the very act of the Logos's self-emptying. This self-giving establishes a human creaturely reality *in distinction from* and *in the closest possible unity with* the Logos. Rahner writes:

> The primary phenomenon given by faith is precisely the self-emptying of God, his becoming, the kenosis and genesis of God himself. . . . Insofar as in his abiding and infinite fullness he empties himself, the other comes to be as God's very own reality. . . . God goes out of himself, he himself, he as the self-giving fullness. Because he can do this, because this is his free and primary possibility, for this reason he is defined in scripture as love.[12]

In Jesus, God communicates perichoresis or kenotic giving-way-to-each-other for human participation. The way we come to know this love, John's first letter says, is that Christ "laid down his life for us" and draws the conclusion, so we ought to lay down our lives

---

[9] *On Care for Our Common Home: Laudato Si'*, Encyclical Letter of the Holy Father Francis (Washington, DC: United States Conference of Catholic Bishops/Vatican City: Liberia Editrice Vaticana, 2015), par. 77.

[10] Jürgen Moltmann, "God Is Unselfish Love," *The Emptying God: A Buddhist-Jewish-Christian Conversation*, ed. John B. Cobb Jr. and Christopher Ives (New York: Orbis Books, 1990), 121.

[11] "God Beyond All Names," © 1990, Bernadette Farrell. Published by OCP. All rights reserved.

[12] Karl Rahner, *Foundations of Christian Faith*, trans. William V. Dych (New York: Crossroad, 1982), 222.

for each other (see 1 John 4:16). To become perfect as God is perfect is to live kenotically. "Beloved, let us love one another, because love is of God; everyone who loves is begotten by God and knows God" (1 John 4:7).

A Way of Living

The kenotic way of Jesus is first of all the way he lives. He lives the way of downward mobility, not grasping at equality with God. In this grasping or exploiting we should hear an echo of the temptation in the garden. Adam and Eve, succumbing to the serpent's promise that "you will be like gods" (Gen 3:5), exemplify grasping at equality with God. The road to hell is paved with promises of upward mobility! We should remember too what Ernest Becker called the *causa sui* project of modernity, the illusory attempt to be one's own god, enacted in personal, communal, and national ideologies.[13] Jesus, the new Adam, counters this fall, emptying himself, taking the form of a slave, humbling himself in lovingly doing the will of the One who sent him.

Sadao Watanabe's print, which graces the cover of this book, shows Jesus seeking the lost sheep. It is emblematic of this kenotic life. Christ is almost bent double, the arch of his back is at the top. His head and arms move downward to lift the lost lamb to his breast. Eventually, the Good Shepherd lays down his life for the sheep. But this is the result of kenotic living, in which he seeks those on the margins, eats with sinners, bends low to lift them up and carry them back from lostness and suffering. Jesus dies because of the way he lives and cares for others.

Michael Downey traces Jesus' kenotic life journey in a series of examples.[14] To name a few, there is the self-emptying in the waters of baptism, in which one must go down in order to come up. There is a premonition of death in this. The waters symbolize life-threatening chaos as well as cleansing and new life. Christ sojourns in the wilderness, where he empties himself in fasting, the paradigm for later monastic and contemplative spirituality. "Empty yourself completely," the Brief Rule of St. Romuald says, "and sit waiting, content

---

[13] The *causa sui* project of modernity was discussed in chapter 2 in relation to Ernest Becker's work, *The Denial of Death* (New York: Free Press Paperbacks, 1997).

[14] Downey, *God's Reach*, 26–34.

with the grace of God."[15] The self-emptying of fasting also sets the stage for Jesus' confrontation with Satan, who tempts him to aggrandize himself materially and spiritually. In the face of these, he empties any shred of self-will for God's will: "One does not live by bread alone, but by every word that comes forth from the mouth of God" (Matt 4:4). Giving himself to God's will is the foundation of his ministry. In this public ministry Jesus repeatedly "bends low to be with the lowly," as Downey says.[16] Nearing the end, he again bends down to wash his disciples' feet, saying: "as I have done for you, you should also do . . . blessed are you if you do it" (John 13:15-17).

Even forceful confrontations illustrate this risk-taking, kenotic love. Take the story of the woman caught in adultery (John 8:1-11). It is not only the woman whose life is under threat. Just before this passage, chapter 7 sounds an ominous note. The religious authorities are looking for a reason to arrest and kill Jesus. When he appears, the people say, "Is he not the one they are trying to kill?" (John 7:25). Killing Jesus might well take the form of stoning, as several later events show (John 8:59; 10:31; 11:8). The controversy swirling about him concerns the interpretation of the Mosaic law: "Did not Moses give you the law?" Jesus asks. "Yet none of you keeps the law. . . . If a man can receive circumcision on a sabbath so that the law of Moses may not be broken, are you angry with me because I made a whole person well on a sabbath? Stop judging by appearances, but judge justly" (7:19, 23-24).

All of this serves as backdrop to our story. The religious authorities make the woman stand before Jesus, hoping to bring a charge against him. Contradicting the law of Moses would be a good one. "Moses commanded us to stone such women. So what do you say?" In the course of this story Jesus bends down twice to write in the sand with his finger. For John Shea, this echoes the story of Moses receiving the law from God. God inscribes the law on stone tablets with his finger (Exod 31:18). Shea observes, "Human authors use quills and parchment. God uses his finger that is capable of carving into the hardness of rock. Jesus also writes with his finger, showing his closeness to God and that he writes for God."[17]

---

[15] Brief Rule of St. Romuald, available online: www.incarnationmonastery.com.

[16] Downey, *God's Reach*, 30.

[17] John Shea, *The Spiritual Wisdom of the Gospels for Christian Preachers and Teachers: Year C, The Relentless Widow* (Collegeville, MN: Liturgical Press, 2006), 91.

Our hearts understandably go out to the woman. After all, whatever her fault, she is a victim. Where is the man caught in adultery? The whole thing is a set-up by hypocritical men who can engage in adultery with impunity. Hypocritical too are the religious authorities. Their apparent devotion to law masks their own unworthy purposes, a temptation that bedevils religious authorities in every age. In this situation, Jesus judges justly and not by appearances.

How does he proceed? Unlike the Hollywood action hero, there is no violence. Jesus does not deter them by displaying more firepower than the would-be stone-throwers. His only weapon in this potentially violent situation is truth. Reaching nonviolently into the very psyche of those wishing to stone the woman, he says, "Let the one among you who is without sin be the first to throw a stone at her." The Word is mightier than the sword! His words compel them to face an undeniable truth and thus think about the law at a deeper level. Paul's self-description in the second reading from Philippians on the Sunday that this gospel is read is true of everyone: "not having any righteousness of my own based on the law" (3:9). The law is God's gift, but no one can claim *not* to have transgressed it. Therefore no one can cast the first stone.

Jesus' risk taking provokes a spiritual struggle, requiring a self-emptying of one's customary posture for something new. One can imagine the resistance: "But we've always done it this way!"

He appeals to the would-be executioners' capacity for self-criticism, as unlikely as this may seem in the situation. He wants to rescue everybody, opening the possibility of new life to those with stones in their hands and the woman they are exploiting for their own purposes. Jesus, authoritative interpreter of the Mosaic law, is also authoritative interpreter/enactor of God's mercy. He enacts it in a self-emptying love that risks all to find and rescue those who are lost. The first reading on the Sunday when this gospel is read anticipates this move. God says, "See, I am doing something new! Now it springs forth, do you not perceive it?" (Isa 43:19). Jesus is doing something new. Can they accept it?

In our own time we have caught glimpses of this in Gandhi and Martin Luther King Jr., putting their bodies on the line, nonviolently provoking a change in the moral consciousness of their oppressors. In the end, Jesus acts with love toward the woman but also toward the men. Both are lost sheep. He enacts a self-emptying love that risks all to find and rescue those who are lost.

How does Jesus' kenotic way of living become ours? In many ways. But foundational for this spirituality is the liturgy itself. From age to age, Word and Eucharist invite participation in the kenotic paschal journey. "It is this mystery of the Christ-event," Henri Nouwen writes, "that is made visible in the liturgical discipline of the church."[18] Living the self-emptying spirituality of Jesus, we must be prepared to honestly accept challenges to our customary understandings and patterns of behavior. Faith is not just reception and preservation of past tradition but openness to the future, to the surprising ways of God. The Greek philosopher Heraclitus once said that unless we learn to expect the unexpected we will miss the truth.[19]

A Way of Building and Performing the Body of Christ

The kenotic spirituality of Jesus is a way of building and performing the Body of Christ. The liturgy's ritual stages display a striking trajectory: more and more toward the *body*. Communion is a sharing in the Body and Blood of Christ. He becomes our food and drink. Though it is a spiritual reception, it is beyond receiving words or ideas into one's head. Reception of the Word comes to ritual completion in a different and intimate mode of presence, a *beyond word* reception *in the body*, which transforms us into the Body of Christ. Chauvet's book, *The Sacraments*, is evocatively subtitled *The Word of God at the Mercy of the Body*. He speaks eloquently of how the Word seeks inscription in the body. God wants to write God's law on our hearts, on the body of a people, on humanity. We must eat the scroll of the Word. We make a beginning by meditating on or chewing the cud of the readings during the Liturgy of the Word. But it must go further. The Word, the Christ, is now literally "in our mouths" as the Bread of Life and the Cup of Salvation. Beyond hearing is ingesting. He writes:

> We must eat, masticate to the point of accepting, in heart and body, the bitter scandal of a God crucified for the life of the world. For John the eucharistic act of eating is the great symbolic experience in which we are given, to feel and live, the scandal of faith until it enters our bodies, that is to say, into our life.[20]

---

[18] Henri Nouwen, *The Selfless Way* (Maryknoll, NY: Orbis Books, 2007), 73.

[19] Philip Wheelright, *Heraclitus* (New York: Atheneum, 1971), 20.

[20] Louis-Marie Chauvet, *The Sacraments: The Word of God at the Mercy of the Body*, trans. Madeleine Beaumont (Collegeville, MN: Liturgical Press, 2001), 50.

Notice how Chauvet equates body with life. Human life in all its dimensions, even the most spiritual, is bodily life. What is the *body* of our life? A whole range of things, it turns out. Chauvet says, "Faith cannot be lived in any other way, including what is most spiritual in it, than *in the mediation of the body*, the body of a society, of a desire, of a tradition, of a history, of an institution, and so on. What is most spiritual always takes place in the most corporeal."[21]

This certainly includes the body/personhood of the individual communicant. Jesus asks, "Can you drink the cup that I drink?" (Mark 10:38). To share Christ's baptism and drink his cup is to be set on the path of his kenosis. But body always includes more than the individual. Christians belong to the corporate Body of Christ. Communion is communal—not a moment in which the communal body evaporates back into private individuals. Ritually, it is the most heightened actualization of Christ's communal Body. In an ongoing act of self-emptying love, the risen Christ communicates life, identity, and unity to the members of his Body. Paul understands the Body's unity as participation in Christic self-emptying, the mutual deference of each to each, so that "the members may have the same care, one for another." This is so much the case that "if one member suffers, all suffer together with it; if one member is honored, all rejoice together with it" (1 Cor 12:25-26; NRSV). The words introducing the Philippians hymn (2:2-4; NRSV) make it clear that practicing kenotic love is a way of building and performing the body of Christ:

> [B]e of the same mind, having the same love, being in full accord and of one mind. Do nothing from selfish ambition or conceit, but in humility regard others as better than yourselves. Let each of you look not to your own interests, but to the interests of others.

But the self-emptying of Christ, given to and making the ecclesial body, has further implications. The whole liturgy, Chauvet says, is a passage or transit beyond itself into the liturgy of life. Christian ethics, compassion, and agapic love in action, the gracious mutual love of sisters and brothers, is to reach and touch the social body of humanity. Evangelization as sharing the Gospel is mediated by a body of practice, personal, communal, social. It becomes credible to

---

[21] Ibid., xii.

the extent that our living really expresses the self-emptying love of Christ. Cardinal Emmanuel Suhard, archbishop of Paris during the 1940s, expressed it well: "To be a witness does not consist in engaging in propaganda, nor even stirring people up, but in being a living mystery. It means to live in such a way that one's life would not make sense if God did not exist."[22]

Pope Francis likens the church to a field hospital tending the wounded in a battle zone.[23] The battle zone is the entire world. All too often, this is not just metaphor but literal truth. Consider the case of the Chilean church under the oppressive Pinochet regime. William Cavanaugh's detailed study titled *Torture and Christ* wrestles with the question: how does the church *perform* itself in relation to society and the state, especially when this state is oppressive to the point of using torture to assert its power?[24] This is not just a political question but a theological and liturgical one, bearing directly on the meaning of the Eucharist. For the object of torture is the body, personal and social. And the object of the Eucharist is the body, personal and social.

There is a strange symmetry here, between something holy and something demonic. On the one hand, there is the church's discipline of self-emptying love, flowing from Christ through the Word and the Eucharist (and other sacraments). On the other, there is the discipline of violence employed by the state, in this case, Pinochet's torture apparatus. The discipline of Christ and the church gathers people together into one body animated by mutual kenotic love; the discipline of the torture state is to scatter and rend the body. Kenotic spirituality is a dying to self that brings greater life; the spirituality of violence is the inflation of the self and/or state by depriving others of life. The discipline of Christ's Body is loving deference to others, not just fellow Christians; the discipline of the torture state vilifies others as enemies for suppression or liquidation.

In the Chilean case, the government was on the attack, using torture to rend the bodies of persons and social organizations, causing them to disappear (in Spanish the verb form is *desaparecer*). How

---

[22] Cardinal Emmanuel Suhard, quoted in *Give Us This Day* (May 2018), 310.

[23] See "A Big Heart Open to God," *America Magazine*, September 13, 2013.

[24] William T. Cavanaugh, *Torture and Christ: Theology, Politics, and the Body of Christ* (Malden, MA: Blackwell Publishers, 1998).

would the Catholic and other churches, as well as all people of good will, handle this? Their joint efforts to aid targets of torture and defend human rights were publicly branded as communism and terrorism by a regime filled with "observant" Catholics. Most of the torturers were also observant Catholics. How does the Body of Christ, to use Cavanaugh's expression, *perform* itself in such a milieu? Would the church let itself be *disappeared* along with those many persons who had been disappeared? Or would it keep *reappearing* despite efforts to make it withdraw? Cavanaugh writes,

> The strategy of torture and disappearance attacks all intermediary organizations between the individual and the state by isolating individuals from one another. The church in Chile resisted this strategy precisely by knitting people back together, connecting them as members of one another. The church thereby undertakes the fundamentally Eucharistic task . . . building up the true body of Christ, a counter-discipline to the discipline of the state.[25]

Because torture aims to rend the very Body of Christ and the body of humanity the church is sent to serve, it contradicts the very meaning of Christ's self-emptying love and the Eucharist that celebrates it. So, in addition to creating social spaces and venues that knit people together in solidarity, the Chilean bishops were eventually compelled to excommunicate these observant Catholic torturers and the regime that begot them. "If torture is essentially an anti-liturgy, a drama in which the state realizes omnipotence on the bodies of others, then the Eucharist provides a direct and startling contrast, for in the Eucharist, Christ sacrifices no other body but his own."[26] Excommunication pronounced these state-sponsored activities incompatible with the self-emptying love of Christ. You cannot be a member *and* a torturer of Christ's Body. The serious step of excommunication was not taken only to condemn the sin but to call the sinners to conversion.[27]

[25] Ibid., 267.

[26] Ibid., 279.

[27] Cavanaugh documents a serious flaw in how excommunication was applied. It was done anonymously; that is, instead of citing specific torturers or Pinochet or others in the regime by name, it said that anyone who engaged in these activities was excommunicated. Given the public nature of state operatives, Cavanaugh maintains that excommunicating them by name would have been more effective and appropriate. See ibid., 253–64.

Such an analysis may seem far from home, but it would be naïve not to realize that any state, any organized body of people, is capable of evil. In recent years our own country became embroiled in controversy around the torture tactic of waterboarding. At the time of this book's writing, we have witnessed the state rending the bodies of families, tearing children from their parents at our southern border, some as young as two and three years old. The difficulty of now reuniting them shows how thoughtlessly and carelessly this policy was undertaken.

Every state, every bureaucracy, has the capacity to become a cold-blooded monster. There may be a variety of views on what a country's immigration policy should be. But using something bordering on torture as a bargaining chip to advance one's political agenda is unacceptable. The outcry, by churches of all stripes as well as nonchurch people of good will, forced public abandonment of this policy. But in its defense the attorney general cited Romans 13:1, in which Paul urges Christians to obey public authority. Aside from the exegetical problems with this interpretation, was there awareness that pastors in Hitler's Germany cited the same passage to urge compliance with the Nazi regime and its policies? Or that slaveholders used the same passage, calling for the return of runaway slaves? Or that Romans 13:1 was cited by defenders of apartheid? The lesson is clear: if the church does not interpret and assert itself, speaking truth to power, the state will tell the church how it should think and what it should do. Against this, the church must be, as Cardinal Suhard said, a "living mystery" of Christ's self-emptying love.

A Way of Dying

To understand the dying of Jesus as self-emptying love and our participation in it, we must have the courage to be truthful and vulnerable in the face of death, even while affirming our faith in the living God. The liturgy impels us to do so because it places the courageous, vulnerable, faithful death of Jesus at the center: *my body given for you, my blood shed for you*. What is most important is the *for you*—the death of Jesus precisely as an act of love. Communing with him, receiving him, we are drawn into the possibility that our dying can be an act of love toward God and others. To appreciate this kenotic character of Jesus' dying, we must recall the unique psychological-spiritual burden death imposes on human beings. Like other animals we are mortal; unlike them we *know* we are mortal. The soaring reach of our transcendence toward the Mystery in which all things abide also discloses our createdness, finitude, and mortality. Though we are a little less than angels, we are also food for worms. This dark shadow of death hovers over our lives and accomplishments.[28]

While death is a psychological burden for everyone, it poses a particular burden for religious faith. It only arises for those who believe that God is love and wishes to impart fullness of life to human beings. Sebastian Moore writes, "Death tries to tell me that I am not God, and that is a good word."[29] To know that one is not God is a good word, the beginning of wisdom. Authentic spirituality lies in acknowledging the Mystery in which all things abide and, even more, living a life worthy of the gift of being. Should this Mystery approach us in self-bestowing love, spirituality consists in still more: a responsive love of God, who has first loved us. And loving God will mean loving the neighbor (everyone) and all creation.

But Moore immediately adds, "Death also tries to tell me that I have no ultimate value, and that is the worst of words." For the believer this means *no value to God*. This "worst of words" sucks the air out of high spiritual aspirations because it calls into question the God of love. If God is the *in every moment* source of our life, how is it that God lets go of us in death? If God is love, as Scripture says, how is it that God abandons us to death? God disappears, as it were, when most needed. This first wounding to faith brings in tow a second. If God is missing in action, at least when it comes to death, then either God doesn't exist or God is a cruel master. Neither an illusory god nor one that wishes us ill deserves our faith, trust, and love. Death, then, really is the last word. Though we may ignore or repress it until it takes us like a thief in the night, we are people who "sit in darkness and death's shadow" (Luke 1:79).

This rehearsal of dark feelings and thoughts is far from the God whom Jesus reveals. It is what remains if we simply put brackets around the Christ story. Jesus does not welcome death, but he does

---

[28] We met the issue earlier in this book. Chapter 1 discussed spirituality as recovering a sense of our createdness. Chapter 2 considered strategies of repressing this sense in favor of an illusory autonomy, characteristic of the enlightenment and modernity.

[29] Sebastian Moore, *The Fire and the Rose Are One* (New York: Seabury Press, 1980), 121.

not hide from it either. He faces the radicality of death full on, something we are loath to do. Our psychological avoidance of death often colors how we imagine his. Overemphasizing his divinity, we place him above death so that he is only play-acting his humanity. He "dies and flies," as Michael Downey says, as though in death he instantly wakes up, alive in God:

> This perception of Jesus as one who dies and flies immediately to heaven blinds us to the reality that this one person, Jesus the Christ, did truly die. Such a view inadvertently undercuts the truth that the Christ was a corpse, was mourned by his followers, and was laid in the tomb. There is silence, grief, desolation, disappointment. The pain of this experience of the followers of Jesus cannot be glossed over.[30]

Hans Holbein's grim painting, *The Body of the Dead Christ in the Tomb*, provides a visual antidote to this "dies and flies" Jesus. It shows Jesus as a truly dead and beginning-to-rot corpse. The painting fascinated Dostoevsky. On seeing it, he became so transfixed that his wife had to pull him away, fearing he might go into epileptic seizure. In his novel *The Idiot*, one of Dostoevsky's characters, mesmerized by the painting, says it can destroy faith.[31] But neither the "dies and flies" Jesus nor the simply dead Jesus is the Christ of the Gospel. Neither one is the Christ we commune with in the Word and the Eucharist. If Jesus, the presence and flow of God's love toward humanity, is simply extinguished, then death indeed has the last word. In fact, as Moore points out, these two mutilations of the Gospel are related. "The radical spiritual sickness of man is not flight from death but his acceptance of death as the last word. It is this that puts him in flight from death."[32] Is there some space here for dying as an act of love?

The raising of Lazarus (John 11:1-45) is of interest because it portrays Jesus' emotions and attitude in the face of death. We know that raising his friend prefigures Jesus' own resurrection. Not surprisingly, preaching often emphasizes this. But if we move too quickly to resurrection, we rob it of its true power because we have robbed death of

---

[30] Downey, *God's Reach*, 46.

[31] The painting may be viewed online at Wikipedia under "The Body of the Dead Christ in the Tomb."

[32] Moore, *The Fire*, 125.

its true radicality. The story actually works in the opposite direction, forcing us, with Jesus and the disciples, to pass *through* the radicality of death on the way to Jesus' life-giving deed. The impending death of Jesus pervades this story. Francis J. Moloney provocatively titles his commentary on this episode "A Resurrection That Will Lead to Death," referring to the Sanhedrin's decision to kill Jesus in response to the raising of Lazarus.[33] This episode is the first of three in John's gospel, all pointing toward the death of Jesus: the Lazarus story, the Sanhedrin's decision to kill Jesus, the anointing of Jesus at Bethany. Gail O'Day describes the series as "The Prelude to Jesus' Hour," meaning the hour of Jesus' death.[34]

The emotions of Jesus in this story are complex. His compassion, like an undertow, encompasses the whole: "Now Jesus loved Martha and her sister and Lazarus. So . . ." (11:5). Love makes Jesus risk his own life, reentering dangerous territory where opponents want to eliminate him. It is a costly love, prompting the Sanhedrin's death verdict for Jesus. Scripture scholar Thomas Brodie writes, "The idea of death is being increasingly confronted by that of love, and there is an implication that it is by some form of love that death is to be overcome."[35] Early in John's gospel, Jesus invites inquiring disciples to come and see. In the imagery of John's Prologue, he invites them to come and see the light that shines in the darkness. But now the mourners invite Jesus to come and see the darkness of death. Through his interaction with Martha, Mary, the mourners, and the dead Lazarus, Jesus also confronts death itself, and his own death.

Faced with the despairing tears of the mourners, different emotions burst forth from Jesus' innermost depths: "he became perturbed and deeply troubled" (v. 33). In the original Greek these words mean profound anger, indignation, and agitation.[36] They are followed by tears. This anger and agitation, Thomas Brodie explains, is not just a passive internal state but an outburst:

---

[33] Francis J. Moloney, *The Gospel of John*, ed. Daniel J. Harrington, Sacra Pagina Series (Collegeville, MN: Liturgical Press, 1998), 322–44.

[34] Gail O'Day, "John 11:1–12:50: The Prelude to Jesus' Hour," in *The New Interpreter's Bible*, vol. 9 (Nashville: Abingdon Press, 1995), 681–718.

[35] Thomas L. Brodie, *The Gospel of John: A Literary and Theological Commentary* (New York: Oxford University Press, 1993), 392. In much of what follows I am especially indebted to Brodie's interpretation, 383–400.

[36] O'Day, "Prelude," 690.

The anger happens *tō pneumati*, "in spirit," meaning that Jesus' breath or spirit goes out in anger. In other words, he breathed angrily. And then he was "disturbed" (literally, "and he troubled himself," or "disturbed himself"). . . . The basic idea, therefore, is of unfolding anger: he breathed angrily and was shaken.[37]

Similarly, the tears of Jesus also burst outward from his inner depths. Literally, he *breaks into* tears. "Thus there are two outbursts—first of anger, and later of tears."[38]

What do these outbursts express? First, if the raising of Lazarus anticipates Jesus' resurrection, these outpourings anticipate Jesus' death. Brodie writes:

> The death of Jesus will be accompanied by the handing over of the spirit and by the outflow of blood and water (19:30, 34). There is a literal emptying. Given that the Lazarus story, from start to finish (11:2, 53), is so closely connected to the death of Jesus, it is appropriate that in this story also, this "rehearsal" of Jesus' passion-glorification, there should be an initial process of self-emptying. The burst of spirit-disturbing anger and the flow of tears suggest such a process.[39]

To what are these outpourings directed? As usual, the bystanders don't understand the depth of Christ's action. They interpret his tears only as compassion: "See how he loved him." Yes, but other emotions are at play. Jesus is angry, indignant, deeply troubled. His outbursts express vulnerability and truthfulness but also protest and resolution. His heart is resolved toward God's will, come what may. He experiences more profoundly than anyone else the vitiating force of death, its power to undermine our relationship to the God of love. Here it is helpful to take a good look at the face of Michelangelo's David. With a David-like determination, Jesus raises the banner of faith, love, and life against the Goliath of death. He does this as an act of love for Martha, Mary, Lazarus, and the mourners in their despairing lostness before death. Whatever faith they and we may have in God's love, the darkness of death always threatens to undermine it. It is the dark night in which we stumble (John 11:10) and easily lose hold of

---

[37] Brodie, *The Gospel of John*, 395.
[38] Ibid.
[39] Ibid., 396.

the light. Death, with its alienating hold over these despairing mourners, is the object of Christ's anger, indignation, tears.

To say that Jesus overcomes death does not mean he removes death from human life. Even the raised Lazarus will die. Even Jesus will die. He overcomes death by passing through it and making it an act of self-emptying love and trust in his Abba. How radical is this clear-eyed self-emptying? How low must Jesus go? In his dying he experiences being abandoned by his Abba: "My God, my God, why have you forsaken me?" (Matt 27:46). In the words of Chauvet, Jesus experiences "the incomprehensible silence of the Father who, allowing him to die, did not intervene to save him."[40] What could be darker or more radical than this, to love and trust even in the face of being forsaken? "Even if Jesus dies under a 'why?' of incomprehension of God's ways, he still makes this agonizing why into a prayer."[41] In this most costly act of faith and love, Jesus goes *with* and *for* us to this darkest of all places: a death undermining faith and love because God is experienced as utterly forsaking us. If the primal sin in the garden was breaking trust with God, Jesus reverses and heals the rupture by keeping trust with God even in the God-forsaken experience of death. Chauvet writes *"The sacrifice of Jesus is thus his 'kenosis'*—the movement which is exactly the reverse of Adam's sin—where he consents to taste humanity to its extreme limit, death experienced in the silence of a God who would not even intervene to spare the Just One this death."[42]

Jesus opens a way beyond either hiding from death or mistaking it for the last and worst word. Ultimately, the victory of this trust can only be assured by his Abba. The raising of Lazarus is not simply an assertion of Jesus' own power but a plea to the Father: "And Jesus raised his eyes and said, 'Father, I thank you for hearing me'" (11:41). Only the God of love whom his living and dying reveals can bring life out of death so that love is the last word. And the God of love answers by raising him from the dead, a resurrection partially glimpsed in the raising of Lazarus.

---

[40] Louis-Marie Chauvet, *Symbol and Sacrament: A Sacramental Reinterpretation of Christian Existence*, trans. Patrick Madigan and Madeleine Beaumont (Collegeville, MN: Liturgical Press, 1995), 301.

[41] Ibid., 497.

[42] Ibid., 301.

This act of love for the One who sent him is at the same time an act of love for us. Jesus' life is taken from him precisely because of the way he cares for others, a way that brings him into conflict with business as usual. Still, in the midst of *being taken*, Jesus freely gives himself. Though "he takes the form of a slave," as Philippians says, his obedience is neither begrudging nor slavish but loving self-donation: "he humbled himself, becoming obedient to death, even death on a cross" (2:8). This is the difficult but grace-enabled path for those who follow him: in the midst of our *being taken*, to freely give and entrust ourselves to the incomprehensible mystery of God.

Because I live in an intentional ecumenical community of retired church workers and social justice activists, I experience death often and intimately. There are roughly three generations living at Pilgrim Place. Every year a number of dear friends whom I have grown to know and love die. I have sat with some in the course of their dying and sung for some at the moment of death. This has taught me a number of things. One is that death is both something we do and something that happens to us. The paradox of our impressive autonomy and yet radical dependence comes to the fore most of all in dying. "Death," Rahner writes, "appears both as act and fate, as end and fulfillment, as willed and suffered, as plenitude and emptiness."[43]

Before my wife and I moved to Pilgrim Place, my first close-up experience with death was with my mother-in-law, Pat. In hospice care for about a week, Pat drifted back and forth between willing and suffering, between acts of love and passivity to forces beyond her control. We prayed, sang, cried, laughed, told stories, and at times were just quietly present in mutual support. I say *mutual* because Pat, a woman of deep faith, was caring for us as much as we were caring for her. At one point, having moved in and out of consciousness and pain over several days, including frightening hallucinations, she insisted on sitting up, putting her arms around her daughters, like a mother hen gathering her chicks, saying, "We've had a good life together." She was *doing* her death as an act of love, even as she was gradually being submerged by forces beyond her control. It was not a case of "rage, rage, against the dying of the light," as in Dylan

---

[43] Karl Rahner, *On the Theology of Death*, trans. C. H. Henckey (New York: Seabury Press, 1973), 41.

Thomas's poem, but "love, love, into the Light." To the extent that she could, Pat made even losing everything an act of love.

A second thing I have learned is that dying is a time for accompaniment. Human persons are not born alone and they are not meant to die alone, though sadly this often happens. Exploring the intercessions in the eucharistic prayer led us to understand all our living as intercession, acting on behalf of others, bearing each other's burdens, standing with Christ in his self-emptying love for all. That is why intercessions go as far as remembering the dead. Our communion with the dead and risen Christ is also communion with those who have died and risen with him. There is a great mystery of mutuality here. The dead have not passed *away* but passed *over* into being with God. They do not become merely a-cosmic or separated from this world but are world-oriented or pan-cosmic. With God, they will what God wills for the living. With God, who holds us in being by remembering and loving us, they remember and hold us in love. This is the "cloud of witnesses" of which Hebrews 12:1 speaks. This is the sentiment at the heart of the *Día de los Muertos*.

But the radicality of death calls forth the self-emptying love of the living for the dying. It is our call as the Body of Christ to receive and surround the emerging fears, sadness, regrets, guilt, and even anger of the dying person with the loving-kindness of God. Such accompaniment continues, even when the dying person is no longer conscious. Connie Green, a Quaker friend and hospice nurse for thirty-five years, shared the following story with me. When she met Claire and her husband Peter, he was in the final stages of dying from a brain tumor, diagnosed nine years before. "Within three days of our first meeting he lapsed into a coma" and "lived for another four days over a long weekend." Her story continues:

> During this time a remarkable thing happened. His old friends came and spent time in his room. They reminisced, cried, laughed, and told wonderful stories. His brothers arrived confessing to having had difficult relationships with Peter, admitting remorse. They came to his bedside and told him they loved him and would miss him. His neurosurgeon, who had treated him for all of the nine years of his illness came and sat at Peter's bedside for a full three hours on that Saturday afternoon. I sensed that this was a deeply needed expression, by the surgeon, of his own feelings and respect for Peter's long journey. The

friends and family helped tend to Peter's needs, turning him, swabbing his lips, tenderly caring for him as well as for Claire. There was a palpable Presence of Love in the room and when anyone entered they commented on the atmosphere. It was like walking into a soothing pool of warm tropical water. There seemed to be golden light suffusing all. Those present were reluctant to leave.

This poignant story ends with an interesting liturgical detail.

> The priest came and performed the Sacrament of the Sick, Last Rites, but he did not have the Host with him so there would be no Eucharistic rite. Claire was saddened by this. I found words come to me suggesting that we had been experiencing Holy Communion during the whole time of our vigil. I said I felt that the Love of Christ was present and we had all partaken. Claire took a deep breath and nodded in recognition and peaceful agreement. At the end, Peter and Claire were alone together when he died. Claire was lying next to Peter in their bed holding him as he slipped quietly away.

Because the grace of God is loose in the world, many people, whatever their religious or nonreligious affiliation may be, implicitly enact God's love toward the dying. Rahner writes, "Many a person has prayed, thank God, without knowing it, because his heart trembled with the anxiety of true love for another and he sent into the silent infinitude of God a general SOS which was only apparently undirected."[44] But in ecclesial accompaniment, Christians bring the "I am with you always" of the risen One to the dying. Feelings of weakness and inadequacy in this accompaniment should not surprise or discourage us. The love we offer and the love enacted by the dying person is a more than human love. The little we have to offer, like the meager offering of a few fishes and loaves, becomes an abundance in the hands of the self-emptying Christ. This difficult, self-giving love is really possible, Paul says, "through him who loved us. For I am convinced that neither death, nor life, nor angels, nor principalities, nor present things, nor future things, nor powers, nor height, nor depth, nor any other creature will be able to separate us from the love of God in Christ Jesus our Lord" (Rom 8:37-39).

---

[44] Karl Rahner, "The Apostolate of Prayer," in *Theological Investigations*, vol. 3, trans. Karl-H and Boniface Kruger (New York: Seabury Press, 1974), 214.

The Communion Rite in Light of the Christ's Kenosis

We began this chapter with the observation that this whole reality of kenotic spirituality, self-emptying love of God and neighbor, uniquely and unsurpassably performed by Jesus once for all, is not only the reality we are plunged into at baptism; it is what we receive in communion. It is what sends us forth. So let us now bring the light of Jesus' kenotic love to our understanding of the communion rite. In the Roman Catholic tradition its structure and flow is as follows:

Lord's Prayer

Sign of Peace

Breaking of the Bread with Lamb of God

Invitation to Communion and Response

Communion with Song

Silence

Option of Communal Song

Prayer After Communion

Protestant versions feature most of these same elements: the Lord's Prayer, the fraction or breaking of the bread, communion, and prayer after communion, often spoken by the minister and people together.[45] Often there is song after communion and before the final benediction. The sign of peace occurs earlier, after the confession of sin or at the conclusion of the Liturgy of the Word. Eastern churches elaborate the rite with many additional prayers. But included are the Lord's Prayer, the fraction with reference to the Lamb of God, reception of communion accompanied by song, and a prayer of thanksgiving.

These texts and actions mutually inform each other. They exemplify intertextuality, which was discussed earlier in chapter 7. As we understand the gospel in light of all the readings leading up to it, we receive Christ as our food and drink in light of the ritual texts leading

---

[45] Regarding the fraction, the Lutheran rite is a significant exception. There is no meaning-laden ritual of breaking the bread. If broken during the rite it is only a functional preparation for distribution.

up to it. This word of the communion rite is a scriptural word. The bulk of its elements either directly quote or paraphrase scripture. The Lord's Prayer quotes Matthew 6:9-13; the ending of the embolism—"Deliver us, Lord, we pray, from every evil, graciously grant peace in our days . . . as we await the blessed hope and coming of our Savior, Jesus Christ"—draws on Titus 2:13. The ritual action of breaking the bread comes from Scripture's description of Jesus' fourfold eucharistic actions: taking, blessing, breaking, and giving. When we exchange the sign of peace we are echoing the words of the risen Christ to his disciples (John 20:19, 21, 26). The Lamb of God brings together numerous biblical sources. To name a few, Isaiah (53:7) portrays God's suffering servant as a lamb led to slaughter, which is quoted in Acts 8:32. In 1 Corinthians 5:7, Paul speaks of Christ as our paschal lamb who has been sacrificed. Lying behind this is the Passover ritual in Exodus 12, with the blood of the lamb applied to the doorposts and the same lamb roasted for the meal. On seeing Jesus approaching, John the Baptist says: "Behold, the Lamb of God who takes away the sin of the world" (John 1:29). Revelation speaks of the Lamb that was slain, now in glory (5:8, 9, 12; 13:8) and the wedding feast of the Lamb (19:7, 9). The invitation to communion combines several of these references: "Behold the Lamb of God, behold him who takes away the sins of the world. Blessed are those called to the supper of the Lamb." Substituting "my soul" for "my servant," the assembly's response cites Matthew 8:8, where the centurion expresses his trust in Jesus' power to heal: "Lord, I am not worthy that you should enter under my roof, but only say the word and my servant shall be healed."[46]

Once again, it is true to say that ritual texts mediate the Scriptures and the Scriptures inform the rite. These ritual texts and actions prepare us for the feast and converge upon it by answering the question: To what does communion with the risen One commit us? What are the contours of becoming ecclesially what we are receiving sacramentally? More specifically, how do these texts summon us toward a spirituality of self-emptying love?

---

[46] Paul Turner provides the scriptural basis of ritual texts for the entire liturgy in *At the Supper of the Lamb: A Pastoral and Theological Commentary on the Mass* (Chicago: LTP, 2011).

The Lord's Prayer

This treasure is so embedded in Christian consciousness that we easily move across the surface of the prayer without realizing its deeper implications. John Shea has noticed how it begins not with us and our needs but from God in heaven: "We do not begin on earth and petition heaven. We begin in heaven and bring heaven to earth."[47] This mirrors the descending movement of the Philippians hymn, a from-God-to-us movement. So we begin *in God above* because we live and move and have our being in God (our createdness). But God holds us not only in being but also in love. So, we begin in the love of God who has first loved us (grace).

This love is named "Father" (we could also say "Mother") to indicate an intimacy deeper than the Creator-creature relationship, the intimacy of parent and child: "Our Father, who art in heaven." That parent-child intimacy is the point of this parental image, because Christ's kenosis makes us adopted daughters and sons. It is not an assertion of male gender in God. The *Catechism of the Catholic Church* is quite clear on this point:

> In no way is God in man's image. He is neither man nor woman. God is pure spirit in which there is no place for the difference between the sexes. But the respective "perfections" of man and woman reflect something of the infinite perfection of God: those of a mother and those of a father and husband.[48]

That we start from God, with the intimacy of a child with its mother or father, is what is meant by being "born from above" from the Nicodemus story: "no one can see the kingdom of God without being born from above" (John 3:3). In this spatial symbolism we are living not from ourselves or our own egos, but from God above. The self and the ego are still operative but as coming from and responding to the God of love. This is how the humanity of Jesus moves with the life of God moving within him. In all he says and does, he starts from God: "I do not seek my own will but the will of the one who sent me" (John 5:30). Leonardo Boff writes, "It is in starting with God,

---

[47] John Shea, *Following Jesus* (New York: Orbis Books, 2010), 60.
[48] *Catechism*, par. 370.

from his vantage point, that we become concerned with our own needs."[49]

To start from God is to see with God's eyes and feel with God's heart. But to do so *humanly* is to see with Christ's eyes and feel with Christ's heart. The response this love evokes in us is Christic: "hallowed be thy name." Jesus is the one who above all hallows the Father's name in word and deed. The liturgy teaches us that through, with, and in Christ we hallow God's name by participating in his self-emptying love.

From hallowing God's name, the prayer moves to petition: "thy kingdom come, thy will be done on earth as it is in heaven." If Jesus is the one who above all starts from and hallows God's name, he is also the one who enacts the kingdom to come here and now: "This is the time of fulfillment. The kingdom of God is at hand" (Mark 1:15). It is in light of this that we "can understand Jesus' exclamation: Happy the eyes that see what you are seeing! (Luke 10:23)," writes Leonardo Boff.[50] Hallowing God's name in Christ takes the form of Chauvet's return-gift. Hallowing as communion leads to practical hallowing, sending us into deeds. We cooperate in building the reign, striving for a culture of compassion, loving one another and God in the pattern of the self-emptying Christ. We live with everyone as sisters and brothers so that no one among us is in need, oppressed, or exploited. However imperfectly and incompletely, we bring the kingdom of heaven to earth. This striving is eschatological, looking toward the future. This is what communing with the risen One commits us to.

Having put on the self-emptying Christ in baptism, we are drawn into his kenotic love through the bread of the word and the bread of the sacrament: "Give us this day our daily bread." Participating in the kenosis of Jesus and the perichoresis of the Trinity, we mutually give way to each other in love: "forgive us our trespasses as we forgive those who trespass against us."

What is the scope of this mutual *deferring to each other*? Biblically speaking, much broader than the individualism of our culture

---

[49] Leonardo Boff, *The Lord's Prayer: The Prayer of Integral Liberation* (Maryknoll, NY: Orbis Books, 1985), 6.

[50] Ibid., 59.

suggests. It cannot be limited to "the small-scale private forgiveness of small-scale private sins," N. T. Wright says.[51] Key to understanding the larger scope of the prayer is the fact that the word "debt" occurs in both Matthew's and Luke's versions of the prayer. Matthew's version says, "forgive us our debts, as we forgive our debtors" (6:12); Luke has "forgive us our sins for we ourselves forgive everyone in debt to us" (11:4). There is no question that debts can be translated more broadly as sins or trespasses. But "debts" in the Bible specifically evokes an economic-political history of debt leading to slavery and attempts to restrict and relieve the slide into crushing debt-slavery. This was the intent of the Jubilee celebration. Pope Francis describes it as "a year of general forgiveness and 'liberty throughout the land for all its inhabitants' (cf. Lv 25:10)."[52] Liberty means slaves set free and debts forgiven. In the words of John Dominic Crossan, "For the biblical tradition, when debt creates too much inequality, it has become sinful."[53] The scope of "forgive us our trespasses as we forgive those" extends to any structures by which some people are kept in oppressive and destructive indebtedness to others. The forgiveness envisioned addresses all that wounds personal relationships but also communities and nations. A compassionate Christ requires a compassionate people who "can stand in awe at what the poor have to carry rather than stand in judgment at how they carry it," as Gregory Boyle writes.[54] It doesn't mean that the fault is not there or is not acknowledged. But in dealing with it the bottom-line is a self-emptying love that secures the well-being of the other. It is like the Father in the story of the prodigal, who emptied himself of his dignity "and ran down the road to welcome his disgraced son."[55]

Persons and communities professing the kenotic way of Jesus are, however, always in danger of going off the rails. In the name of religion, including Christian faith, people have done the most horrible things to each other. Self-will, whether of the individual or of the community, can mask itself in religious guise. So, we pray: "And lead

---

[51] N. T. Wright, *The Lord and His Prayer* (Grand Rapids, MI: Eerdmans, 1996), 36.

[52] *Laudato Si'*, par. 71.

[53] John Dominic Crossan, *The Greatest Prayer: Rediscovering the Revolutionary Message of the Lord's Prayer* (New York: HarperCollins, 2011), 160.

[54] Gregory Boyle, *Tattoos on the Heart* (New York: Free Press, 2010), 67.

[55] Wright, *The Lord and His Prayer*, 38.

us not into temptation but deliver us from evil." In English translation this sounds as though we are asking God to hold back from pushing us toward temptation. But God tempts no one (Jas 1:13). The original Greek means two things at once, "do not allow us to enter into" and "do not allow us to yield to" temptation.[56] Some translations render it differently as "save us from the time of trial." In Luke's account of the agony in the garden Jesus says to his disciples: "Pray that you may not come into the time of trial" (Luke 22:40; NRSV). What is at stake here?

Everyday temptations are certainly included, but a more radical trial is envisioned. When the time of trial comes for the disciples, they abandon Jesus. Peter follows him after his arrest only to deny him. On the way to Gethsemane, he warns them, "This night all of you will have your faith in me shaken" and quotes Zechariah 13:7, "I will strike the shepherd and the sheep of the flock will be dispersed." In effect, we are praying that we may not abandon or betray the self-emptying way of Jesus but endure with him. We ask God to keep us faithful, not only as individuals but as church. Psalm 16:1 captures the sentiment well: "Keep me safe, O God; in you take refuge."

All these dimensions of the prayer reveal what it means to commune with the risen One. Communion means hallowing God's name, working for God's reign, being a force for reconciliation in our divided world, persevering in the face of powerful temptations and trials. All of these call for the practice of kenotic love toward God and neighbor. It follows that communion is inherently communal, never a private affair. It is not *my* Father but *our* Father. Speaking from her Buddhist tradition, Christina Feldman writes, "The saboteurs of compassion are doubt and fear, born of a belief in self and separation."[57] Christ's kenosis enacts the opposite spiritual posture, rejecting the illusion of separateness: love of God and love of neighbor.

In the Roman Rite, the Lord's Prayer is not a standalone element. It is part of a larger unit including a bridge prayer (embolism) by the presider and a doxology said by all:

---

[56] *Catechism*, par. 2846.

[57] Christina Feldman, *The Buddhist Path to Simplicity: Spiritual Practice for Everyday Life* (New York: Metro Books, 2006), 101.

Deliver us, Lord, we pray, from every evil,
graciously grant peace in our days,
that, by the help of your mercy,
we may be always free from sin
and safe from all distress,
as we await the blessed hope
and the coming of our Savior, Jesus Christ.

For the kingdom,
the power and the glory are yours
now and forever.

The Sign of Peace

Starting from this point and looking ahead, one is struck by the recurring theme of peace. The embolism above asks for "peace in our days." The next moment in the rite's flow is the sign of peace, which the presider introduces with the words:

Lord Jesus Christ, who said to your Apostles,
Peace I leave you, my peace I give you,
look not on our sins,
but on the faith of your Church,
and graciously grant her peace and unity
in accordance with your will.

Exchanging a gesture of peace, usually a handshake, then flows into the fraction or breaking of the bread. Here again we find the theme of peace.

The Fraction and Lamb of God

The assembly accompanies this action by singing the Lamb of God, ending with the petition, "grant us peace." This is the Lamb who takes away the sins of the world. As in "thy kingdom come," a request is also a call. Communing with the risen One commits the person and community to peacemaking, which promotes unity between human beings. Receiving him, we go with him in taking away the sins of the world. Peace is Christ's gift and we are not the Christ. But we are his Body, and peacemaking is a task he gives not only by his word but by giving himself to us in communion. John Paul II spoke eloquently to this theme:

> The Eucharist is not merely an expression of communion in the Church's life; it is also a *project of solidarity* for all humanity. . . . The Christian who takes part in the Eucharist learns to become a *promoter of communion, peace and solidarity* in every situation. More than ever, our troubled world, which began the new Millennium with the spectre of terrorism and the tragedy of war, demands that Christians learn to experience the Eucharist as *a great school of peace,* forming men and women who, at various levels of responsibility in social, cultural and political life, can become promoters of dialogue and communion.[58]

Two images from this moment in the rite underscore its kenotic meaning—the *lamb* and the *breaking* (and related to this, the *pouring* of the consecrated wine). These are images of self-sacrifice. The metaphor of sacrifice should, however, be understood in terms of self-emptying love. The sacrifice of Christ is not the violence visited upon him but the free act of resolute love by which he undergoes and absorbs violence in fidelity to his mission. God neither wills violence upon Jesus nor that human beings perpetrate this violence in order to accomplish the divine will. This cannot be what we celebrate in the words of the gospel acclamation for Easter Sunday morning: "Christ, our paschal lamb has been sacrificed; let us then feast with joy in the Lord." Rather, we celebrate the victory of self-emptying love over all the death-dealing strategies of fallen humankind. This very love is the gift of God. The kenotic love of Jesus does not reveal a *wrath* in God to be placated but the kenotic love of the One who sent him: "For God so loved the world that he gave his only Son" (John 3:16).

Singing the Lamb of God and breaking the bread interpret each other. In Paul, the breaking signifies communal sharing, affirming the essentially communal-ecclesial nature of the Eucharist. For it is by sharing in the one loaf that we become one body in Christ (1 Cor 10:17). So, as Chauvet says, the Eucharist is essentially "bread-as-food, bread-as-meal, bread-for-sharing."[59] Interpreted by the Lamb

---

[58] Apostolic Letter, *Mane Nobiscum Domine* of the Holy Father John Paul II for the Year of the Eucharist, October 2004–2005, 27; emphasis in original.

[59] Chauvet, *Symbol and Sacrament*, 406.

of God, it also symbolizes the breaking of Christ's body, his self-emptying on the cross. Rahner understands this self-emptying as cosmic as well as historical: "When the vessel of his body was shattered in death, Christ was poured out over the whole cosmos."[60] Because this breaking signifies the self-emptying of Christ upon the whole cosmos, the whole cosmos is transformed by his resurrection. Pope Francis writes, "Christ has taken unto himself this material world, and now, risen, is intimately present to each being, surrounding it with his affections and penetrating it with his light."[61] This taking of the world unto himself in his death is the embrace of kenotic love. Interior to *breaking as sharing* is *breaking as kenosis*, a dying that brings new life. That is why Paul can say, "For as often as you eat this bread and drink the cup, you proclaim the death of the Lord until he comes" (1 Cor 11:26).

Kenosis answers the question: What makes the meal truly communal? Meals need not be. They can instead manifest relations of inequality, subordination, and domination. A striking moment from the life of Gandhi, portrayed in the movie of the same name, shows him gathering with the most important political leaders. A servant comes in to serve food and drink. Gandhi horrifies his colleagues by insisting on taking the servant's role and waiting on them. His action reveals their hypocrisy. Their collective effort to rid India of British domination is marred by their own cultural forms of domination and subordination. Paul forcefully criticizes such meal abuses at Corinth: "in eating, each one goes ahead with his own supper, and one goes hungry while another gets drunk"; the affluent make "those who have nothing feel ashamed" (1 Cor 11:21-22). What makes us truly one body in Christ is *being* his self-emptying love toward one another. "It is thus from *the very heart of the break*," Chauvet writes, "that the Eucharist above all speaks."[62] Among the various Protestant rites, there is an option to sing or say the Lamb of God at this point.[63] But

---

[60] Rahner, *Theology of Death*, 66.

[61] *Laudato Si'*, par. 221.

[62] Chauvet, *Symbol and Sacrament*, 407.

[63] Holy Eucharist I of the Episcopal Church; Service of Word and Sacrament I of the United Church of Christ; Service of Word and Table IV of the United Methodist Church. The rite of the Evangelical Lutheran Church says that the bread may be broken at this point. But it does not really have a fraction rite. The Lamb of God is featured as an optional first song to accompany communion.

other texts are featured, such as "Christ our Passover is sacrificed for us" or the Corinthians text cited above (1 Cor 10:16-17).[64] The option for this passage in the Presbyterian *Book of Worship* is interwoven with bread and cup actions:

> Because there is one loaf, we, many as we are, are one body, for it is of one loaf that we all partake.
>
> *The minister takes the loaf and breaks it in full view of the people, saying:*
>
> When we break the bread, is it not a sharing in the body of Christ?
>
> *Having filled the cup, the minister lifts it in the view of the people, saying:*
>
> When we give thanks over the cup, is it not a sharing in the blood of Christ.[65]

Invitation to Communion

In the Roman Rite, the invitation to communion carries forward the lamb imagery: "Behold the Lamb of God, behold him who takes away the sins of the world. Blessed are those called to the supper of the Lamb." During the fraction, *lamb* coupled with *breaking* signified the downward movement of self-emptying even unto death. Here, the coupling of *blessed* with *supper of the Lamb* implies the upward exaltation of Jesus and the pledge of our participation in it. We can discern in the movement from one to the other the trajectory of Philippians, the "clear pattern of descending and ascending not only in the text but in the person of Jesus Christ," as Laura Reece Hogan says.[66] The Lamb once slain is now risen. It is the risen Christ who gathers us together, speaks to our hearts in the proclamation of the Word, and nourishes us with the bread of life and the cup of salvation.

Christian kenosis, then, is not simple loss or self-negation but life in abundance coming out of love and fidelity to God and neighbor.

---

[64] Holy Eucharist II of the Episcopal Church; Service of Word and Sacrament II of the United Church of Christ; Service for the Lord's Day of the Presbyterian *Book of Common Worship*; Service of Word and Table I of the United Methodist Church.

[65] *Book of Common Worship*, 74.

[66] Laura Reece Hogan, *I Live, No Longer I: Paul's Spirituality of Suffering, Transformation, and Joy* (Eugene, OR: Wipf and Stock, 2017), 34.

It is not just losing but losing in order to find. Yes, carried out to the full it carries one into death, even a violent death, as in the case of Jesus, or, in our own time, the deaths of Mahatma Gandhi, Dietrich Bonhoeffer, Martin Luther King Jr., Dorothy Kazel, Ita Ford, Maura Clark, Jean Donavan, Oscar Romero, and many others who remain unacknowledged. We do not have to subscribe to unacceptable atonement theories to see that loving fidelity to God, neighbor, and God's good earth will bring one into conflict with worldly powers. The violence undergone is the world's, not the will of God. The will of God is the noble courage of fidelity and love even in the face of violence. It is God in Jesus absorbing the violence of this world, siding with victims, disrupting the old pattern, so that something new and redemptive can break through: "See, I am doing something new! Now it springs forth, do you not perceive it?" (Isa 43:19). Are not yesterday's and today's martyrs, all holy women and men, icons of Christ precisely because the new thing God has done and offers to all shines forth in their living and dying?

The initial words of assembly's response to the invitation may feel negative: "Lord, I am not worthy that you should enter under my roof." But the emphasis of the biblical story from which these words are drawn is not on unworthiness but on the great faith of the centurion. This faith expresses a spiritual posture. The centurion, a man of authority, opens and entrusts himself to an authority greater than his own. Matthew rarely talks about Jesus' emotions, but here he does: "he was amazed and said to those following him, 'Amen, I say to you, in no one in Israel have I found such faith'" (8:10). For Jesus this Gentile is an object lesson in true spirituality—openness, trust, and faith in the God of love Jesus makes present. Praying these words, we take this centurion's kenotic faith as model of our own.

Communion:
Processing, Singing, Receiving, Silence, Prayer after Communion

Communion, as was said earlier, is not a moment in which the corporate body evaporates back into private individuals. Ritually, it should be the most heightened actualization of Christ's corporate Body. The procession expresses this communal dimension. The persons in front of and behind me are not strangers but sisters and brothers, members of my ecclesial family. Together we are on an ecclesial family outing, on parade to dine in the kingdom of God, even here and now. We sing together along the parade route. Speaking of the processional song, the General Instruction of the Roman Missal says: "Its purpose is to express the communicants' union in spirit by means of the unity of their voices, to show joy of heart, and to highlight more clearly the 'communitarian' nature of the procession to receive Communion."[67] Additionally, the song text interprets the meaning of communing with the risen Christ and so plays its role in the intertextual experience of the rite. The communion song extends this process of interpretation either by echoing the Word of the day or biblically expressing the implications of communing with the risen Christ.

Bernadette Farrell's "Bread for the World" speaks to the word in the rite. Like a good homily, it links the biblical world (the supper and the washing of the feet) to the human world of our time:

> *Refrain:* Bread for the world: a world of hunger. Wine for all peoples: people who thirst. May we who eat be bread for others. May we who drink pour out our love.

> *Verse 1:* Lord Jesus Christ, you are the bread of life, broken to reach and heal the wounds of human pain. Where we divide your people you are waiting there on bended knee to wash our feet with endless care.[68]

On the other hand, the communion song may mirror the word in the day's readings, so that the Christ we receive is the Christ we have met earlier in the day's Scriptures. Quoting the gospel's temptation scene, the Roman Missal's communion antiphon for the First Sunday of Lent is: "No one lives by bread alone, but by every word that comes forth from the mouth of God." Songs elaborating this text return us to the gospel story during communion.[69]

Many parishes and dioceses have initiated the beautiful custom of having everyone stand until all have received, reinforcing percep-

---

[67] *General Instruction of the Roman Missal*, Third Typical Edition (Washington DC: United States Conference of Catholic Bishops, 2011), par. 86.

[68] "Bread for the World," Bernadette Farrell © 1991. Published by OCP. All rights reserved. Used with permission.

[69] Additional examples include: "Beyond the Days," Ricky Manalo © 1997. Published by OCP. All rights reserved; "Not on Bread Alone Are We Nourished," The Collegeville Composers Group, *Psallite* (Collegeville, MN: Liturgical Press, 2006).

tion of the communitarian nature of receiving. Ritually it signals that my experience of communion is not over when I alone have received—it is over only when all my sisters and brothers have also received. That all remain standing has the added benefit of encouraging assembly song during communion.

These ritual signals and actions are important because the consumeristic individualism of our culture prejudices us in the other direction. To put it crudely, in communion each individual receives and takes away a piece of Jesus. It is not unlike getting a "happy meal" at a fast-food restaurant. Having little to do with each other, consumers drop in to get their meal and go their separate ways. But in truth, communion is not each of us taking away a bit of Christ; it is Christ drawing us into union with himself and each other. It is completion of gathering and of finding ourselves in the Word. In the *Confessions*, Augustine reports hearing a voice say, "You will not change me into yourself like bodily food: you will be changed into me."[70] By sharing the one loaf, Paul says, we are made one body (1 Cor 12:17). This embodiment of Christ in people—yes, as persons but as persons belonging to Christ and each other—is the meaning of the ancient saying, "The church makes Eucharist and the Eucharist makes the church."

Communally processing, singing, and receiving do not eliminate the contemplative dimension from the liturgy. Just as earlier there are silences following the readings, there is silence after reception and before the prayer following communion. It is communal because, though deeply personal, it is not private. Being in silence with others is qualitatively different from being in silence alone. This ritual silence should not be shortchanged. It signifies the *beyond words* character of union, corresponding to *contemplatio* in the fourth stage of *lectio divina*. Having passed through many words, one arrives at companionable silence with God. Because Christ is the Word *of God*, communing with him is entry into *the* Mystery. This is especially so because it is the *risen* Christ with whom we commune. Are we sufficiently aware of how mysterious this is? Is not our talk about real presence always in danger of reducing the sacramental presence of Christ to possession of a physical object?

[70] *The Confessions of St. Augustine*, trans. Maria Boulding (New York: Random House, 1997), 134–35 (7.10.16).

Even the most traditional Catholic explanation—transubstantiation—is more mysterious than people often imagine. Despite what many Catholics and Protestants alike may think, it does not equate *real presence* with *physical presence*. Christ is not present *physically* or *corporeally* "inside" the consecrated bread and wine. A possible source of this common misunderstanding is that we believe we are receiving the *body and blood* of Christ (in fact his whole person) and *body-blood* suggests *physicality*. But Aquinas presents transubstantiation as an alternative to such crude physicalism, charting a middle course between physical presence and weakly spiritual presence in the sense that the bread and wine are only psychological reminders of something absent. Catholic theologians agree on this interpretation across the conservative-liberal spectrum.[71] All analogies limp, but Aquinas's best analogy for Christ's presence—body-blood-soul-divinity—under the appearances of bread and wine is the way in which the human soul animates the body. The soul is not a physical body inside our body but the spiritual life-force that *intimately* informs, sustains, and makes the living body *what* it is, therefore functioning as its *substance* while remaining itself nonphysical.

The original Greek for the Latin word *sacramentum* is *mysterion*. A sacrament is a mystery because through something finite and perceptible the nonperceptible infinite mystery of God is given. It is simultaneously revealed and hidden—not one or the other but the tension of the two. To commune with Christ in sacrament is to inhabit this tension that stretches us toward mystery. It is also to accept his hiddenness. The real presence of Christ in sacrament includes a real absence. He is no longer present as he was during his earthly exis-

---

[71] For a very clear presentation from a conservative-leaning perspective, see Avery Cardinal Dulles, "Christ's Presence in the Eucharist: True, Real, and Substantial," *30Giorni*, no. 9 (2005): 1–8; available online at www.30giorni.it/archivo_anno_2005. David Power presents more theological background and nuance in "Thomas Aquinas on the Eucharist: Focal Point of Medieval Thought," in *The Eucharistic Mystery: Revitalizing the Tradition* (New York: Crossroad, 1995), especially 219–26. What he says echoes Dulles: "Christ's presence is in no way a localized presence, a hidden presence, a presence beneath or in the accidents of any physical being. As Aquinas says, it is a spiritual presence, one that defies imagination, one inconceivable to reason alone, one not to be found in the order of nature" (223). By clarifying the theory of transubstantiation, I am not suggesting that newer and more adequate approaches might not emerge, an ongoing task for theology as faith seeking understanding.

tence. Otherwise there is no resurrection, no ascension. John Shea gives a humorous gloss on the ascension story. As Jesus ascends the disciples stand looking intently at the sky, even after he is taken from their sight in a cloud (Acts 1:6-12). Two white-garmented men suddenly appear and ask, "Why are you standing there looking at the sky?" In other words, it's time for them to stop gawking and get on with the mission. But getting on with the mission is just what they are worried about. Shea writes,

> If the mission is more than just telling people about Jesus, if it entails initiating people into the relationship with God that Jesus made possible, then how is this going to be done if Jesus is not here to do it? To extend the image of ascension, one can fantasize that it was not curiosity that made them stare but panic. If they could have, they would have reached up and pulled Jesus back to earth by his heels. What they were watching move ever farther away from them was the One who made it possible for them to love one another. What will happen now that he is gone?[72]

Chauvet too speaks of the absence that belongs to the sacramental presence of Christ. He writes, "Now as risen, Christ has departed; we must agree to this loss if we want to be able to find him."[73] The real presence of Christ in sacrament includes this *not-present-in-an-earthly-way* absence.

Consenting to this real absence goes against the grain. We are like Thomas, who wants to put his finger into the nail marks and wounded side of Jesus before he will believe. Jesus says, "Have you come to believe because you have seen me?" (John 20:29). Looking ahead, as it were, to his ascension, Jesus concludes, "Blessed are those who have not seen and have believed." Believing without seeing corresponds to recognizing the *absence in the presence*. The doubting Thomas story, which the Lectionary presents on the Second Sunday of Easter in Cycle A, is preceded by 1 Peter 1:8, which concludes with: "Although you have not seen him you love him; even though you do not see him now yet you believe in him, you rejoice with an indescribable and glorious joy."

---

[72] John Shea, *An Experience Named Spirit* (Chicago: Thomas Moore Press, 1983), 29.
[73] Chauvet, *Symbol and Sacrament*, 177.

The Emmaus story shows that we encounter the risen One only through mediation. There are in fact many mediations. There is the mediation of his ecclesial body, the church; his word, the Scriptures; his supper, the Eucharist, and, by extension, the other sacraments. Primary among these is baptism, which plunges us into the kenotic mystery of the Christ: "Can you be baptized with the baptism with which I am baptized?" (Mark 10:38). By living the kenotic love of Jesus, we mediate him to each other. We find him wherever we find agapic love in action. To commune with him in all these ways, but preeminently in the Eucharist, is a letting go of the self toward the Mystery of God. So, it is ritually fitting that all our words and actions lead into the silence of this Mystery before we conclude the rite and are sent forth. The prayer after communion reiterates the request the church has been making throughout the entire liturgy: transformation. We ask that we truly become ecclesially what we receive sacramentally. And this means that we actualize our return-gift by living Christ's self-emptying love beyond ritual in the liturgy of life. We are sent.

Sending

The sending rite in most Western church traditions, Catholic and Protestant, is more like the period at the end of a sentence than a new sentence. That is because to commune with the risen Christ is to be sent. Our communing with him in the Word comes to completion in communing with him in the Eucharist. Then, by going forth to love with the self-emptying love of Christ, we give witness to his Abba who has first loved us. Of God's love, Rahner writes,

> This love is precisely the descending love, the love that communicates itself to the world, the love that, as it were, loses itself in the world, the love that brings about the becoming-flesh of the Word, the love that means the abiding of the eternal Word in his creature, and that therefore means a divinized world and Church.[74]

---

[74] *Karl Rahner: Spiritual Writings*, ed. Philip Endean (New York: Orbis Books, 2008), 58.

Borne by God's self-communicating grace, we are offered the real possibility of bringing all that is conflicted and unresolved in our hearts to the resolved heart of Christ. In him and the Spirit, "our 'ascending' love to God is always participation in God's descent to the world." It must be "service-with-God-in-descent, descent into otherness, the lostness, the sinfulness of this world."[75] In light of this, the sending rite, as the culmination of all that has gone before, poses a question: To whom are we sent? Wither does sending send us? To our homes, our neighbors and colleagues, our extended families, our communities, our nation, our world. This ever-widening circle, encompassing what Jesus meant by one's neighbor (everyone), means we are sent not only to comfortable places but to hard places of lostness and suffering. These can be as close as one's family, spouse, children, or parents. Sometimes they are farther afield. Because liturgy is foundational for the Christian who is *sent* we also take the liturgy with us to such places.

One example is the church at the US-Mexican border, south of San Diego, California. I learned of it from my friend, Elizabeth Moore, Methodist minister and abbot of the ecumenical Order of St. Luke. From time to time, she and others from our Pilgrim Place community make the journey down to El Faro Park for the Sunday service. People gather on each side of the border wall, barely able to see each other through the thickly interlaced rebar. At most they can reach a little finger through to touch someone's pinkie finger on the other side. They call it a "pinkie kiss." But they can at least speak to each other through the fence, with an American pastor on one side and a Mexican pastor on the other. Some of those who regularly gather are families separated by the border fence. An excerpt of Elizabeth's eloquent description, given in a Vesper service at Pilgrim Place, follows:

> When you reach this inner fence, John introduces you to Guillermo— the Mexican pastor. Who introduces a U.S. Army veteran, deported after being in the U.S. over 30 years for a crime he admits to—but not a crime that deserves the loss of his family and livelihood. We hear the story of many American veterans who have been deported after fighting in a war that broke their minds and bodies. And, in their brokenness, we sent them back to a place that was never their home. The church service begins. John on one side. Guillermo on the other. Prayers

---

[75] Ibid., 57–58.

are said. Songs of praise are sung. The Word is proclaimed. And bread is broken. Not one loaf, because passing it through the fence is not allowed—a violation of U. S. Customs law. But it is one loaf in spirit. The Body and Blood of Christ are shared. And the Peace is passed by "pinkie kisses" through the fence. Pinkie kisses must suffice, even though the heart cries out for hugs; even though tears run down the faces looking through the tiny holes, faces gazing at mothers and fathers and cousins and brothers. We go quietly back through the outer fence and begin our walk to the car. Our pilgrimage has not brought us to a magnificent cathedral or a distant holy island. Instead it has brought us to this place close to home. To this park at the end of a dirt road. To these families who cannot embrace one another. To this place where we are forced to acknowledge that walls can divide nations. But it is also a place that by its very being declares that the Church of Jesus Christ cannot be divided. Songs and prayers flow through that wall. Love flows through that wall. Christ flows through that wall.

We return home changed. Pilgrimage does that to a person. Thanks be to God.

Conclusion

This book began with an evocation of mystery. In Wilder's words, we live "the life of the village against the stars."[76] We experience the holy Mystery in which all things abide in the interplay of transcendence (to the stars) and immersion (village concerns). By its very transcendence this Mystery is also immanent, closer to us than we are to ourselves. For Christian spirituality it is the closeness of God as self-communicating love or grace. Coming near in redemptive love, always and everywhere, it is fully actualized in an earthly time and place in Jesus of Nazareth.

God is self-emptied, that is, given into our humanity. And Jesus, the humanity of God, in his truly human knowing, willing, and loving, pours himself out in a return of love for love. His divinely born humanity expresses both God's love for us and humanity's return of love for God. Because it is love of God, it is love of neighbor as well as all creation. You cannot love the God whom you do not see unless you love the sister and brother whom you do see (1 John 4:20). In Jesus, this return, this moving with the life of God moving within

---

[76] Thornton Wilder, "A Preface for Our Town," in *Thornton Wilder: Collected Plays and Writings on the Theater* (New York: The Library of America, 2007), 659.

him, takes the specific form of kenosis or self-emptying love. Such love is not cheap, not to be sentimentalized or romanticized. Jesus' courageous fidelity to the One who sent him brings him to a violent end. Leonardo Boff writes,

> His court-ordered assassination is the result of his life, his preaching, his liberating practice, the consciousness that he had developed of his connection to the *Abba*-Father, and his connection to the reign, something that very much scandalized the religious authorities and placed him under suspicion as a subversive by the representatives of the roman Empire.[77]

So Jesus' self-emptying life leads to self-emptying death, a final act of fidelity and love: *my body given for you, my blood shed for you.* In this he keeps trust with the One who sent him, even in the experience of being God-forsaken. The resurrection announces that his Abba-Father keeps trust with him and the reign he inaugurates, a reign that continues to grow in our midst, animated by the Pentecost sending of the Spirit.

This is the paschal mystery and its spirituality. It is mediated from age to age by the church and its liturgy. Through it we learn to have the mind of Christ. The ritual stages of worship progressively induct us into the kenotic pattern of Philippians. Gathering us, the risen One gives himself in the bread of the word and the bread of the table, that we may become his word, his bread, his self-emptying love for the world.

> The grace of the Eucharist is finally our own becoming *eucharistic people*, that is, our becoming sons and daughters for God and brothers and sisters for others, in communion with the Son and Brother whose memory we celebrate here.[78]

This *more than human love*, which nonetheless gives itself for human participation, involves dying to the small self, losing one's life to find it, opening to the fullness of the Mystery that we cannot control, creating communities of care and kinship, speaking truth to power,

---

[77] Leonardo Boff, *Christianity in a Nutshell*, trans. Phillip Berryman (Maryknoll, NY: Orbis Books, 2013), 81.
[78] Chauvet, *Symbol and Sacrament*, 314–15.

giving the self to and for others, even one's enemies and even at risk of one's life. There is no greater love than this (John 15:13). It is not a neurotic, grim, guilt-laden duty but fullness of life and joy, even in the midst of suffering and hard patches. It is being *like* Christ, which flows from abiding *in* Christ and his Spirit, both the gift of God: Compassionate Christ, compassionate people.

Index of Persons

Index of Subjects